Systems Economics

Systems Economics

Concepts, Models, and Multidisciplinary Perspectives

EDITED BY **KARL A. FOX** AND **DON G. MILES**

IOWA STATE UNIVERSITY PRESS AMES

1. Chapter 7 is a revised version of Karl A. Fox, "The Eco-behavioral View of Human Societies and Its Implications for Systems Science," *International Journal of Systems Science* 14:895–914, 1983. Used with permission.

2. Chapter 8 includes materials from Karl A. Fox and Paul van Moeseke, "Derivation and Implications of a Scalar Measure of Social Income," pp. 21–40 in H. C. Bos, H. Linnemann, and P. de Wolff, editors, *Economic Structure and Development: Essays in Honor of Jan Tinbergen,* Amsterdam: North-Holland Publishing Company, 1973; and Paul van Moeseke, "Socio-economic Interface and Social Income," *Mathematical Social Sciences* 9:263–273, 1985. Used with permissions.

3. Chapter 9 is a revised version of James R. Prescott, "A Behavior Setting Approach to Microanalytical Simulation Models at the Community Level," pp. 132–149 in Karl A. Fox, *Social Systems Accounts: Linking Social and Economic Indicators Through Tangible Behavior Settings,* 1985. Copyright © 1985 by D. Reidel Publishing Company, Dordrecht, Holland. Used with permission.

Printed in the United States of America from camera-ready copy provided by the editors

First edition, 1987

Library of Congress Cataloging-in-Publication Data

Systems economics.
Includes indexes.

1. Economics. 2. Agriculture—Economic aspects. 3. Equilibrium (Economics) I. Fox, Karl August, 1917– . II. Miles, Don G.
HB171.S99 1987 330 86-27586
ISBN 0-8138-1738-2

TO KENNETH E. BOULDING

Economist, social scientist, and humanist;
cofounder of the Society for General Systems Research;
and world citizen

CONTENTS

PREFACE

This book is addressed to economists and agricultural economists. It advocates a systems approach to many of the problems with which members of these disciplines are concerned and presents major innovations. These are mentioned in the introduction and summarized in Chapter 10.

The volume is of potential interest to all economists and agricultural economists, but some of the contributors are well known only in portions of these communities. We have therefore included a short statement in the contributor list about each of the nine authors, emphasizing aspects of his career that are particularly relevant to his contribution.

The authors are independent and original thinkers and in no sense constitute a school. Their chapters reflect the many different ways in which the economy interacts with other systems and (hence) the many different ways in which economists must learn to combine their skills with those of other professionals. It appears that the most promising frameworks for multidisciplinary cooperation can be expressed in the language of general systems theory, broadly conceived.

We hope that some university and college teachers of economics and agricultural economics will use this book as the primary text for new and experimental courses in "systems economics" or "systems approaches to multidisciplinary research," choosing additional readings from references cited in the various essays.

The book can be used for supplemental reading in a wide range of courses. Boulding's essay should be exciting to many students, even at the introductory level. Courses in labor economics, public finance, industrial organization, comparative economic systems, national income accounting, natural resource and environmental economics, economic theory, mathematical economics, history of economic thought, economic development, urban economics, regional economics, quantitative methods, and research methodology should all find one or more of the essays valuable for supplemental reading.

The editors knew and admired the work of each of the other authors. Each received the same letter of invitation and each was enthusiastic about the proposed volume; each designed his essay to enhance the usefulness of the volume to its intended readers. However, when all the essays were in hand, the other authors decided that the work should be dedicated to Kenneth Boulding.

Kenneth Boulding had a brilliant early career in the mainstream of economics. He published his first article in the *Economic Journal* in 1932 (when he was 22) and the first modern textbook on economic theory in 1941. In 1949 he became the second person ever to receive the John Bates Clark Medal of the American Economic Association, for outstanding contributions to economics prior to age 40; five of the first six medalists subsequently received the Alfred Nobel Memorial Prize in economic science.

During 1943-1949, Boulding taught labor economics at Iowa State College and found that it involved much more than economics. He found the accepted theory of the firm unrealistic and formulated a dynamic theory in terms of stocks, flows, and the transformation of assets. He also experimented with ecological formulations of interactions among firms in his 1950 book, *A Reconstruction of Economics*.

During the early 1950s at the University of Michigan, Boulding presided over a Seminar in the Integration of the Social Sciences; in the mid-1950s he became a cofounder of the Society for General Systems Research. He served as president of the American Economic Association in 1968 and president of the American Association for the Advancement of Science in 1979. His career symbolizes the scope and intent of systems economics.

The editors received helpful suggestions from at least three anonymous reviewers and accepted most of them; the overall sequence of chapters and the functions assigned to the introduction and to Chapter 10 reflect their advice. Charles W. Meyer gave wise counsel on two versions of the manuscript and particularly on the contributions of the editors themselves.

The original version of the manuscript was typed by Carolyn Millage, and much of her work on the word processor survives in portions of the book. Sue Streeter has handled the new and revised materials since July 1985 and the very demanding work of putting the entire manuscript in camera-ready form. The accuracy and consistency of the text and its format and appearance also reflect the care and high standards of manuscript editor Carla Tollefson and production editor Carol Sanderson of the Iowa State University Press.

Karl A. Fox
Don G. Miles

CONTRIBUTORS

KENNETH E. BOULDING is Distinguished Professor Emeritus, University of Colorado, Boulder. He has served as president of the American Economic Association, the American Association for the Advancement of Science, the Society for General Systems Research, and several other national and international associations. Among his many notable books are *A Reconstruction of Economics* (1950), *The Organizational Revolution* (1953), *The Image* (1956), *Conflict and Defense* (1962), *The Meaning of the Twentieth Century* (1964), *Ecodynamics* (1978), *Evolutionary Economics* (1981), and *The World as a Total System* (1985). His awards include the John Bates Clark Medal of the American Economic Association (1949), the American Council of Learned Societies prize for distinguished scholarship in humanities (1962), the Frank E. Seidman Distinguished Award in Political Economy (1976), and the Rufus Jones Award of the World Academy of Arts and Sciences (1979).

KARL A. FOX is Distinguished Professor in Sciences and Humanities and Professor of Economics, Iowa State University, Ames. He is a Fellow of the Econometric Society, the American Statistical Association, the American Association for the Advancement of Science, and the American Agricultural Economics Association (AAEA). He received the AAEA's awards for Outstanding Published Research (1952, 1954, 1957) and Outstanding Doctoral Dissertation (1953); his first book, *Econometric Analysis for Public Policy* (1958), received the association's award for Publication of Enduring Quality in 1977. His subsequent books include *The Theory of Quantitative Economic Policy* (1966, with J. K. Sengupta and Erik Thorbecke), *Social Indicators and Social Theory* (1974), and *Social System Accounts* (1985).

ROY J. GARDNER is Professor of Economics, Indiana University, Bloomington. He completed his B.S. degree *summa cum laude* at Bradley University in 1968. At Cornell University he was successively Andrew D. White Fellow (1971) and National Science Foundation Fellow, completing his Ph.D. in 1975. He received the Duncan Black Award of the Public Choice Society in 1977, was a Visiting Research Economist at CEPREMAP (Paris) in 1979-1980, and is currently (1985-1986) a Humboldt Foundation Research Fellow at the University of Bonn. He has published pathbreaking articles on the Borda game, core and value for a public goods economy, wealth and power in a collegial polity, and other topics in economic theory, social choice, comparative systems, and mathematical economics.

GLENN L. JOHNSON is Professor of Agricultural Economics, Michigan State University, East Lansing, and holds a Distinguished Faculty Award from that institution. He has published extensively on production economics, farm management, agricultural policy, agricultural development, agricultural sector analysis, and more recently on research methodology and philosophic issues relevant for economists and agricultural economists. He is a Fellow of the American Agricultural Economics Association and received the association's awards for Outstanding Published Research in 1953 and 1959. He served as vice president for program of the International Association of Agricultural Economists from 1976 to 1979, president-elect from 1979 to 1982, and president from 1982 to 1985. He has organized and directed multidisciplinary studies of the agricultural sectors of Nigeria, Korea, and the United States, using general systems simulation and other approaches. His book *Research Methodology for Economists* was published in 1986. He was awarded the Theodor Brinkman Prize of the University of Bonn in 1985.

MICHAEL S. LAWLOR is Assistant Professor of Economics, Wake Forest University, Winston-Salem, North Carolina. He received his B.A. from the University of Texas at Austin in 1981, and his Ph.D. from Iowa State University at Ames in 1986. His current research interests are in the history of economic theory and monetary economics.

DON G. MILES is a Lecturer in Agricultural Economics at the Muresk Institute of Agriculture Campus of the Western Australian Institute of Technology (W.A.I.T.). He received a Diploma in Agriculture in 1971 and a Bachelor of Business Degree with

Distinction in 1981, both from W.A.I.T. In 1981, Mr. Miles was recipient of the Wansbrough Prize for the paper, "Rice: A World Food," and was Dux of the Muresk Degree. He received a Master of Science from Iowa State University in Economics during 1983. The creative component for his M.S. degree was described as "highly original and profound" by the examining committee, and was titled "Wholistic Analysis, Problem Shifting Analysis, and Systems Economics." He is completing his doctoral studies under Professor John Dillon at the University of New England in New South Wales, Australia. Mr. Miles is currently Head of Agricultural Economics and Marketing at the Muresk Institute of Agriculture, Muresk, 6401, Western Australia.

JAMES R. PRESCOTT is Professor of Economics at Iowa State University, Ames. He was a junior year Phi Beta Kappa at the University of California, Berkeley (1956), and received the Economics Department Prize in 1957. At Harvard he was successively Woodrow Wilson Fellow, Amelia Earhart Fellow, I.B.M. Fellow, and Teaching Fellow in the university computing center, completing his Ph.D. in 1964. He has collaborated on land use and transportation planning models for several metropolitan regions and a large-scale systems simulation model for Iowa in terms of 120 counties and small cities. His books include *Economic Aspects of Public Housing* (1974), *Urban-Regional Economic Growth and Policy* (1975, with W. Cris Lewis), and *An Economic Simulation Model for Regional Development Planning* (1975, with Herbert H. Fullerton). He has consulted on regional planning and central place systems in several countries.

JATI K. SENGUPTA is Professor of Economics and Operations Research, University of California, Santa Barbara. He received the Duff Scholarship (1951-1953), Jubilee Scholarship (1955), and University Gold Medal (1955) from Calcutta University. In 1960 he received a Fulbright Scholarship to study in the United States and was designated a Centennial Scholar at Iowa State University in 1962. He has published extensively in the fields of econometrics, operations research, and mathematical economics, and has made significant contributions in stochastic economics, including stochastic programming and the economics of uncertainty. His books include *The Theory of Quantitative Economic Policy* (1966, with K. A. Fox and Erik Thorbecke), *Economic Analysis and Operations Research* (1969, with K. A. Fox), *Stochastic Economics* (1972, with Gerhard Tintner), *Stochastic Programming: Methods and Applications* (1972), *Decision Models in Stochastic Programming* (1982), *Optimal Decisions under Uncertainty* (1985), *Information and Efficiency in Economic Decision* (1985), and *Stochastic Optimization and Economic Models* (1986).

PAUL VAN MOESEKE is Professor and Head, Department of Economics, Massey University, Palmerston North, New Zealand. He received degrees "with great distinction" from Ghent University (1956) and Louvain University (1959). He was a CRB Fellow and Woodrow Wilson Fellow at Yale 1960-1962 and received his Ph.D. at Yale "with distinction" in 1964. In 1969 he received the Alumni Award in the Social Sciences of the Belgian Science Foundations, their highest award for university scientists under 37. He has published pathbreaking articles on stochastic and parametric linear programming, homogeneous programming, the Le Chatelier principle in convex programming, value cores for finite agents, the theory of efficiency, and scalar measures of social income; he also edited _Mathematical Programs for Activity Analysis_ (1974). He was decorated an Officer of the Order of Leopold (Belgium) in 1976.

INTRODUCTION

KARL A. FOX and DON G. MILES

The objectives of this book are to describe, develop, and advocate a systems approach to economics and to illustrate the prospective scope and power of this approach. The essays by Boulding, Lawlor, and Gardner are general in nature; those by Miles, Fox, van Moeseke, and Prescott are applied. The chapters by Sengupta and Johnson have both general and applied aspects; somewhat arbitrarily we have included Sengupta's in the former category and Johnson's in the latter.

We believe there is an urgent need for graduate instruction in a new field which we call *systems economics*. This volume of essays is an initial contribution to the literature of the field. Most of the essays cite other references which also belong in the systems economics literature.

We hope this volume will encourage some readers to experiment with courses or seminars in systems economics or systems approaches to multidisciplinary research. Such experiments will give shape and content to the field and determine its place in the graduate (and advanced undergraduate) training of economists and agricultural economists.

Many of the noneconomic concepts would be introduced or adapted from general systems theory. Several chapters of *Systems Economics* contribute to this objective. Other chapters are designed to facilitate communication between economists and other social and behavioral scientists. All chapters should encourage recognition that cooperation between economists and other scientists can be mutually advantageous and communication natural and relatively easy in a systems framework.

How fast and how far systems economics will develop depends on the quality and enthusiasm of those who are attracted to the field. Shackle (1967, pp. 2-3) describes three episodes in which economics happened to attract a particularly able group of young contemporaries:

> In the mid-eighteenth century economics was founded as a systematic discipline by Cantillon, the Physiocrats and Adam Smith. In the last third of the nineteenth, it suddenly took on a new unity and elegance in the hands of a very remarkable group of men of many countries, all born in the years 1840-51, who founded the notion of general equilibrium on the three pillars of a subjective theory of value, the application of the differential calculus to moral science, and the conception of the universal inter-penetrating influence of every economic quantity on every other. Their work and outlook were dominant for more than half a century, and, of course, it lies still at the heart of economics. But in the 1920s and 1930s it was suddenly found to be not enough. Attention was called by contemporary fact to the vagaries of money and the general price level, and then to the bewildering phenomenon of general heavy unemployment. These problems attracted a number of highly gifted minds from diverse scholarly beginnings, not only economics itself but mathematics, classics, and physics, and the result was a great ferment of new work at the heart of economic theory.

Shackle's second group, which included Walras, Pareto, Jevons, Menger, Marshall, Wicksteed, Wicksell, and John Bates Clark, constructed "the Great Theory" of general equilibrium economics which Shackle (p. 290) also refers to as "the Economics of Tranquillity, that is, of Confident Foresight." Its assumption of a stable, knowable, and foreseeable world seemed tenable as a first approximation to reality during 1871-1913 while Western Europe was at peace. The cataclysm of World War I, followed by hyperinflation in some countries and (later) by mass unemployment in nearly all, dramatized the irreducible lack of knowledge and the impossibility of perfect foresight among human decision makers. Shackle's third group, including Keynes, Kahn, Joan Robinson, Harrod, Hicks, Meade, Kalecki, Lerner, Myrdal, Lindahl, Lundberg, Frisch, Alvin Hansen, Samuelson, Kaldor, and others, created a new theory of general output and employment and a new economics of uncertainty. From 1926 through 1939 this younger group, including Leontief, Chamberlin, Tinbergen, Sraffa, and Allen in addition to those already named, made at least six major innovations in economic theory and econometrics. Collectively, they brought economic theory into much closer conformity with contemporary facts.

Can systems economics provide the impetus for another wave of innovations in the formulation and solution of current problems? While Shackle's third group worked <u>within</u> economics, many of our current problems will require us to go <u>beyond</u> economics and to cooperate on equal terms with scientists from other disciplines. We believe that general systems theory provides the most promising framework for such cooperation.

Systems theory will certainly aid in the reformulation of

many problems which are wholly economic, as illustrated in Gardner's essay (Chapter 3). To that extent, systems economics can be developed as a special field within economics having close ties to mathematical economics and econometrics and paying little attention to other disciplines. However, we believe systems economics will be particularly important in conceptualizing problems which include social and/or environmental as well as economic components.

Johnson (Chapter 5) presents this view convincingly and illustrates it from his own extensive experience with systems simulation models of the agricultural sectors of less-developed countries. Miles (Chapter 6) gives a concrete application of the systems approach to a small enterprise involving biological, physical, economic, and sociopolitical aspects. Fox (Chapter 7) proposes a system of social accounts based on people's allocations of time among units of their immediate social and physical environments called _behavior settings_. This "eco-behavioral view of human societies" has interfaces with nearly all social and behavioral sciences and is inherently multidisciplinary. Prescott (Chapter 9) outlines a dynamic microanalytical simulation model of a small community which would use behavior settings as basic units and yield in each period a set of time-allocation matrices and other social accounting tables for the community.

Sengupta devotes the bulk of his Chapter 4 to problems of modeling eco-behavioral systems, which include both economic and noneconomic behavior settings. van Moeseke (Chapter 8) crosses disciplinary lines with two models for estimating the dollar values of social variables. Lawlor (Chapter 2) contends that the economy must be modeled as an open system if we are to account for the sources and distribution of information used by economic agents; hence (implicitly) we must go outside the economy to develop a realistic explanation of economic events. Boulding (Chapter 1) takes a universal view of "economics in the general system of the world."

Given these examples and others cited in the chapter references, it seems best (taking our cue from Viner) to define systems economics provisionally as "what systems economists do." The contributors will speak for themselves without further introduction. Chapter 10 attempts a summary and overview of the contributions. Appendix 1 (Miles) gives additional background on the development of systems economics, and Appendix 2 (Fox) discusses classic examples of systems thinking in several sciences.

REFERENCES

Shackle, G. L. S. 1967. _The Years of High Theory: Invention and Tradition in Economic Thought, 1926-1939_. Cambridge: Cambridge University Press.

PART 1

General

1

The Economy as an Ecosystem: Economics in the General System of the World

KENNETH E. BOULDING

This beautiful planet on which we live is a subset of the universe. It is indeed an open system with inputs of energy from the sun and outputs of transformed energy and heat to space, a few inputs of matter from the solar system and outputs of human artifacts in space vehicles. Nevertheless, this world is still a very self-contained general system in three dimensions of space and one of time. The human mind has an extraordinary capacity for forming images, imperfect though they may be, of total systems, even those which lie far beyond immediate personal experience. The formation of images of the larger system is, indeed, one of the principal interests of the scientific community.

DESCRIPTION

The question of how we describe a system in its totality in a way that can be transmitted from one human mind to another is perhaps the most fundamental problem of human learning and epistemology. We start off with a state description of the system at a given moment of time. This might be called a "frame," a flashlight photograph, and a succession of frames forms the description of the system in space and time, like a movie. The total system is so large and so complex that it cannot possibly be described completely, and the question arises as to how we map the system in models, which can be described and which characterize what we think of as the significant structures of the system. Ordinary maps, indeed, are good examples. A globe gives us a general picture of the distribution of the earth between land and water, mountains and plains, rivers, cities, political boundaries, and so on. It contains an enormous amount of human knowledge, accumulated very painfully over many centuries and summarized in a remarkably succinct form. Furthermore, there is a hierarchy of maps on different scales. For many areas of the world we can get large-scale topographical maps, even detailed maps of our own house, and an X ray or a CAT scan of our own body. In a way we really do not understand, our capacity for consciousness and reflection enables us to map even our mind and the structures which lie within the body, particularly within the skull.

Another way of mapping is by enumeration, measuring, and aggregation. When we take a census, we get a good deal of information about almost every person in the census area, and we can manipulate this data statistically into categories and taxonomies, proportions, correlations, and so on. We do accounting and make a balance sheet, which summarizes the assets and liabilities of an organization or a person, aggregating values into monetary units, like the dollar, without regard to the type or location of the items involved.

In our state description, we can also identify changes which are going on, even though these do not appear until the next frame in the time sequence as described. We can state that a particular object is moving with a certain velocity, has a certain acceleration. We can state that some things are growing, some are declining, some things are being added, some subtracted, and some transformations are going on. Wheat, for instance, is being ground into flour. I am in the middle of dictating this paper. All of these things are part of the state description, though they will not be observable until subsequent states in the future.

Now we introduce time into the picture and examine two successive state descriptions, or frames. We can describe the change that has happened between the first and the second. We can actually make a map of these changes, like a time chart. We can even make one in three dimensions. Suppose, for instance, we made a transparent map of the world for each day of a person's life, put a dot on it to indicate where the person was, and then pile these maps in chronological order, perhaps from birth or even conception right through to death. Then we would have a kind of transparent cube within which the path of the individual would be seen as a kind of worm rising through the time dimension, shooting around the world as the person travels, and then ending at death. We usually think of it as rather insulting to call a person a worm, but in the four-dimensional space in which we really live the analogy is not altogether unfounded. We can see all of human history as a vast pattern of worms in our space-time cube, originating, perhaps, in a thin stream coming out of Africa and looking a bit like a nuclear explosion as we spread around the world and multiply. Where two of these worms of opposite sexes intersect and an egg is fertilized, one, or occasionally more, of these worms start off from the point of intersection.

The cube map, however, also illustrates the inadequacy of maps to express the totality of the system. Each point in the "worm" which represents a single human being, in reality represents an organization of quite literally inconceivable complexity, composed of billions upon billions of atoms and molecules, some ten to a hundred billion neurons, knowledge structures, emotions, desires, values, and so on, which it certainly seems almost indecent to represent by a point on a map. We could add one more dimension to the map by coloring the point on it, but this is about as far toward _n_ dimensions as we can get in maps.

PREDICTION

The situation is further complicated by the fact that we are looking for something beyond description into prediction or at least projection. From our description or image of the past, we want to be able to make predictions of the future. The main reason for this is that we are decision-making organizations, and every decision is a choice among an agenda of images of the future. Therefore, we have a very strong interest in having these images of the future realistic--that is, capable of being realized when we choose one. This is why we have to go beyond maps, even in four or five dimensions, because if we are to form reasonably accurate images of the state description of tomorrow, we must have models which relate at least two successive frames of state descriptions.

In order to predict, therefore, the state description of today, we must include a description of change. A tennis player perceives a ball not only in its position in the air at a moment in time, but also in terms of its velocity and perhaps its deceleration, or even the change in its rate of deceleration, if he is a real champion. So he is able to make a decision which involves a future in which his ball hits his racket and rebounds within the limits of the other side of the court.

It is an interesting question as to whether all the information that is necessary to make the best possible prediction of tomorrow can be contained in the state description of today, or whether we also have to have state descriptions of yesterday, the day before, and so on. If our model is one of difference equations, a first-order equation enables us to predict tomorrow from today, whereas if we have a second-order equation, we have to know yesterday and today in order to predict tomorrow, and so on. If we have differential equations, however, which include such things as velocity and acceleration, we only need today's description in order to characterize tomorrow's. This looks like a fairly simple question, but I am not sure there is any easy answer to it. Certainly things that happen between today and tomorrow may depend on other things which happened a long time ago. Between today and tomorrow I am going to age, and probably lose a few neurons, but how much I will age may depend on the particular combination of chromosomes that happened when my egg was fertilized in 1909. On the other hand, the genetic patterns that were formed when my egg was fertilized are still around in my body today, though perhaps modified by things that have happened since. Perhaps my current genetic structure is all I really need to know in order to predict how much I am going to age, even though this kind of knowledge is far beyond our present capability.

Just as there are hierarchies of maps, there are hierarchies of models. The simplest model is that where nothing is happening at all, in which case prediction is remarkably easy. The probability that a salt crystal in an abandoned salt mine will be there tomorrow is so close to 1.0 as to be virtually identical with it. Of course, even there, there is some probability, however small, that the mine might be hit by a meteorite large enough to vaporize it. Even this improbable example illustrates a fundamental principle which might be called the "third law of epistemological dynamics"--that absolute certainty is unobtainable. The third law of thermodynamics is that absolute zero can never be reached because the closer we get to it, the harder it is to get any further. Similarly, the closer we get to absolute knowledge about the future, the harder it is to get any further. There is always an irreducible minimum of uncertainty.

The next level of models is those that have constant parameters. With the possible exception of the expansion of the universe (I do not know whether this has constant parameters--I rather doubt it), virtually all the systems of this type with which we are familiar are cyclical; otherwise, they would either expand or contract beyond our means of perception. A good example is the rotation of the earth, the cycle of day and night; the probability that the sun will rise tomorrow is, again, extremely close to 1.0. The cycle of the seasons which results from the rotation of the earth around the sun is highly predictable: "If winter comes, can spring be far behind?" The cycle of the planets makes very accurate prediction possible, for instance, of eclipses, although it did take us a long time to catch on to how to do it in the more complex systems. It is important to realize, however, that the success of prediction in celestial mechanics is a result of the fact that evolution of the solar system has virtually ceased and that nothing is really happening. This is only a slightly more sophisticated form of prediction than the one that the salt crystal will be around tomorrow.

EQUILIBRIA

Perhaps the next level of model, which I suspect is only found in rather rough approximations in the real world, might be called the "ergodic system," in which the individual components change but the system does not. An equilibrium population is a very good example in which age distributions are constant, age-specific birth and death rates are constant, total births are equal to total deaths, and every year there are the same number of people of each age and sex. In such a population, the age distribution is exactly the same as the survival distribution of a cohort of births over time.

Cross-sections are the same as time patterns. We see this perhaps most clearly in an organization that sustains a given role structure. In a college, for instance, seniors graduate, juniors become seniors, sophomores become juniors, freshmen become sophomores, and a new class of freshmen is admitted. As faculty retire, new younger faculty are appointed. A president leaves, retires, or dies; a new president is appointed; and so on. Wherever there is a role structure and an apparatus for sustaining it, individuals change but the organization does not. However, this is never the case in practice. All organizations tend either to grow or to decay, as do individual organisms. Homeostasis as described, for instance, by the great physiologist, Cannon, is a quasi-ergodic process. Breakfast depreciates and we replace it with lunch, cells abrade from our skin and are replaced, we get sick and recover, we get hot and cool off, we get cold and warm up, and so on. On the other hand, these equilibrium processes are imperfect, for the organism continually ages irreversibly. It is rather interesting that of two recently competing theories of cosmology, the more ergodic theory (which is Hoyle's)--that the universe maintains a steady state through the constant creation or destruction of something or other--as over against the "big bang" and expanding universe theory, which is strictly nonergodic, the latter seems to be winning out.

Nevertheless, there are enough quasi-ergodic systems around to make the concept of equilibrium useful, even though in a strict sense equilibrium is unknown in the real world. Heraclitus was supposed to have said, "You cannot step into the same river twice," but it might be more accurate to say you cannot step into the same water twice, but you can step into the same river. A section of the river that is flowing at a constant velocity and volume of water is a very nice example of an equilibrium population of water molecules, although it will exhibit some unpredictable turbulence and, of course, it may possibly flood. It is rare even for a flood, however, to completely change the course of the river. Here again, we run into the principle that only stabilities enable us to predict, perhaps even to perceive.

Ecosystems are again very nice examples of quasi-equilibrium systems. They are a little more complex than an equilibrium population, as they consist of many different populations in interaction with each other. If we suppose, however, in an isolated system that the birth and death rate of the population of each species is a function of the set of all populations in the system, including, of course, its own population, we have a nice system of *n* equations and *n* unknowns, which economists will recognize immediately. This system may have a solution, which, again, with a bit of luck, may represent a stable equilibrium within certain limits. If we take 25 percent of a given kind of fish out of a lake, it is highly probable that the population will recover in three or four mating seasons, if nothing else happens. If we take 90 percent of the fish out, of course, it may not recover. If we take 100 percent out, it will certainly not recover.

NICHES AND PARAMETRIC CHANGE

The species of an ecosystem include not only biological species but populations of water molecules, soil particles of various kinds, chemicals, air, and certain underlying parameters, like temperature, cyclical changes, and so on. Any change in the parameters of such a system will change the position of the equilibrium. This can happen through genetic mutation which creates another biological species, climate change, soil erosion, drought, and so on. An equilibrium population of a particular species is perhaps the best definition of a niche and, of course, these niches are constantly changing. One important concept here is that of the empty niche--that is, a species which would have an equilibrium population if it existed.

Evolution, which is next in the hierarchy of models, then consists in the filling of empty niches through parametric change. This may be either by migration, as, for instance, when rabbits were introduced into Australia, where there was clearly an empty niche for them, or it may be by genetic mutation. Since the advent of the human race, human artifacts, which are as much species in the world ecosystem as anything else, are created by invention and may expand into an empty niche if one exists for them. If an empty niche is filled, of course, all the other niches change. Some may shrink to zero, in which case the species that corresponds to it becomes extinct.

Whether the evolutionary process itself has patterns, even if only in the sense that some patterns are more probable than others, is a question that only admits a very imperfect answer in our present state of knowledge. The record of the past certainly suggests that, on this earth at least, evolution has certain directionalities or "time's arrows." One is towards greater complexity. I have little doubt that I am more complex than a virus or an amoeba, which have been around much longer as species. One can detect also a movement to what might be called control--the ability of the organism to change its environment or to sustain desirable environments, whether internal or external. The development of the senses, mobility, warm-bloodedness, and in the human race, its extraordinary capacity to create artificial environments, even on the moon, are all examples of this process. Perhaps linked with this there is the movement toward cleverness or consciousness, the development of structures within the organism which map, as we have seen, into its total environment, including itself. I think we still do not understand how these directionalities come about, but perhaps one hint is that there are more likely to be empty niches in an ecosystem at higher levels of complexity, control, or cleverness than there are at the lower levels, for the lower levels are likely to have been filled already.

What is clear, however, is that the pattern of evolution in space/time is a highly indeterminate system. It is not merely stochastic in the sense of the law of large numbers, where random elements cancel themselves out in favor of an overall pattern. The probability that an empty niche will be filled before it closes is never equal to 1.0. If it is filled, the history of the world will be very different from what it would have been if it were not filled. The evolutionary process is studded with the actual happening of very rare events at particular times and places. _When_ rare events happened makes an enormous difference to the overall dynamics of the system.

Even here, there may be patterns which are somewhat independent of the timing of these rare events. We do seem to perceive, for instance, something like what has been called _emergent evolution_--that there may be different paths toward some goal that is a very good idea. The development of the eye of vertebrates and of the invertebrates, ending up with the mammals on one side and the octopus on the other, is perhaps an example. A somewhat similar niche structure, for instance, of birds in the Oceanic islands, where reptiles and mammals never reached, or among the marsupials in Australia or the placentals in the rest of the world, suggests that there may be some basic pattern of niche structures which will be filled in some way or other with fair degrees of probability.

COMPLEXITY, PREDICTABILITY, AND CONSTRAINTS

The more complex the system we are considering, the more difficult it is to apply any simple concepts of cause and effect. When everything depends on everything else, as it does in ecosystems, it is by no means easy to discover exactly what depends on what. Systems of this kind particularly are also what I call "echo-systems," in which a particular event echoes and re-echoes all over the system. Something which happens to A affects B, which affects C, which affects D, and so on all through innumerable alphabets. It is often very hard to tell where the final result comes out. This is especially true, of course, in systems that have fundamental indeterminacy, as evolutionary systems have and, indeed, any system has which involves information or its derivatives as an essential feature. The old story that if we had tomorrow's newspaper it would not happen is a good illustration of the problem of the fundamental unpredictability of systems involving information, which is not mere ignorance but a property of the system itself. No amount of increase in human knowledge can turn an essentially indeterminate system into a determinate one, unless, of course, the system itself is changed.

We must not rule out the capacity of human beings to change systems in directions that make them more predictable. A good example of this, of course, is the thermostat. We can predict the temperature of a room with a thermostat as long as the system functions properly much more successfully than we can predict the temperature outside. The development of increasing control in the evolutionary process indeed might be thought of as involving a move toward greater predictability. I can predict my own blood temperature tomorrow more successfully than I can the temperature outside because I too have a thermostat, even though it may occasionally break down when I get a fever and will break down completely in death, when I go to the temperature of the environment as a corpse.

Increased knowledge in systems of this kind involves much more knowledge about limits and constraints than it does about cause and effect. A system may have strong random elements in it and yet may exhibit constraints beyond which it cannot go, at least without changing the system. The body is a case in point. Every system is constrained by its potentials, although even here we cannot rule out the re-creation of potential as it is exhausted. Conservation principles impose important limits. Physical laws, indeed, may be thought of as limits on biological and social systems rather than as causes. These limits often take the form of identities, or near-identities. It is one of the functions of mathematics to search for new identities, for mathematics in a sense is the study of identities--that is, of relationships which cannot be otherwise from what they are. A good deal of experience and empirical knowledge consists of finding where in the real world the essential identities and limitations apply.

THE ECONOMY AS AN ECOSYSTEM: PART OF THE GENERAL SYSTEM

How, then, does economics fit into all this? Like all important sets, it is fuzzy, but we can identify it roughly as that part of the world system which consists of those human artifacts that are actually or potentially exchangeable and human activity, insofar as it is directed toward the production, transportation, utilization, exchange, and consumption of exchangeable human artifacts. Human artifacts, it should be noted, consist not only of material artifacts like houses, automobiles, and teacups but of organizational artifacts like families, governments, and firms, (some of which, especially firms, are occasionally exchanged); and also human capital or human persons (who are partly biological artifacts from the fertilized egg but also partly artifacts of the human society around them in terms of language, learning, skills, even nutrition and health up to a point). If we define economics as the study of that subset of the world system which consists of commodities, we have at least covered a good deal of it, even though we cannot always be sure what is a commodity and what is not. Among the human artifacts that are commodities we have to count money, debt, financial instruments, stocks, obligations, promises of various kinds, and so on.

We start off, then, with the state description of the economy. This consists in the first instance of real capital--that is, the itemized list or position statement of all elements of economically significant sets. This includes consumer capital--the clothes on my back and in my closet, houses, furniture, books, automobiles--which constitutes my household environment and which in developed societies is probably the larger part of real capital as a whole. We must list also all buildings, stores, factories, inventories, machines, railroads, airplanes, land, materials (even in the mine), the fish in fishing boats (more doubtfully perhaps the fish in the sea), forests, growing plants--the list is very long.

In a system of widespread exchange, we can add the system of relative prices and of valuation coefficients to the physical stocks and get a value for each item in terms of some measure of value or money of account. Someone may have a hundred bushels of wheat. If this is valued at $4 per bushel, the total value is $400, $4 per bushel being the valuation coefficient. It is usually related somewhat to some exchanges which have gone on or are expected to go on. We can group these items a number of ways, first of all into balance sheets which list all the items which are in some sense the property or obligations of a particular organization or person. Balance sheets will contain items, like debt, which are negative assets--that is, liabilities to the debtor and positive assets to the creditor. There is a certain law of conservation here that when we add up all the balance sheets of the world, debts should cancel out, though it is not always clear that they do, which is perhaps why we have financial crises. Balance sheets usually have a "bottom line" of the net worth of the person or organization associated with it, which is simply the positive assets minus the negative ones. If the net worth is negative, the person or organization is insolvent. This does not necessarily mean that it cannot function, but it does mean that it is a little threatened.

When we look at the total list of assets, valuations, and balance sheets of the following day, we will find they have changed. Some, perhaps, are unchanged. One hundred dollars in cash or bank deposit today is $100 tomorrow if nothing has happened to it, although this may be just a misleading accounting convention, especially if there is inflation or deflation. All physical capital, including human bodies and minds, have aged by one day. In most cases, this means that their value in the unit account has diminished. There are exceptions to this, as in the maturing of wines, perhaps even in the maturing of minds (who knows?), the evaluation of rare paintings, and so on. It is a tricky question whether depreciation is in the quantity or price or valuation coefficient, and we can put that one aside. The relative price structure will have changed, although perhaps not all the items in it. And insofar as valuation coefficients are linked to the relative price structure, those stocks of things that have gone up in relative price will have increased in value, those that have gone down will have decreased, and this will produce changes in virtually all bottom lines or net worths.

Other important changes involve production and consumption. Production is equivalent to the birth and consumption to the death of assets. Production, however, nearly always involves various transformations, the death of some things and the birth of others. When wheat is ground into flour, wheat diminishes and flour increases. If money is used to pay labor to do the grinding, money and wheat diminish and flour increases. If the mill wears out, its value as an asset is diminished. Production, therefore, always involves asset transformation, the diminution of some assets and increases in others. According to cost accounting conventions, the value of what is produced is equal to the value of what has been destroyed in the course of its production. What is destroyed is a cost of what is produced. There is, however, a form of consumption which does not produce anything else. If my clothes wear out, the energy and materials in my body are used up keeping me warm and have to be replaced by food, and so on. The tricky problem here is whether there is a real distinction between goods and services; it can be argued that services are merely goods of short length of life or that services create psychological goods. When I go to an opera, a psychological good is created in my mind called "just having gone to an opera." If this depreciates very rapidly, I may have to go to another opera next week; if I am not an opera buff, it may take years to depreciate. This is in principle no different from the fact that lunch restores the energy and materials I have lost since breakfast.

What we are describing here begins to look a little bit like an ecosystem of commodities, but it also looks like a quasi-ergodic system. Each commodity has a stock which is a population, which is added to by production and subtracted from by consumption. If consumption equals production, the stock of commodities will be stable. If consumption exceeds production, it will decline. If production exceeds consumption, it will increase. The equilibrium of the price system, which economists are very fond of, certainly corresponds to something in reality and is a kind of intermediary in this ecological equilibrium of commodities. If we postulate an equilibrium set of relative prices, any other set will have some prices that are "too high" and some that are "too low." If a price is too high, then the terms of trade of the producers of the item in question will be "too favorable"--that is, they may be perceived as getting too much for what they give. This will attract other people into that occupation, production will increase, stocks will increase, and this will bring down the price. A similar line of argument says if the price is too low, it will rise. This is very similar to the principle in ecosystems that if a species has a population less than its niche or equilibrium level, conditions will be favorable for it, births will exceed deaths, and the population will rise. If the population exceeds the equilibrium, conditions will be harsher, deaths will exceed births, and the population will fall. Adam Smith's famous Book I: Chapter 7 of The Wealth of Nations, indeed, could well be listed as the first clear statement of an ecological equilibrium.

The economic system, however, is an evolutionary system as well as an ecological one because, as in the biosphere, in the ecosystem of commodities the parameters change. The most striking change, of course, is that of technical innovation which lowers the cost of a particular commodity--that is, reduces what has to be sacrificed in order to produce a unit. This will have two effects: It will diminish the equilibrium relative to price; it will also expand the production, consumption, and stock of the commodity if its durability has not changed and, depending on the extent of this expansion (which as all economists know depends largely on the elasticity of demand and perhaps on the elasticity of supply of the cost elements), there may be a release of resources and populations, so that stocks, production, and consumption of other commodities may also increase. On the other hand, there may also be a diminution in commodities that are competitive. If so, the whole structure of niches will change.

The models of the classical economists, especially Adam Smith and David Ricardo, were perhaps even closer to ecological models than are those of modern economics, especially since Walras, because classical economics had a very clear notion of the food chain, a concept beloved of ecologists. Those commodities the diminution of which constitutes costs are, in a sense, the food of the product, often in a fairly literal sense. We feed grass to a cow and we get milk and meat. We feed grain to farm laborers and farmers and they produce more grain than they eat. The surplus grain can be fed to shoemakers, along with leather, and turned into shoes. We feed wool and food to weavers and it produces cloth. We feed iron ore and food to iron founders and it produces steel, and so on. What increases the niche of a species tends to be a change in parameters which makes for a more efficient utilization of food and other inputs into the organism and also, of course, changes which increase the survival rate of individuals and their capacity to reproduce.

The concept of the empty niche is very useful in explaining the particular forms which economic development takes. An element in the economic system which is found only in very primitive forms in the biosphere is that of demand as a niche creator.

Niches are created by the willingness of people to buy things, and this goes back to certain structures of wants, for the satisfaction of which various substitutes may be available. My favorite example is the chain of events which begins with the demand for artifical illumination, as humans do not seem biologically to be timed to going to bed and getting up with the sun, especially in winter. This made for niches for primitive oil lamps and for candles. As candle wax was rather scarce and it was hard to increase its output very much, this created a niche for whale oil in the nineteenth century once shipbuilding had got to the point where whales could be caught. The continuing increase in population, however, led to overkilling of whales and a scarcity of whale oil. It is not surprising that this created a niche for kerosene, which was distilled from oil after 1858. This, however, produced gasoline as a by-product, which was mostly burned off. This, in turn, opened up a niche for the internal combustion engine, which certainly had not existed in, say, 1830, when there was no gasoline. It is not surprising that the automobile was invented and moved rapidly into an ever-expanding niche and created niches for gas stations, repair shops, iron ore mines, rubber plantations, shopping malls, and emergency wards in hospitals. It is a good example of how an empty niche that is filled creates large numbers of other empty niches and, of course, may diminish some of those that are already filled.

Another feature in which the economy has something in common with the biosphere is in the nature of production itself. Production in both cases not only involves transformation of materials but also requires a genetic factor that might be called "know-how," which may, however, be limited in its realization by the absence of appropriate materials, energy, or even space and time. All production, whether from the divided cell or the fertilized egg, or the blueprint or plan for a house or an automobile, begins with some kind of know-how structure. This has to be able to direct energy and information to the selection, transportation, and transformation of materials into the probable structures of the product. The main difference between human artifacts and biological products is that human artifacts are "multiparental" in that the know-how structures which produce them are embodied in large numbers of different human beings and human artifacts. Thus, an automobile is produced by the knowledge contained in innumerable planners, draftsmen, researchers, coal and iron miners, shippers, assembly-line workers, executives, lawyers, and so on for a very large list. The genetic structure that produces the automobile is not contained in the automobile itself, as it is in biological artifacts. This is a fairly fundamental difference and, of course, accounts for the extraordinary proliferation of human artifacts and the tremendous speedup in the evolutionary process that has taken place since the advent of *Homo sapiens*, but the production process is essentially very similar.

Another feature of the economy which is not found in the biosphere is money and the specialized parts of the economy, including human artifacts, which are specialized in the process of exchange itself. Something like exchange is present in the biosphere in terms of organisms taking things in and giving things out, but there is practically nothing that looks like barter. Trees give off oxygen and take in carbon dioxide, and the animal kingdom takes in oxygen and gives off carbon dioxide. This is a kind of exchange, but it certainly does not involve "trade." There is no consciousness on the part of any of the participants as to what is taking place, and there is certainly no negotiation of the terms. Another feature of economic life not found in the biosphere is debt (negative assets), which permits an enormously complex structure of property. There are primitive forms of property in the biosphere in terms of the parental care of children, quarreling over territory, and so on, but these nowhere begin to approach the immense complexity of property relations in the economy.

Because of all this complexity, the economy is capable of pathologies and perversions that are virtually unknown in the biosphere. The most striking of these are inflation, deflation, and unemployment, for which it is hard to think of any biological parallel. A biological ecosystem, indeed, is free private enterprise beyond the dreams of Milton Friedman and exhibits an "invisible hand" in ecological equilibrium, even in recovery from catastrophe, like a forest fire, but it has no government and evidently does not need one. The economic system, however, can hardly exist in the absence of government, although Hong Kong certainly shows that it can exist quite successfully when government is minimal. It is hard to visualize exchange, however, without the institution of property, for we cannot exchange what does not belong to us, and property is essentially more a creation of the legitimated threat system than it is a creation of exchange itself. There are examples of things like silent trade, where two tribes who have no common government and hate each other so much they cannot even meet without fighting conduct trade by some convention which is beneficial to all parties and therefore continues. But any elaborate system of trading, and certainly any system of finance, would be impossible in the absence of the sanctions of the law and the protection of property from too much theft and dishonesty.

There are certain parallels to the property concept in the biosphere in territoriality, nests, beaver dams, termite colonies and the like, but they are not related to any real system of exchange, though they may be an important regulator of population. There is a great deal to be said for a housing shortage rather than a food shortage as the limit which creates the niche.

Two phenomena in the economy for which it is hard to find any parallel in the biosphere are unemployment and inflation and, of course, a combination of them that we call "stagflation." Where there is no money, there can be no inflation or deflation; and it is tempting also to regard employment as something which would be most unlikely to occur in the absence of money, for instance in a pure barter economy, but which is also related to other elements in the system besides the monetary aspects. There is involuntary unemployment when the quantity of labor demanded by employers is less at the existing wage structure than employees and potential employees would like to supply. Economists being brought up on price theory are tempted to explain this in terms of either money wages or real wages that are in some sense too high and where there are institutional obstacles to lowering them. This is, however, too simple a picture. In the first place, as Keynes pointed out, the labor market usually determines only money wages, and a fall in money wages does not necessarily involve a fall in real wages if the price of wage goods falls as fast.

The situation is complicated also by the fact that demand for labor is affected both by the existing stock of inventories and also by the difference between rates of interest and rates of profit. Whenever an employer hires an employee, two things happen in the employer's balance sheet: Cash goes down as the wage is paid out, and inventories or capital values of some sort, which is the product of the work, go up. This may not take the form of saleable goods; it may involve the restoration of depreciated fixed capital, even just the maintenance of a plant or the disposal of garbage. In any case, there is a change in the structure of real capital in the employer's balance sheet, and it is a commonplace of economics that a rational employer will not hire somebody unless the diminution in cash is more than offset by an increase in the value of real capital produced by the work. Marginal productivity theory, of course, assumes that the quantity of labor employed will be that at which an additional unit of labor adds the same amount to the value of the capital that is subtracted from the money spent in the wage. The assumption here is that as any kind of labor is employed, the more that it is employed, the less the marginal product, and only when the marginal product equals the marginal wage will the increase in employment stop.

Another factor in the situation which is often neglected is the fact that hiring somebody means not just a sacrifice of cash but a sacrifice of what the cash might have bought, particularly in terms of interest-bearing securities. The increase in the value of the product, therefore, which is marginal profit, must be at a rate at least equal to (and presumably a little greater than) the rate of interest which could be earned by putting the money spent on the wage out to interest. Because of time lags, habits, and custom, this relationship between profit minus interest on the one hand and employment is a loose one. In the years 1932 and 1933, for instance, profits in the United States were about minus 3 percent, and real interest was still about 3 percent. In those years it was not surprising that unemployment was 25 percent. What is surprising is that it was not 75 percent, as almost literally anybody who hired anybody in those years was bound to lose money by it. One can argue that it was only habit that held 75 percent of the economy together and prevented a total collapse.

These considerations do raise some very interesting questions about the future of capitalism as a social system. The Marxian predictions were certainly wrong and Marx's analysis was totally inadequate. This does not mean to say that there might not be a more adequate analysis which would throw light on the potential futures of capitalism. A great deal depends here on what it is that really determines the distribution of national income as between labor income, profit, and interest. Economics still has not really come to grips with this problem. I have made some suggestions about it myself, but these on the whole have been rejected by the profession, which still clings to what seems to me a completely inadequate marginal productivity theory of macro-distribution. My conclusion is there is no nonexistence theorem about the survival of capitalism, but that under some rather improbable circumstances, capitalism could get into conditions that could be even worse than the Great Depression of the 1930s and could easily destroy it.

There are some parallels to these problems in the biosphere. The facts that the oxygen that most living organisms breathe today was the excrement of the first anaerobic organisms and its accumulation certainly killed most of them off suggest that in the evolutionary process biological ecosystems do not have to be stable and may easily contain within themselves the seeds of their own destruction. There is an alarming possibility indeed that the human race itself might destroy this planet on which it has developed and the whole evolutionary process in this part of the universe would come to an end. Every dismal theorem, however, should have a cheerful lemma, which is that if the system learns fast enough, the dismal theorem does not have to be true. Evolutionary systems have been quite clever at avoiding the Malthusian trap. Very few species are really limited by the food supply, and there is certainly no theorem that says we cannot avoid the trap now threatening to engulf us in the breakdown of national defense with the advent of the nuclear weapon. It is an important principle of systems economics that all systems can get into strange and unfamiliar regions and that something can go wrong with anything. I have sometimes called this the "Three Mile Island principle," for that nuclear power station was a good example of it. There are also, however, very powerful dynamic processes of a long-run cybernetic nature that seem to diminish the probabilities of irretrievable disaster. And if disaster is not irretrievable, it will be retrieved, and may even be an important precondition of further evolution.

The parallels between biological evolution and societal evolution--a subset of which is economic development--are striking and not accidental, even though there are also important differences. Both involve ecological interaction (selection) and constant change in parameters (mutation). Both involve entropic processes--the exhaustion of potential--soil erosion, climatic and geological change, the using up of potentials for mutation, the exhaustion of exhaustible resources, and so on. Both must have some mechanisms for limiting populations of species to some ecological niche, whether robins, humans, or automobiles. Both involve anti-entropic processes in the re-creation of potential: Plate tectonics restores eroded mountains. The throughput of energy from the sun restores thermodynamic and gravitational potential as rain falls upstream. Mitosis and fertilization restore biological potential. The increase in human knowledge and discovery restore economic and social potential. Because one of the major human artifacts is images of the future in human minds, societal evolution is teleological in the way that biological evolution is not; our images of the future change the future, though not always in ways that we expect. Societal evolution is overwhelmingly "noogenetic" (learned structures and behaviors transmitted from one generation to the next by a learning process); biological evolution has some noogenetic elements (birds learn some of their birdsong) but is overwhelmingly biogenetic (DNA and all that). This perhaps explains the much more rapid pace of societal evolution, but in spite of these important differences, the basic processes of biological and societal evolution are remarkably similar.

2

Is the Economy a Closed System? General Equilibrium and General Systems Theory

MICHAEL S. LAWLOR

INTRODUCTION

The history of social analysis in general, and economics in particular, exhibits a persistent fascination with attempts to make social theory "scientific."[1] Comte[2] issued the original call for a "Positive Philosophy" of society that would develop general laws of prediction and control to enable the emergent industrial society of the 19th century to realize the same benefits of rationalization at a cultural level that science was already providing at the technological level. After Comte, this matter of fact approach to society is observed as social practice from the elaborate schemes of the Utopian Socialists in the 19th century down to the present in the form of the detailed records of the social accountants more appropriate to a computerized age. Likewise, in the more theoretical work of such diverse thinkers as Mill,[3] Marx,[4] and Samuelson,[5] there runs the common quest for scientific status.

It would, of course, be a mistake to see this cult of science as anything less than the pervasive feature of western civilization. Thorstein Veblen pointed this out 80 years ago:

> On any large question which is to be disposed of for good and all the final appeal is by common consent taken to the scientist. The solution offered in the name of science is decisive so long as it is not set aside by more searching scientific inquiry. . . . There are other, older grounds of finality that may conceivably be better, nobler, worthier, more profound, more beautiful. . . . But whatever the common-sense of earlier generations may have held in this respect, modern common-sense holds that the scientist's

---

The author is grateful to Karl Fox, Robert Hollinger, Bobbie Horn, Tom Kompas, and Charles Meyer for helpful comments and discussion.

answer is the only ultimately true one. (Veblen 1906/1919, pp. 3-4)

It was part of Veblen's genius to work out some of the sociological implications of this exalted "place of science in modern civilization." He also had distinct views on the further question of exactly what standard of scientificity we are to subscribe to in this quest for respectability. Veblen was the unchallenged master of bringing the latest advances in biology, psychology, and anthropology to bear upon his unique analysis of society. Yet, as the unflinching analyst of the outmoded ("pre-Darwinian") scientific preconceptions of economics, he would be the first to admit that science advances unceasingly in scope and conception. For although both Marx and Samuelson have called for scientific analysis in economics, their conceptions of science may in the end make them more different than alike.

It is in the spirit of Veblen's unorthodox range of scholarship that this essay will attempt to show how one of the latest mutations of scientific outlook, the work of the general systems theorists, might shed some light on the problems of orthodox economic equilibrium theory.

The plan of the essay is as follows: In Part II, I will survey the development of a new scientific outlook, general systems theory, that has arisen in the life sciences (like Veblen's "evolutionary point of view") in the last 30 years. Part III will be devoted to a brief review of the theory of general economic equilibrium, which seems to be the perfect example of an economic system in the sense of the general system theorists. In Part IV, I will point out that the fundamental anomaly general equilibrium theory presents from the general systems viewpoint, that of being both a closed and an open system, is a result of defects in the framing of the general equilibrium problem from Walras on. In particular, I will argue that explicit recognition of the lack of any theory of the process by which Walras's equilibrium might actually come about and be maintained explains some well-known puzzles of the general economic equilibrium. Drawing on the work of F. A. Hayek, I will suggest that the problem essentially boils down to one of social-level facts concerning the processes by which knowledge and information are acquired in a social setting. Recognition of these shortcomings of equilibrium theory is forced upon us by the insights of general systems theory. With this recognition, though, comes a rationale for breaking out of the scholastic confines that the modern state of mathematical equilibrium analysis presents to the economic theorist without having to abandon its useful insights.

THE METHODOLOGY OF SYSTEMS THEORY

A simple example conveys the essence of the system theorist's view of scientific investigation. If asked to explain the operation of an internal combustion engine, there are two methods open to you. First, you could proceed to disassemble the engine and investigate separately the operation of the carburetor, pistons, valves, and camshaft. You would then reassemble the parts and reference your explanation of the engine by your investigations of the individual components. This method is called the analytic method. It is opposed to the holistic systems method where explanation of the engine would involve observation of the complete engine. In this approach, explanation of its operation would follow the path of the gasoline. From the tank, fuel is mixed with air by the carburetor and forced into the cylinders by the first valve, where it is ignited to drive the pistons which turn the drive shaft and ultimately the camshaft, so that the next valve is opened; and the process repeats itself.[6] Here the engine is analogous to the system theoretic concept of an open system operating via negative entropy (the injection of fuel) with a simple feedback mechanism (the camshaft). It is the contention of the systems theorists that there are certain "complex interrelated wholes" which can be understood by the second procedure, but not by the first.

The case which gave rise to the modern version of systems theory is attributed to von Bertalanffy's use of the system concept to settle a long-standing dispute in the life sciences.[7] Stemming from certain developments in cellular biology[8] that appeared to contradict the mechanical application of physical laws to living beings, the organistic school of biology argued that the study of life was a "sui generis" phenomenon. This ran counter to the analytic approach whereby physical/chemical explanations were sought for biological phenomena. In claiming that the "emergent" properties of life were not reducible to physical laws, the organicists were rejecting the dominant reductionist research program of Enlightenment science. For the "vitalist" biologists, the attempt to reduce all science to the level of the ideal rational science, physics, was a misguided one.

von Bertalanffy attempted to solve this apparent methodological contradiction while retaining the validity of physical laws by using them to explain the uniqueness of living beings. His explanation centered around the distinction between closed and open systems. He began by defining a system at the most general level as "complexes of elements standing in interaction" (von Bertalanffy 1968, p. 33). Closed systems are those which are isolated from their environment. For this reason, given initial conditions and the laws governing the interaction of the system elements, a final equilibrium will be reached which is completely specified by the initial givens. This is the paradigm of physical and chemical experiments which operate in vacuums or closed containers. Physically, such systems seek the most probable state of maximum disorder through entropy since a more ordered state would imply the incomplete expression of the second law of thermodynamics and thus be improbable. But von Bertalanffy noted that we observe systems in biology "which by their very nature and definition are not closed systems" (p. 39). Such living organisms are characterized by highly improbable states of organization from a physical standpoint. This seems to contradict those very physical laws that defined closed systems. It was von Bertalanffy's insight to show that this contradiction disappears when it is realized that

> every living organism is essentially an open system. It maintains itself in a continuous inflow and outflow, a building up and breaking down of components, never being, so long as it is alive, in a state of chemical and thermodynamic equilibrium but maintained in a so-called steady state which is different from the latter. (P. 39)

Since this vital distinction was not made in the vitalist debate, says von Bertalanffy, it seemed that physical laws did not apply to living systems since conventional physics was designed to explain closed systems. He claims two major general conclusions are to be learned here. First, that the characteristics of an open system lead to the "principle of equifinality." By this is meant the fact that an open system can reach its particular steady state "from different initial conditions and in different ways." This is in contrast to a closed system where "the final state is unequivocally determined by the initial conditions" (p. 40). Mathematically, this distinction between equifinal steady states and unequivocally reached equilibriums can be shown to depend on the definition of a system as open or closed.[9]

The second general property he derives from this distinction is that it offers an explanation of "the apparent contrast between inanimate and animate nature," whereby the physical law of dissipation to the most unorganized state of matter conflicts sharply with the biological evidence of evolution toward more complex forms. Again appealing to the distinction of closed versus open systems, von Bertalanffy claims that closed systems obey this law of dissipation since there can only be positive entropy in such irreversible processes as closed systems represent. Open systems, though, can forestall this tendency to decay by importing energy in the form of negative entropy and "may even develop toward states of increased order and organization" (p. 41).

From this amazingly simple and powerful distinction blossomed a revolution in biology that eventually grew into a scientific outlook that cut across disciplines.[10] The rapid spread of the appeal of systems theory was the result of a coincidence of diverse developments of which I can only sketch the barest outline. Simultaneously with the growth of the systems view in biology, Norbert Wiener was extending his wartime work in mathematical self-guidance systems for armaments into a new science of information and control that he dubbed "cybernetics."[11] A child prodigy with an early education that seems to have surpassed even that of John Stuart Mill in bizarre precociousness,[12] Wiener thought that his basic insight into "feedback loops" as the model of self-control had radical implications for thinking about such complicated "systems" as computers, language, sociology, and psychology.[13] In the more extreme flights of philosophical rhapsody of some of its proponents, cybernetics served as the symbolic manifestation of the complex information-oriented social control that was then beginning to characterize so much of modern life.[14] It captured the spirit of the earliest enchantment with the hope of solving all social ills through the collection and management of vast data bases to be used for social engineering purposes.[15] In practice, its major impact seems to have been on the design and use of complex computer and technological systems.[16]

For the growth of systems theory as a policy approach, this information-theory work pioneered by the cyberneticists was combined with operations research tools such as linear programming to set large-scale data collections into action. Also a product of the war effort,[17] linear programming found its perfect operational use in the applications of the prewar work of Leontief in data organization and Tinbergen in design of policy models.[18] Leontief's organization of economic data into "input-output tables" was successfully married to Tinbergen's policy planning models utilizing the optimization techniques of linear programming. Despite Lord Keynes's early dismissal of Tinbergen's work as "black magic,"[19] it was the political acceptance of Keynes's demand management policy recommendations that provided the fertile ground for the spawning of the "quiet revolution" in mathematical-statistical economics that we now know as econometrics.[20]

Furthermore, as these initially economic-based system analyses gained recognition and (perhaps more importantly) public funding, they became the paradigm of applied social science to which other disciplines aspired. Consequently, attempts were made at data collection and statistical analysis of a wide range of "social indicators" that were to parallel the impact of the purely economic accounts.[21] Combined with the postwar concern with "development," these "systems" of data collection and analysis spread geographically as well. Especially in the area of development aid to the Third World, the attempt to operationalize a system-wide view of society led social scientists throughout the sixties and seventies to the construction and analysis of ever more complex data systems. Uses ranged from long-term macroeconomic policy planning to developing social accounting frameworks for analyzing development across cultures and over time. While most of these extensive pragmatic uses of systems concepts are not directly related to the abstract systems theory of von Bertalanffy and Wiener, they share a common outlook of complex interrelatedness with the former, conscious attempts at control with the latter, and appeals to span traditional categories of knowledge with both.

The interface where the abstract theorists of systems met with the social engineers is symbolically represented by the founding of the Society for General Systems Theory in 1954.[22] Growing out of the multidisciplinary milieu of the Center for Advanced Study in the Behavioral Sciences, this society was the brainchild of the biomathematician Anatol Rapoport, the physiologist Ralph Gerard, the economist Kenneth Boulding, and L. von Bertalanffy, a biologist. The latter recalls that system theory at the time "responded to a secret trend in various disciplines." This secret trend was toward "attempting scientific interpretation and theory where there was none and higher generality than that in the special sciences" (von Bertalanffy 1968, p. 14).

The original program of the society reveals the manner in which this secret trend was to be nurtured:

> The Society for General Systems Research was organized in 1954 to further the development of theoretical systems which are applicable to more than one of the traditional departments of knowledge. Major functions are to: (1) Investigate the isomorphy of concepts, laws, and models in various fields, and to help in useful transfers from one field to another; (2) encourage the development of adequate theoretical models in fields which lack them; (3) minimize the duplication of theoretical effort in different fields; (4) promote the unity of science through improving communication among specialists.[23]

The work of the Society has been carried out in the <u>General System Yearbook</u> and the journal <u>Mathematical Systems Theory</u>. In general, the literature on systems theory has remained true to the society's original program. Work alternates from further developments of abstract, metascientific models of general interaction to trying to use these models to clear up difficulties in specific fields or span traditional categories through applications of homologous models in each. Despite early hopes of widespread impact, though, the traditional barriers to cross-disciplinary research have proved more formidable than might have been predicted. This seems to be especially so in the more rarifed pure-theory work of the various disciplines. Faced with more practical exigencies, the social engineers outpaced their theoretical counterparts in opening their eyes to other sources of knowledge.

This last distinction, between policy practitioners and professional theorists, has been especially marked in the field of economics. As we have seen, the econometricians were pioneers in the systems approach to policy planning and this has led many of them to reach out toward other disciplines more recently.[24] Despite the practical economists' growing catholicism, though, the mainstream economic theorists of the last 50 years have taken little notice of outside influences. Instead, at the hands of the mathematicians that turned to economics from the 1930s on, economics has, if anything, narrowed its focus, at least so far as the problem addressed by the most abstract theorists, the problem of general economic equilibrium, is concerned.

I would argue that there were two reasons for this theoretical narrowness. First, as in the case of many scientific advances in history, the transformation of economic theory into a mathematical-based discipline that has taken place in the last 50 years has involved a large measure of work to translate old theory into a new language, here a mathematical one. Consequently, much of the work of general equilibrium theorists, for example, has been to prove the logical possibility of the existence of a state of equilibrium under ever more general assumptions. At its greatest degrees of abstraction such a search became an end in itself. In fact, so abstract was the language of these topological investigations that the proofs often took years to be translated back to a more pedestrian level that would make them available even to trained economists. Thus, secondly, the mathematical economic theorists became isolated by their own success. Working with their given problem led to more and more complicated self-generated puzzles. So numerous were these self-generated puzzles that they had little need to look beyond their system, much less at the economy itself, for further topics of research. The next section will be devoted to looking at this enthralling system in more detail.

THE WALRASIAN SYSTEM

In 1974, writing in the _International Journal of General Systems_, Kenneth Boulding expressed his dismay that economists had hardly noticed the development of general systems theory:

> Just why the economics profession has viewed general systems theory with such a massive indifference I really do not know. Like the physicists, the economists are so bound up within the elegant framework of their own system that they find it hard to break out into broader interests. Economists, indeed, may be a good example of a principle I have sometimes enunciated that "nothing fails like success." (p. 67)

Over 10 years later, it must be admitted that the situation is much the same.

In order to redress that massive indifference somewhat, the next two sections will be devoted to analyzing the relationship of general systems theory concepts to what Boulding thought was its most analogous field of study in economics, general equilibrium theory.[25] Along the way, we may gain some insight into what the terms of that dubious success that Boulding refers to really are and of what use the systems theorists can be to guide the further development of general equilibrium theory.

The now highly complex literature on general equilibrium

theory in economics seems at first glance to represent a textbook case of a "system." The general formulation of the problem is as follows: The "economy" consists of large numbers of atomistic producers (with given techniques of production) and consumers (with given preference orderings of goods and endowments of resources). Each react parametrically to prices and attempt to maximize their constrained objectives of profit and utility in a mutually consistent way.[26] Since producers' profits depend on sale of their production, sales depend on demand, demand depends upon incomes, and incomes depend on the sale of resource endowments to producers, the individual agents' behaviors are complexly interrelated.

Historically the first problem addressed, by Walras in 1873,[27] was, "does there exist, in principle, a set of prices, one price for each good, that will simultaneously allow producers to maximize profits and consumers to maximize utility given the constraining interrelatedness between the actors?"

Combining his father's passion for the economics of exchange with training in mathematics and physics, Walras naturally saw this complex issue as a mathematical one.[28] Imbued with the spirit of the Enlightenment,[29] he saw his task as grounding the science of economics in the same bedrock upon which the Newtonian physics he knew so well was founded, the concept of equilibrium.[30] In so doing, he formulated the basic conceptual framework in which the theory of general economic equilibrium is still organized today, despite a century of improvement in the mathematical tools applied to it. Basically this conception is that equilibrium in each market implies the equality of supply and demand. When supply and demand functions are defined with sufficient generality to include as arguments the resource endowments and the prices of all goods simultaneously, the complex interrelationships of production and consumption can be conceived of as a system of simultaneous equations.

Walras's feat was to formulate this system and derive such insights from it as his mathematical training would permit.[31] Having determined that the system contained a sufficient number of equations to determine the unknowns, Walras took "existence" for granted. Assuming a state of equilibrium, he could then go on to characterize an elegantly synchronized system:

> Equilibrium in production, which implies equilibrium in exchange, can now be easily defined. First, it is a state in which the effective demand and offer of productive services are equal and there is a stationary current price in the market for these services. Secondly, it is a state in which the effective demand and supply of products are also equal and there is a stationary current price in the products market. Finally, it is a state in which the selling prices of products equal to the costs of the productive services that enter into them. The first two conditions

relate to equilibrium in exchange; the third to equilibrium in production.[32]

This integrative view of the economy as a complex system of interdependent markets and the insights that are to be had from such a "vision" have only been incrementally improved by the rarified analysis Walras's system has received at the hands of the pure mathematicians for the last 50 years.[33]

The history of Walras's system from 1874 down to our own time has been a curious combination of ups and downs on the tide of theoretical favor. Several lines of influence can be traced. In his own day, the vision that Walras formulated in his _Elements_ was to inspire many diverse thinkers. Schumpeter, who considered Walras to be the greatest economist in the history of the discipline, would claim that his treatise represented the "Magna Carta of exact economics."[34] One line of influence that would run through Wicksell, H. L. Moore, Schumpeter, Leontief, and J. R. Hicks down to much of present welfare economics, international trade, monetary theory, and growth theory is concerned with elaborating the economic content of this Magna Carta. This path to modern economics, though, was not a direct and unwavering growth of influence.

In the English-speaking countries, Walras's _Elements_ remained a little-read book for decades and was not even translated into English until 1954.[35] The path of its influence in English-speaking circles took a circuitous route. Having been eclipsed by the dominance of Marshall for 60 years, the reentry of discussion of general equilibrium theory was most influenced by the publication of J. R. Hicks's _Value and Capital_ in 1939.[36] Interestingly enough, Hicks's introduction to Walras was through Pareto, whose _Manual_ he was assigned to teach by Lionel Robbins in his first year at the London School of Economics.[37] This lapse of 65 years of attention within the Anglo-American world was not helped as it might have been by a knowledge of Wicksell since his work, as well, remained neglected until Kahn translated it in the thirties. Instead, it was through the enormous influence of _Value and Capital_ that what Hicks called "the method of General Equilibrium" has become a pervasive influence on modern economic theory. In both its microeconomic specification of the individual actors via indifference curve analysis and its system-wide "temporary equilibrium" model, _Value and Capital_ set down the foundation for most of what is taught in a modern principles of economics class: consumer theory, production theory, and (Hicksian) Keynesian macroeconomics. E. Roy Weintraub argues that "from this perspective, it can be suggested that the decade of the 1930s saw the degenerative Marshallian program replaced with two competing programs, the macroeconomic and microeconomic, or the Keynesian and Hicksian."[38]

But at the same time that Keynes and Hicks were brewing theoretical revolutions in England, another group of disciples was extending Walras's work on more explicitly formal grounds. This second line of influence stemming from the Elements was to catch that wave of interest in mathematical formulations of economic theory that the English tradition had been opposed to at least since Marshall[39] but which swamped economics beginning in the 1940s. The intellectual object of this second line was a concern not so much with the economics of Walras's system but the analytics. In particular, the concern of a generation of mathematically trained theorists, culminating in Arrow and Debreu's (1954) proof of existence of a general equilibrium price vector,[40] was to rigorously dress Walras's crude existence argument in more elegant mathematical garb.[41] Since it is the work of these mathematical theorists that provides the modern version of Walras's formulation of an economic system, the results of their work must be mentioned to bring our specification of the general economic equilibrium up to date.

Using more sophisticated mathematics, modern general equilibrium theorists have set out more precisely just what conditions are sufficient for the simple static case to hold. Generally, it has been found that Walras's insights hold but his mathematics were not very elegant. With the sparest assumptions of nonincreasing returns to scale in production, convex preference orderings, and continuity in actors' reactions to prices,[42] modern theorists have shown that the existence proof holds, but significantly for us, in general the solution is not a unique one.[43] This means that given the same primitive assumptions, more than one set of prices can satisfy the general equilibrium solution. In its traditional form, the theory cannot specify which will occur.

Additionally, as a result of recent debates between neo-Walrasian theorists and the Cambridge school devotees of Sraffa's[44] system, the sensitivity of the solution vector to the given endowments of the system has been more explicitly recognized. Frank Hahn's attempt to show that the Sraffa system is nothing but a special case of the more general neo-Walrasian model led him to the conclusion that any specific solution to the general system depends on a "unique history" of the system.[45] By history he refers to the fact that endowments or income distribution (which are explicitly "givens" to the problem) affect the whole equilibrium price vector through their influence on demand patterns. Hahn's contentious style in a highly charged debate obscures this fact with his argument. C. J. Bliss, though, is less coy on the subject than Hahn. He forthrightly admits the fact that in general the solution vector is nonunique and critically depends on what he calls "the primitive postulates of the system" (basically those assumptions given as data from without the economic system).[46] Finally, it is Bliss, again, who has no delusions about the neglect in even the most modern formulations of the system of any dynamic behavior of the economy. A rather extensive quote from him at this juncture will serve to introduce the very themes to which a systems-theoretical account of general equilibrium compels us.

Bliss urges the following strategy for the theoretical use of the neo-Walrasian's proof that existence of a general equilibrium is logically possible:

> It may seem more sensible to simply assume that equilibrium will prevail and to thus confine our investigations to the equilibrium state. We could regard the object of our investigations not as "the economy" but as "economic equilibrium" and we could attempt to justify this procedure as a useful starting point to what one might eventually hope to see realized in a complete account of the behavior of the economy, including a full specification of its disequilibrium dynamics. . . . The awkwardness of proceeding in this manner is that we are introducing assumptions of a rather special, perhaps even dubious, character. (Bliss 1975, p. 28)

From the standpoint of general systems theory, the attempt to formulate the economic equilibrium without reference to the underlying dynamics would seem dubious indeed if we conceive of the economy as an open system.

GENERAL EQUILIBRIUM THEORY AS GENERAL SYSTEMS THEORY

What is the relationship of the economists' general equilibrium theory and general systems theory? In its traditional form given above, the existence of a general economic equilibrium seems to contradict the insights of von Bertalanffy. First, it is simultaneously conceived of as an open system that takes inputs from the environment (both physical and social) and transforms them into outputs to the larger social system, as well as a closed system whose final equilibrium (a vector of relative prices) is completely determined by its initial conditions (endowments, technology, and preferences). Second, it seems to contradict the systems theory view that the elements of a complex interrelated whole cannot be understood in isolation from the whole system. For it is the hallmark of this approach that the theory is "built up" from the analysis of individual behavior of the maximizing agents in isolation from the whole. This is the meaning of making prices parametric to the agents. The whole then is conceived of as some complex sum of the parts with the parts clearly dominating the analysis. In other words, partial equilibrium modeling of consumers and agents seems to apply the analytic method with particular force. Yet the usual argument for the extra insight gained in going from this partial approach to the general equilibrium is usually seen to be more in the spirit of systems theory in that it purports to show how everything depends upon everything else.[47] How can general equilibrium theorists have it both ways?

This contradiction is explained by two interdependent failings of the general equilibrium theory of economics which, when recognized, make Boulding's claim for the applicability of general systems theory to economics more understandable. These failings are the lack of an adequate dynamic underpinning to explain the process by which such general equilibrium prices will be arrived at and maintained, and the general neglect of the knowledge assumptions necessary for such an equilibrium. We will take up each in turn and then try to show how they are related to each other and to the work of the systems theorists.

As should now be clear, the main focus of the development of general equilibrium theory has been on the specification of equilibrium states. The question of the conditions necessary for the equilibrium prices so defined to come about from any set of initial conditions has progressed little since Walras's own formulation. Walras resorted to a fanciful story about a "tatonnement" process whereby some fictional "auctioneer" would call out prices to the economic actors. The auctioneer then compares supply and demand for each good given to him by the agents in the form of tickets ("sur bons") and raises the price in markets with excess demand and lowers it in markets with excess supply. Only when he has stumbled upon a set that would allow the simultaneous equilibrium of supply and demand on all markets to occur, would he allow actual trades to take place.[48]

In the modern literature, the investigation of the conditions for "getting into equilibrium" has been subsumed under the mathematical rubric of "stability" of the system.[49] Again, although the mathematical techniques for defining the conditions of stability have advanced, the schema still belongs to Walras. Bliss is candid on this topic as well:

> The investigations that have been undertaken into the stability of general equilibrium have admittedly been largely confined to investigating the stability of the Walrasian tatonnement--the adjustment process under which no actual trades take place until the equilibrium prices have been attained. (Bliss 1975, p. 28)

Thus, while all of the elements of the proof for existence of equilibrium prices depend analytically on the character of the individual actors in the system, the method by which the prices are assumed to occur has been seen as involving something over and above these individual actors. Bliss (1975, p. 16) quotes Koopmans (1957, p. 179) on this: "If, for instance, the net rate of increase in price is assumed to be proportional to the excess of demand over supply, whose behavior is thereby expressed? And how is that behavior motivated?" It is here that the system more faithfully resembles the systems-theoretic claim of the whole of a complex system adding up to more than the sum of its parts. Stability concerns render the apparently most rationalistic and reductionist of all social scientific models dependent in the end upon an inexplicably social- or structural-level concept. But here that concept is anthropomorphically transformed into a being of such fantastic omniscience that it resembles Hegel's ideal spirit more than rational economic man!

Of course, it would be misleading to suggest that the general equilibrium theorists themselves have not been aware of this failure of general equilibrium theory. In the tradition of general equilibrium economists, Hicks noted this problem explicitly. In Value and Capital, Hicks states that the problem of "trading at false prices" could lead to an unstable equilibrium of the system.[50] But instead of retaining Walras's tatonnement process, he opted for a scheme whereby equilibrium analysis is confined to an elementary time period, the Hicksian "week," during which stocks of production are given and demand determines prices "temporarily." This "temporary equilibrium" was a bow to his interpretation of Keynes's (1936) view of a monetary economy as a system in which the tatonnement process would be so time consuming that conditions would change before equilibrium could be established. During a Hicksian week, prices are not allowed to change within the week but only at the start (Monday) of the next week when expectations and plans are revised and new conditions prevail in the market.[51] His analytical argument, though, was deficient in rigor, essentially assuming that since "we may reasonably suppose that the transactions which take place at 'very false' prices are limited in volume,"[52] we can assume prices don't change within a week.

It was this analytical looseness that set the stage for the modern mathematical treatment of tatonnement in the work of Samuelson (1947). Essentially, Samuelson's work involved specification of the underlying dynamic properties that were necessary to ensure that small movements away from an equilibrium would result in reestablishment of the equilibrium. From Samuelson's work stems the whole modern treatment of stability. Firmly within the analytic tradition, the problem is conceived as trying to use differential equations to more rigorously specify the mathematical properties of the auctioneer process that will ensure stability.[53] The only new economic insight that seems to have come out of this work is that even utilizing the fictional tatonnement process the requirements for stability are very restrictive. Weintraub (1979, p. 33) sums up the results of this highly technical literature with a theorem:

> For the linear tatonnement system . . . the equilibrium is asymptotically stable, if the excess demand functions are continuously differentiable, are homogeneous of degree zero in prices, satisfy Walras' Law, and exhibit gross substitutability.

It is noteworthy that these conditions are much more stringent than the sparse assumptions necessary for existence. Since it is hard to imagine an economy which exhibits gross substitutability in all commodities (no shoelaces allowed), the implication is that "instability seems to be a universal phenomenon in competitive economies, rather than an exceptional one."[54] So what do we throw out: equilibrium theory (if equilibrium is not stable, what sense is there in pursuing it?) or the fictionalized process by which this alleged instabllity has been pointed out? Both Weintraub and Bliss seem to think the safest bet is to throw out the auctioneer. To Weintraub this traditional approach to stability was "singularly maladapted to the sort of decentralized decision-making that lay at the center of the static ADM (Arrow-Debreu-McKenzie) concept (and) . . . could potentially distract general equilibirum theorists from more comprehensive investigations."[55] For Bliss the stability issue involves "work which may turn out to be singularly unrewarding to a scholar who would like to arrive at the conclusion that his model is a stable one which the economy will tend to approach."[56]

As we have seen, Bliss thinks the proper alternative strategy involves simply assuming equilibrium exists and concentrating analysis on "economic equilibrium" rather than "the economy." Weintraub remains less insulated within his own "elegant framework" but retains his faith in the general equilibrium approach, which he considers to be the "hard core" (in the sense of Lakatos) of orthodox economics.[57] In the spirit of the Lakatosian view of a rationally progressing science, Weintraub argues that the future of economics involves subsuming "the elements of post-war monetary theory and macroeconomics"[58] into the protective belt of the neo-Walrasian paradigm. By so doing, he claims that the traditional division of macroeconomics and microeconomics will not be bridged; they will both become part of one coextensive research program.[59] Interestingly enough, he makes an analogy at this juncture between von Bertalanffy's GST and general equilibrium theory: "A general systems theory, like the neo-Walrasian ADM model in economics, is more than a particular structure to model a particular situation . . . neo-Walrasian general equilibrium theory is not a theory in the same sense as, say, 'the theory of the second-best' or the 'theory of demand.' . . . Instead, we are suggesting that general equilibrium theory, the kind of general systems theory that economists have developed, is the appropriate logic to investigate the compatibility between microeconomics and macroeconomics."

A "kind of general systems theory," yes, but not a consistent, well-posed one if von Bertalanffy's work has any relevance for economic systems. Ultimately, the fiction of the auctioneer and the tatonnement process of getting into equilibrium obscure the very dynamic elements which confirm the insight that Boulding sensed systems theory held out to general equilibrium theory, but was being ignored. Further, this insight helps to explain not only the paradox of reductionism and holism coexisting in the general equilibrium setting but also a further anomaly from the systems theory standpoint. How can a supposedly closed system admit multiple equilibria? Like the vitalist debate before it, these anomalies also disappear when it is realized that the economic system is not, indeed, a closed system but an open one. As a subsystem within a total social system, it imports data from the larger society in the form of raw materials, technology, income distribution, and tastes. With these it produces goods defined in quantities and prices which in turn enter into that larger social system but in a nonunique manner. Given the extreme generality and lack of institutional structure in the general specification of economic equilibrium, it is not surprising that it should be amenable to a number of solutions once it is filled with a bit more reality.

Unfortunately, it is at this point that both general equilibrium theory and the general systems view of society generally break down. In the case of the theory of general economic equilibrium, the specific context for this breakdown can be described as an insufficient theory of economic knowledge. All of the elements of the functions of a capitalist economy are critically dependent on the knowledge available to the individual acting agents. Even the most static analysis of firm supply and consumer demand depends critically on the presumption that producers and consumers have knowledge of market conditions in the form of prices of inputs, relevant techniques of production, competitors' prices, and prices of substitutes. In the more explicitly dynamic contexts of investment and capital theory, it is the treatment of knowledge in the form of expectations that distinguishes all modern approaches from one another. In the yet more complicated setting of a general economic equilibrium, then, the knowledge available to individuals becomes all the more important for any adequate description of how such a system-wide equilibrium will come about. Yet it is precisely this domain into which orthodox economic theorists have been reluctant to tread until very recently. And when they have, the results have been dramatic departures from the mainstream neoclassical vision.[61]

But although this problem is just now being treated by the formal mathematical general equilibrium theorists, its implications for standard equilibrium theory were pointed out half a century ago by F. A. Hayek. An examination of his "Economics and Knowledge" (Hayek 1937) provides an interesting glimpse into the depth of the knowledge problem for orthodox equilibrium theory.

Hayek's paper is concerned with "the role which assumptions and propositions about the knowledge possessed by different members of society play in economic analysis."[62] He points out that the usual descriptions of formal equilibriums are essentially "tautologies" and "can be turned into propositions which tell us anything about the real world only in so far as we are able to fill those formal propositions with definite statements about how knowledge is acquired and communicated."[63] As evidence of this view, he points out that attempts to push economics beyond these formal tautologies toward causal explanations of such behavior as business cycles, interest rates, or oligopoly behavior typically involve assumptions about "foresight and expectations."[64]

For Hayek this is due to the fact that the analyses of equilibriums which are defined for given data are properly applicable only to single individuals as a consistent explanation of behavior.[65] "Actions of an individual can be said to be in equilibrium in so far as they can be understood as part of one plan."[66] Only if the actions are based on one set of data and assumptions about knowledge and preferences of the person can they relate to the same equilibrium. But Hayek, in good Austrian tradition, emphasizes that these "so-called 'data'" are subjectively given to the actor and "not in any sense objective facts."[67] Only in the subjective sense is there a logical a priori consistency of the tautologies we derive from these data.

It is this distinction between objective and subjective givens that forms the crucial link in Hayek's argument that the method of equilibrium of the individual "does not immediately admit of applications to the relations between actions of different people."[68] The difference lies in the nature of the "givens" in a social setting as opposed to a personal one. If a general equilibrium is to be considered, it must involve two types of mutual compatibility of actions. First, there must be a compatibility of the different actions of the different actors in the system since "the plans of the one contain exactly those actions which form the data for the plans of the other." But there must also be a compatibility of these subjective plans with the objective data of the environment. Hayek claims that it is confusion over these different conceptions of givens that is "at the bottom of so many of our difficulties."[69] For in the equilibrium of the individual, we could unequivocally define the givens as any conception that the subject (subjectively) held when he made his plan of action. For Hayek "only this subjective interpretation of the true datum made these propositions (of individual equilibrium) necessary truths." However, in the more general equilibrium setting, this concept of datum becomes a much more problematic assumption. Since the data for one actor consist partly of the plans of other actors and, moreover, all of these individual plans must in some sense correspond to a given physical/social reality, the concept of what the data are in defining a general economic equilibrium becomes much more problematic. "The data which now are supposed to be objective facts and the same for all people are evidently no longer the same thing as the data which formed the starting point for the tautological transformations of the pure logic of choice."[70] For Hayek there is an "insidious change of meaning" in the concept of datum between these respective situations that forms the basis of the difficulty in giving general equilibrium theory any meaning.

Basically the data problem consists of the confusion in stating for the givens of our "system" to whom these data are given and whether everyone in society is given the same or different data. The question of to whom the data of our analysis are given involves the distinction of objective and subjective data already mentioned. When we define a general economic equilibrium, we take the physical, technological, and taste data as given to the economist making the analysis. But, surely, this is different than the data given to the actors in the system. Hayek claims it is essential to clearly distinguish the two types of data since they lead to two different conceptions of equilibrium.

First, we might define equilibrium as the mutual compatibility of "the subjective data, given to the different persons, and the individual plans which necessarily follow from them."[71] This mutual consistency of individual plans is separate from, and prior to, the further requirement that these mutually compatible plans are in agreement with the objective data which are given to the society. Hayek claims that, as opposed to the forward-looking, expectation-based equilibrium of the first type, for correspondence with objective data, "it would never be possible to decide otherwise than ex-post at the end of the period for which people have planned, whether at the beginning the society has been in equilibrium."[72] One implication of this distinction is that the only "changes in data" relevant to the definition of a general equilibrium are those which change the expectations of the individual actors in some way such that they alter their plans. In this light, the famous assumption of "full knowledge" on the part of some past and present theorists[73] becomes a crude attempt to cover up this problem by assuming everyone knows everything.[74]

Hayek goes on to point out that the important element left out of traditional equilibrium theory is the crucial link between these two types of data. In short, how do economic actors acquire knowledge of both the objective and subjective data that cause them to change their plans? This link between the subjective and objective data of the system brings us full circle to our original problem with defining a general economic equilibrium and its relation to systems theory.

In the context of the auctioneer problem, we can now see that this crucial theory of economic knowledge was subsumed there under an analytical contrivance out of touch with the individualist statement of the original problem. Since the Walrasian equilibrium of equality of supplies and demands must come about through the dynamic interaction of individual actors adjusting their own plans, both to the rest of the actors' plans and to some external data, we see that it is not possible to define the parts in isolation from the whole. This anomaly, from a systems theory perspective, falls away when we realize that it is a classic case of missing variables that cause the general form of general equilibrium models to yield nonunique solutions. Moreover, it seems necessary to assume that these extra variables that would enable us to tie down the solution must in general be social-level facts such as Comte thought social science should proceed from. It cannot be another dimension of subjective minds but some social mechanism that structures the process by which this knowledge acquisition comes about.

Hayek hints at this conclusion when he points out that the lack of attention paid to this knowledge problem by economists "would go far to account for the fact that pure analysis seems to have so extraordinarily little to say about institutions, such as the press, the purpose of which is to communicate knowledge. And it might even explain why the preoccupation with pure analysis should so frequently create a peculiar blindness to the role played in real life by such institutions as advertising."[75] In full accordance with the systems theorists' emphasis on the value of homologies to span the work of different disciplines, a complete system specification of a general economic equilibrium, one that included a social-specific role for knowledge acquisition (or control), could possibly clear the theoretical ground for that union of economists and other social theorists that has been called for so many times since Comte first proposed a science of society. This is one way of viewing Fox's[76] work on a theoretical framework for social data and Boulding's[77] attempts to formulate systems of knowledge transfers through grants economics and conflict resolution theory.

In a wider sense, the questions this analysis has revealed can be seen as an organizing node for the increasing dissatisfaction with orthodox equilibrium analysis that has cropped up in the economics profession in the last 20 years. Analysts attracted by the system theory approach are but one sect of a variety of heterodox thinkers active today. Although their motivation, politics, and methodology exist in a multivectored space, one predominating influence on the original impetus for these schools was a rejection of pure equilibrium analysis as sterile and useless. Nevertheless, when it came time to formulate new work, a complete divorce from equilibrium theory has not seemed possible. Without some kind of structure or centering, such necessarily vague views as "process analysis" or "social economics" seem to degenerate into storylike descriptions at best or obscurantism at worst. I think this loss of an "analytical engine" involved in the rejection of orthodox equilibrium analysis, the same engine which had given economics its however dubious claim to analytical superiority within the social sciences, explains the recent attempts by nonorthodox theorists to embrace some variant of equilibrium in their analysis.

A prominent example of this trend would be the latter-day Cambridge school. These theorists start their analysis, just like a good neoclassical economist, from an equilibrium framework. In fact, in a manner reminiscent of Hayek's critique of orthodox theory, this framework has been criticized as consisting of little more than ex-post accounting identities. But the growing number of adherents to the Cambridge approach conceive of this Sraffa price system as a superior system of equilibrium "tautologies." In terms of our analysis, one distinctive feature of this system that could make it more appealing than the orthodox variety of equilibrium theory is that it explicitly makes note of the necessity of specifying some extra-economic social process to close the system. But this is not distinctive in itself since, as we have seen, the same interaction with the social environment is implied by a complete closure of the neo-Walrasian system.[78] What ultimately distinguishes the two approaches on this matter is the Cambridge theorists' insistence that the manner in which this admitted openness is to be closed must come through specification of the income distribution between profits and wages. Moreover, the fact that they conceive of this distribution as an antagonistic social process that is logically prior to price determination makes it totally opposed to the noncoercive image of distribution as an extension of free exchange that forms the basis of the Walrasian tradition.[79]

For our purposes, the very fact that the Cambridge approach takes explicit cognizance of the social environment provides an example of a more throughgoing systems theoretic view of economics. That such a view calls for extra-economic investigation points out that the ultimate significance of general systems theory for economics may be just exactly what its founders had in mind when they called for a bridging of disciplines. To break out of the vice-grip of pure equilibrium analysis involves explicit attention to the institutional details of the case. This is something that applied economists have always recognized. An explanation of the demand for oranges in California would be deficient indeed if it merely reproduced a supply and demand graph. The implication of the systems view of economics is that the abstract theorists of economics, also, have a responsibility to formulate models which acknowledge institutions in a nontrivial manner.

Essentially what is required of economic theorists is an attempt to recognize their environment, not ignore it. It is useful to note in this context that the essence of von Bertalanffy's insight lies in a precise recognition of a system's boundaries and its interaction with the environment. The very distinction of a closed versus an open system depends on this recognition. In fact, one of the most influential system-sociologists in recent years, Niklas Luhman, builds his analysis on the intricate boundary relations, both intersubjective and subjective-objective, that form the social environment.[80] But since this is an essay in system "economics," not "sociology," I propose to round out our critique of equilibrium theory with a final speculative look at the methodological implications of the view of equilibrium proposed above for economics. We do so by concluding with a brief look at the work of two of the 20th century's most original minds: Ludwig Wittgenstein and Piero Sraffa.

In his youth, Ludwig Wittgenstein spent his considerable

intellectual powers in trying to fulfill to its ultimate end the positivist program of grounding language to empirical reality in strict logical terms. His Tractatus Logico-Philosophicus,[81] written in the trenches of World War I, was considered by the then towering figures of Western philosophy to have fulfilled this goal. Yet, later in life, Wittgenstein came to consider the whole idea of a logical relationship of language (and hence thought) with reality as a peculiar form of "philosophical disease" of which modern thought needed to be cured.[82] In his later work,[83] Wittgenstein argued that all of the most interesting aspects of language and thought were the ones which could not be so logically treated. Instead of trying to force the actual functioning of language into a narrowly preconceived positivistic framework, Wittgenstein came to believe that we should recognize it for the richly complex social enterprise that it is. Thus his later work attempts to show, through the analysis of "word games," how socially relative and contextual language actually is as a form of human activity rather than as "the petrified fallacies of reason" that analytic philosophy made of it.[84]

I think it would be possible and informative, although beyond the scope of this paper, to draw a parallel between the transition Wittgenstein's thought took over his life with the transition that is now and has for the last century been taking place in economists' conceptions of the relationship between pure economic (equilibrium) theory and the economy it provides a picture of. A key figure in this story could turn out to be Piero Sraffa. For, his interesting influence on Wittgenstein's reversal[85] aside, Sraffa's work in economic theory provides an object lesson in how such a transition might take place.

Sraffa, like Wittgenstein, started his theoretical career in an attempt to show the consequences of making the dominant orthodoxy logically consistent with itself.[86] He then came to reject that orthodoxy completely, at least by the time of his arrival in Cambridge in the late twenties. This is evident in his terse comments in the "Symposium on the Representative Firm" in the Economic Journal (Sraffa 1930, p. 93) where, in reply to D. H. Robertson's criticism of his view of Marshallian economics, Sraffa states his position most clearly:

> We seem to be agreed that the theory cannot be interpreted in a way which makes it logically self-consistent and, at the same time, reconciles it with the facts it sets out to explain. Mr. Robertson's remedy is to discard mathematics, and he suggests that my remedy is to discard the facts; perhaps I ought to have explained that, in the circumstances, I think it is Marshall's theory that should be discarded.

If it is possible to make the metaphorical leap to "Marshall's Theory" as a symbol of the tension between equilibrium theory and reality, I think it is possible to make the case that Sraffa's later life work (Sraffa 1960) represents an attempt to show how vacuous a pure, logically consistent, equilibrium system really is. For, like Hayek's characterization of the orthodox general equilibrium theory, the major calumny that has been heaped upon Sraffa's equilibrium system is that it is little more than a set of "ex-post accounting identities" and explains no real behavior of agents. "Well, if so, so be it," Sraffa might say. "Now go look for the real social processes and institutions by which agents learn and are controlled in society to flesh out this bare positivistic system that is only one of many 'life forms' of society." If this speculation has any basis,[87] Sraffa, in a much more subtle and involuted manner, can be attributed with the same prescriptive intention that Hayek (1937, p. 68) claimed as the aim of his work:

> All I have tried to do has been to find the way back to the common-sense meaning of our analysis, of which, I am afraid, we are apt to lose sight as our analysis becomes more elaborate. You may even feel that most of what I have said has been commonplace. But from time to time, it is probably necessary to detach oneself from the technicalities of the argument and to ask quite naively what it is all about. If I have only shown that in some respects the answer to this question is not only not obvious, but that occasionally we do not even quite know what it is, I have succeeded in my purpose.

NOTES

1. For a recent review of the history of the idea of a "social-science," see Keat and Urry 1982.

2. Auguste Comte 1853. See Kolakowski 1968 for a modern treatment of Comte's thought and its influence.

3. A statement of Mill's methodological views in the context of economics can be found in the essay "On the Definition of Political Economy; And On the Method of Investigation Proper to It" in Mill 1897.

4. The issue of Marxism and "science" has grown into an immensely complicated literature. All that can be safely said is that on any interpretation, Marx (early or late) was very concerned that his analysis be perceived as science. His well-known polemics on the distinctions of Utopian socialism versus scientific socialism and "vulgar" economics versus scientific political economy turn on just this point. While numerous citations could be made in this context, two that illustrate his life-long concern with scientific analysis are the discussions of political economy in the 1844 manuscripts, especially pp. 90-93 of Marx 1978 and the "Preface to the First Edition" of *Capital* in Marx 1977, pp. 88-93.

5. An account of Samuelson's methodological views is

available in Samuelson 1963. This short paper evoked a comment from Fritz Machlup (1964) and a reply by Samuelson (1964), which make interesting reading and might be given as a prime example of the difficulties of methodological discussions. All of these are reprinted in Caldwell 1984, who has this to say about Samuelson's methodological position: "How could such a renowned theorist be such an awful methodologist? Was his problem that he paid too much attention to the writings of philosophers, or not enough? Is there no interface between the scribbling of methodologists and the practice of economics?" (p. 137).

6. Muir 1969, Chapter 2.

7. See von Bertalanffy 1968, pp. 10-17, for a discussion of the early development of systems theory.

8. Phillips 1976, Chapter 2.

9. See von Bertalanffy 1968, pp. 75-80.

10. Rapoport (1968) provides a short history of the growth of the systems theory point of view.

11. Wiener 1948.

12. Wiener, like Mill, was the subject of experiments by a father with singular views on education. Perhaps instead of this resulting in a nervous breakdown, as in Mill's case, Wiener dreamt up cybernetics. For an account of Wiener's training, see Wiener 1953.

13. von Bertalanffy (1968, pp. 17, 21-22) claims that cybernetics is just a special case of general systems theory.

14. As an example of this view, we can quote R. Theobald:

> Man will no longer need to toil: he must find a new role in the cybernetics era which must emerge from a new goal of self-fulfillment. He can no longer view himself as a superanimal at the center of the physical universe, nor as a super-efficient taker of decisions self-fashioned in the model of the computer. He must now view himself as a truly creative being in the image of a creative God. (In Dechert 1966, p. 69)

15. This spirit is captured in the very etymological roots of Wiener's choice of appellation for his new outlook. "The term 'cybernetics' derives from the Greek word kybernetes, which means steersman. Plato used it to describe the prudential aspect of the art of government" (Dechert 1966, p. 11).

16. Paradoxically, this seems to have been Wiener's greatest fear. See further: Maron 1968, p. 547.

17. See Dorfman, Samuelson, and Solow 1958, pp. 1-5, for a short historical sketch of the development of linear programming from a Western perspective. We now know that the same technique was discovered independently, at a much earlier date, by the Russian mathematician Leonid Kantorovich. For a historical account of Kantorovich's work, see Katsenelinboigen 1980, pp. 33-35.

18. J. Tinbergen 1956 and W. Leontief 1951.

19. The correspondence in Keynes 1973, pp. 285-306, and his well-known exchange with Tinbergen, in the *Economic Journal* of

1939-1940 (Keynes's side is reprinted in Keynes 1973, pp. 306-320), reveal Keynes's trepidation at endorsing statistical operationalizations of his work. The relevant passage I refer to in the paper is from the latter exchange:

> No one could be more frank, more painstaking, more free from subjective bias or parti pris than Professor Tinbergen. There is no one, therefore, so far as human qualities go, whom it would be safer to trust with black magic. That there is anyone I would trust with it at the present stage or that this brand of statistical alchemy is ripe to become a branch of science, I am not yet persuaded. But Newton, Boyle, and Locke all played with alchemy. So let him continue. (Keynes 1973, p. 320)

This is Keynes's polemical skill at its most biting. For a more straightforward account of his views and a defense of Tinbergen by Roy Harrod, see the correspondence referred to above.

20. See Fox 1969 for a short discussion of the early history of the econometrics revolution.

21. For an early and influential statement of the objectives of the social indicators movement, see R. A. Bauer 1966.

22. See von Bertalanffy 1968, pp. 14-15, for his recollections of the founding of this society and Boulding 1974, p. 67, for his.

23. von Bertalanffy 1968, p. 15.

24. Leamer (1983) provides a critical view of the usefulness of econometrics from within the ranks. See Fox and Kaul 1980, pp. 4-33, for a review of the multidisciplinary influences on modern econometric work.

25. On this point Boulding stated that:

> Many and perhaps all of the theoretical systems of economics would qualify as general systems, for they are certainly relevant to other disciplines. The theory of the general equilibrium of prices and outputs of commodities, for instance, as originally developed by Walras, and made operational by Leontief in his input-output analysis in the 1930s, is clearly a special case of a general system of the utmost importance, for it is a special case of the general equations of ecological equilibrium. (Boulding 1974, pp. 67-68)

26. See Bliss 1975, Chapter 2, for a complete analysis of the general setup.

27. While Walras's classic _Elements d' economie politique pure_ was finally published in 1874, the original debut of his system seems to have taken place a year earlier in a paper presented to the Academie des Sciences Morales et Politiques entitled "Principles of a Mathematical Theory of Exchange." It was completely ignored. See further: Walsh and Gram 1980, pp. 146-147.

28. "We should never forget, however, that Walras' formal

schooling had been mainly in the natural sciences and mathematics, and this was available to him when, later, he needed it" (Ibid., p. 144).

29. See Walsh and Gram 1980, pp. 144-145.

30. "Walras is interested in the attainment of equilibrium in the market--in the pure theory of exchange" (Ibid., p. 147).

31. See Arrow and Hahn 1971, p. 4, for a discussion of the enduring insights of Walras's analysis.

32. Walras 1954, p. 224, quoted in Walsh and Gram 1980, p. 153.

33. Consider the following passage from the locus classicus of the modern neo-Walrasian literature:

> To be precise, an economy is defined by m consumers (characterized by their consumption sets and their preferences), by n producers (characterized by their production sets), and the total resources. A state of the economy is a specification of the action of each agent, and a state is said to be attainable if the action of each agent is possible for him and if their (m+n) actions are compatible with the total resources. The set of attainable states plays an essential role; its properties are therefore studied. A special class of economies is then considered, namely the private ownership economies where consumers own the resources and control the producers. Given a price system, each producer maximizes his profit, which is distributed to consumers-shareholders. The wealths of the latter are thus determined, and they satisfy their preferences under their wealth constraints. As a result of this process, each agent chooses an action. These (m+n) actions are not necessarily compatible with the total resources. Can one find a price system which makes them compatible? An answer is given in section 5.7 in the form of an existence theorem (for which way is prepared by the result of section 5.6). This fundamental theorem of the theory of value explains the prices of all commodities and the actions of all agents in a private ownership economy. (Debreu 1959, p. 74)

While there may be some reason to doubt the sweeping contention of the last sentence, it cannot but be noticed that, as far as the economics goes, Debreu is merely decanting Walras into a more recondite vessel.

34. "However, so far as pure theory is concerned, Walras is in my opinion the greatest of all economists. His system of economic equilibrium, uniting as it does, the quality of 'revolutionary' creativeness with the quality of classic synthesis, is the only work by an economist that will stand comparison with the achievements of theoretical physics. . . . It is the outstanding landmark on the road that economics travels toward the status of a rigorous or exact science and, though outmoded by now, still

stands at the back of much of the best theoretical work of our time" (Schumpeter 1954, p. 822). The comment on Walras's system as the "Magna Carta of exact economics" is found on p. 968.

35. The remarks of Walras's translator, William Jaffe, on pp. 7-9 of the preface to Walras 1954, shed some light on the neglect of the _Elements_ for so long in the English-speaking world.

36. Mark Blaug (1978, p. 617) claims that _Value and Capital_ is "a book which was largely responsible for the revival of Walras in modern economics."

37. See Chapter 1 of Hicks 1982 for an account of the formative influences on his thinking and p. 29 for the role of Pareto.

38. E. Roy Weintraub 1979, p. 16.

39. "The great economists of earlier generations--Alfred Marshall, A. C. Pigou, and Lord Keynes--thought that mathematical economics had a slim past and no future at all. Time makes fools even of great men. In the middle third of the 20th century, mathematics has everywhere swept through economics like an epidemic of measles sweeping through a new continent" (P. Samuelson in the forward to Georgescu-Roegen 1966).

40. Arrow and Debreu 1954.

41. For a very complete historical account of the development of the neo-Walrasian "existence" literature, see E. Roy Weintraub 1983.

42. See Bliss 1975, Chapter 2, for a readable exposition of the modern existence literature.

43. "It is important to note that the existence proof shows that at least one equilibrium exists. It does not, and could not, show that only one equilibrium exists. The possibility that there will be multiple equilibriums cannot be excluded" (Ibid., p. 30).

44. P. Sraffa 1960.

45. See section 5 of Hahn 1982.

46. See further: Bliss 1975, pp. 25-37.

47. "Someone who demands of a model as complicated as the atemporal equilibrium model what causes a particular value to be what it is should normally expect to be told that everything, meaning all the primitive specifications of the model, have played a part in causing the variable concerned to take whatever value has arisen" (Bliss 1975, p. 36).

48. Walras (1954) describes this process succinctly on p. 172.

49. For a nontechnical review of the stability literature, see Weintraub 1979, Chapter 7. Arrow and Hahn (1971, Chapters 11-13) provide a complete technical account.

50. See Hicks 1946, pp. 127-129, 245-272, 333-337.

51. See Ibid., pp. 131-140.

52. Ibid., p. 129. When Hicks returned to the stability issue in his "additional notes" of the 2nd edition of _Value and Capital_, he bowed to Samuelson's superior mathematical treatment

of the stability problem, but retained an interesting skepticism:

> By my hypothesis of essentially instantaneous adjustment, I reduced the purely mechanical part of my dynamic theory to the simplest terms--it is now quite evident that I over-simplified it. But in so doing, I did leave myself free to make some progress with the less mechanical parts--expectations and so on. I still feel that this procedure has its uses, and I should be sorry to abandon it altogether in favor of a pure concentration on mechanism . . . for the understanding of the economic system we need something more, something which does refer back, in the last resort, to the behavior of people and the motives of their conduct. (P. 337).

53. See Weintraub 1979, Chapter 2.

54. Nikaido (1969, p. 337) quoted in Weintraub 1979, p. 35.

55. Weintraub 1979, p. 35. ADM is the generally accepted adjective for neo-Walrasian theory.

56. Bliss 1975, p. 28.

57. Weintraub 1979, p. 37.

58. Ibid., p. 37.

59. Ibid., p. 71.

60. Ibid., p. 73.

61. Two extreme examples of the powerful role knowledge assumptions play can be seen in the work of the rational expectations theorists, on the side of complete omniscience, and the work of G. L. S. Shackle (1972), on the side of crippling ignorance.

62. Hayek 1937, p. 45. He continues: "But this is by no means unconnected with the other question which might be discussed under the same title, the question to what extent formal economic analysis conveys any knowledge about what happens in the real world."

63. Ibid., p. 45.

64. Ibid., p. 45. To a modern economist this is a surprisingly up-to-date list to which we might want to add macroeconomics and forecasting of all types.

65. "I have long felt that the concept of equilibrium itself and the methods which we employ in pure analysis, have a clear meaning only when confined to the analysis of the action of a single person" (Ibid., p. 47).

66. Ibid., p. 48.

67. Ibid., p. 48.

68. Ibid., p. 49.

69. Ibid., p. 51.

70. Ibid., p. 51.

71. Ibid., p. 52.

72. Ibid., p. 53.

73. Hayek cites Kaldor (1934) in this context, but the

description would equally well apply to the rational expectations school.

74. See Burmeister 1980 and Frydman 1982 for some conceptual problems such full knowledge assumptions can create.

75. Hayek 1937, p. 67. For an attempt by two modern "Hayekians" to elaborate on the economic role such knowledge institutions play, see O'Driscoll and Rizzo 1985.

76. Fox 1983.

77. Boulding 1945, 1981.

78. Bliss 1975, p. 32, makes note of this openness of the neoclassical system:

> Economic theories that attempt to explain prices or distribution from the postulate of a general equilibrium of supply and demand have sometimes been criticized for neglecting the influence of sociological and historical factors as though the "laws of supply and demand" embodied only the working out of purely economic forces. Plainly this is a misunderstanding. If there is a valid explanation of prices and distribution in terms of an equilibrium of supply and demand (always remembering that this may or may not be the correct theory--it is not a matter of logical necessity) then the influence of sociological and historical factors will be channelled through the excess supply functions of the various actors and in that sense the operation of these influences will be direct. To say that many factors will operate indirectly is not to devalue their importance. It is, of course, largely "non-economic" factors that will give to any particular case its particular character.

79. See Dobb 1973, pp. 247-266, on the significance of the Sraffian treatment of distribution.

80. See Luhman 1982.

81. Wittgenstein 1922.

82. See Janik and Toulmin 1973, pp. 202-238, for a brief account of Wittgenstein's intellectual turnaround.

83. Pears 1970 provides a comprehensive survey of Wittgenstein's thought.

84. Quoted in Heller 1965, p. 218.

85. See Roncaglia 1978, pp. 121-124.

86. See Sraffa 1926.

87. Support for this view can he found, among other places, in an elliptical reading of Sraffa's review of F. A. Hayek's <u>Prices and Production</u> (Sraffa 1932). The content of most of the review consists of Sraffa's attempt to demonstrate logical inconsistency in Hayek's theoretical polemic for a "neutral" monetary policy. But after having spent considerable energy in this pursuit, Sraffa implies that the whole exercise is a misguided one in that the model's premises exclude all of the truly interesting features of a monetary economy from the start. This compares interestingly with Wittgenstein's attitude that his

Tractatus work was not wrong but just misguided in its aim; i.e., that, in fact, the most interesting elements of language were those that his positivistic system were forced to be silent about.

REFERENCES

Arrow, K. J., and G. Debreu. 1954. "Existence of an Equilibrium for a Competitive Economy." *Econometrica* 22: 265-290.

Arrow, K. J., and F. H. Hahn. 1971. *General Competitive Analysis*. San Francisco: Holden-Day.

Bauer, R. A., ed. 1966. *Social Indicators*. Cambridge: MIT Press.

Blaug, M. 1978. *Economic Theory in Retrospect*. 3rd ed. Cambridge: Cambridge University Press.

Bliss, C. J. 1975. *Capital Theory and the Distribution of Income*. Amsterdam: North-Holland.

Boulding, K. E. 1945. *The Economics of Peace*. New York: Prentice-Hall.

______. 1974. "Economics and General Systems." *International Journal of General Systems* 1: 67-73.

______. 1981. *A Preface to Grants Economics: The Economy of Love and Fear*. New York: Praeger.

Burmeister, E. 1980. "On Some Conceptual Issues in Rational Expectations Modeling." *Journal of Money, Credit, and Banking* 12: 800-816.

Caldwell, B. J., ed. 1984. *Appraisal and Criticism in Economics*. Boston: Allen and Unwin.

Comte, A. 1853. *The Positive Philosophy of Auguste Comte*. Translated and condensed by Harriet Martineau. London: Chapman.

Debreu, G. 1959. *Theory of Value*. New York: Wiley.

Dechert, C. R. 1966. "The Development of Cybernetics." In C. R. Dechert, ed., *The Social Impact of Cybernetics*. Notre Dame, IN: University of Notre Dame Press.

Dobb, M. 1973. *Theories of Value and Distribution Since Adam Smith: Ideology and Economic Theory*. London: Cambridge University Press.

Dorfman, R., P. A. Samuelson, and R. M. Solow. 1958. *Linear Programming and Economic Analysis*. New York: McGraw-Hill.

Fox, K. A. 1969. "The Invisible Revolution in Economics: Emergence of a Mathematical Science." In K. A. Fox, J. K. Sengupta, and G. V. L. Narasimham, eds., *Economic Models, Estimation, and Risk Programming*. New York: Springer-Verlag.

______. 1983. "The Eco-Behavioral View of Human Societies and Its Implications for Systems Science." *International Journal of Systems Science* 14: 895-914.

Fox, K. A., and T. K. Kaul. 1980. *Intermediate Economic*

Statistics. Volume II. Huntington, NY: Robert E. Krieger Co.

Frydman, R. 1982. "Towards an Understanding of Market Processes Individual Expectations, Learning, and Convergence to Rational Expectations Equilibrium." American Economic Review 72: 652-668.

Georgescu-Roegen, N. 1966. Analytical Economics. Cambridge: Harvard University Press.

Hahn, F. 1982. "The Neo-Ricardians." Cambridge Journal of Economics 6: 353-374.

Hayek, F. A. 1937. "Economics and Knowledge." Economica 4: 33-54. Reprinted in J. M. Buchanan and G. F. Thirlby, eds., 1981, L.S.E. Essays on Cost. New York: New York University Press.

Heller, E. 1965. The Artist's Journey Into the Interior and Other Essays. New York: Harcourt Brace Jovanovich.

Hicks, J. R. 1946. Value and Capital. 2nd ed. Oxford: Oxford University Press.

Hicks, J. 1982. Money, Interest, and Wages. Oxford: Basil Blackwell.

Janik, A., and S. Toulmin. 1973. Wittgenstein's Vienna. New York: Simon and Schuster.

Kaldor, N. 1934. "A Classificatory Note on the Determinateness of Equilibrium." Review of Economic Studies I: 123.

Katsenelinboigen, A. 1980. Soviet Economic Thought and Political Power in the USSR. New York: Pergamon Press.

Keat, R., and John Urry. 1982. Social Theory as Science. 2nd ed. London: Routledge and Kegan Paul.

Keynes, J. M. 1936. The General Theory of Employment, Interest and Money. New York: Harcourt, Brace and World.

______. 1973. The Collected Writings of John Maynard Keynes 14. London: Macmillan.

Kolakowski, L. 1968. The Alienation of Reason: A History of Positivist Thought. Translated by Norman Guterman. New York: Doubleday.

Koopmans, T. C. 1957. Three Essays on the State of Economic Science. New York: McGraw-Hill.

Leamer, E. E. 1983. "Let's Take the Con out of Econometrics." American Economic Review 73: 31-43.

Leontief, W. W. 1951. The Structure of American Economy, 1919-1939. New York: Oxford University Press.

Luhman, N. 1982. The Differentiation of Society. New York: Columbia University Press.

Machlup, F. 1964. "Professor Samuelson on Theory and Realism." American Economic Review 54: 733-736.

Maron, M. E. 1968. "Norbert Wiener." International Encyclopedia of the Social Sciences 16: 545-547.

Marx, K. 1978. "Economic and Philosophic Manuscripts of 1844." Reprinted in Robert C. Tucker, ed., The Marx-Engels Reader. 2nd ed. New York: W. W. Norton.

______. 1977. Capital. Translated by Ben Fowkes. New York: Random House.

Mill, J. S. 1897. "On the Definition of Political Economy; and on the Method of Investigation Proper to It." Reprinted in J. W. M. Gibbs, ed., Early Essays by John Stuart Mill. London: George Bell and Sons.

Muir, J. 1969. How to Keep Your Volkswagen Alive. Santa Fe, NM: John Muir Publications.

O'Driscoll, G. P., Jr., and M. J. Rizzo. 1985. The Economics of Time and Ignorance. Oxford: Basil Blackwell.

Pears, D. 1970. Ludwig Wittgenstein. New York: The Viking Press.

Phillips, D. C. 1976. Holistic Thought in Social Science. Stanford, CA: Stanford University Press.

Rapoport, A. 1968. "Systems Analysis." International Encyclopedia of the Social Sciences 15: 452-458.

Roncaglia, A. 1978. Sraffa and the Theory of Prices. New York: Wiley.

Samuelson, P. A. 1947. Foundations of Economic Analysis. Cambridge: Harvard University Press.

______. 1963. "Problems of Methodology-Discussion." American Economic Review Papers and Proceedings 53: 211-219.

______. 1964. "Theory and Realism: A Reply." American Economic Review 54: 736-739.

Shackle, G. L. S. 1972. Epistemics and Economics. Cambridge: Cambridge University Press.

Schumpeter, J. A. 1954. History of Economic Analysis. New York: Oxford University Press.

Sraffa, P. 1926. "The Laws of Returns Under Competitive Conditions." Economic Journal 36: 535-550.

______. 1930. "'A Criticism' and 'Rejoinder,' Interventions in the 'Symposium on Increasing Returns and the Representative Firm.'" Economic Journal 40: 89-93.

______. 1932. "Dr. Hayek on Money and Capital." Economic Journal 42: 42-53.

______. 1960. Production of Commodities by Means of Commodities. Cambridge: Cambridge University Press.

Tinbergen, J. 1956. Economic Policy: Principles and Design. Amsterdam: North-Holland.

Veblen, T. 1906/1919. "The Place of Science in Modern Civilization." The American Journal of Sociology 11 (March). Reprinted in Thorstein Veblen, The Place of Science in Modern Civilization and Other Essays. New York: Russell & Russell.

von Bertalanffy, L. 1968. General Systems Theory. New York: George Braziller.

Walras, L. 1954. Elements of Pure Economics. Translated by William Jaffe. London: George Allen and Unwin Ltd.

Walsh, V., and H. Gram. 1980. Classical and Neo-Classical Theories of General Equilibrium. Oxford: Oxford University Press.

Weintraub, E. Roy. 1979. Microfoundations. Cambridge: Cambridge University Press.

______. 1983. "On the Existence of a Competitive Equilibrium: 1930-1954." Journal of Economic Literature 21: 1-39.

Wiener, N. 1948. Cybernetics. New York: Wiley.

______. 1953. Ex-Prodigy. New York: Simon and Schuster.

Wittgenstein, L. 1922. Tractatus Logico-Philosophicus. London: K. Paul, Trench, Trubner, and Co.

3

Systems Theory in Mathematical Economics

ROY J. GARDNER

INTRODUCTION

A system is any process that transforms inputs into outputs.[1] At this level of generality, a theory of systems would appear to apply to everything that economics studies; production, exchange, distribution, and class struggle are all systems. Paradoxically, it is possible to get a Ph.D. in economics and never hear of systems theory. Yet the major concepts of this theory have had an enormous influence on economics, and particularly on mathematical economics, in the course of the twentieth century, or so I shall argue. The argument will draw on major theoretical advances, each of which illustrates central ideas of systems theory. Before turning to the economic applications, however, it is first necessary to define a system more formally and introduce some of its major properties.

A LEXICON OF SYSTEMS AND THEIR PROPERTIES

This section considers the general definition of a system and nine major properties systems may have.

Let X be a vector of inputs and Y a vector of outputs, with F denoting the transformation of input into output. Then the system consisting of this transformation process can be represented as

$$Y = F(X) \tag{3.1}$$

For instance, a production function is a paradigm case of a system. One adds structure to this general framework by imposing some or all of the following properties.

Memory

A system has memory if any of the inputs X are dated earlier than the outputs Y. For example, take the scalar system (3.2),

$$y(t) = x(t-1) \tag{3.2}$$

This system has memory since it is past, rather than current, values of x which determine y. By contrast, the system

$$y(t) = 2x(t) \tag{3.3}$$

is memoryless. Output only depends on current values of inputs.

Discrete

A system is discrete if the dynamics of the system are described by difference equations. A system is continuous if its dynamics are described by differential equations. The system (3.4),

$$p(t+1) = F[p(t)] \tag{3.4}$$

describing the law of supply and demand, where F is a sign-preserving function of excess demand, is discrete: trading takes place at discrete intervals. By contrast, the system (3.5),

$$\frac{dp}{dt} = F[p(t)] \tag{3.5}$$

is continuous. System (3.5) describes the same system as (3.4), only with continuous trading. System (3.5) is also memoryless (recontracting).

Invertibility

A system is invertible if the roles of inputs and outputs can be reversed. For instance, the system (3.2) is invertible, with its inverse being

$$x(t) = y(t+1) \tag{3.6}$$

Invertible systems offer great flexibility in modeling. A system which cannot be inverted is

$$y(t) = x(t)^2 \tag{3.7}$$

Causality

A system is causal if Y depends only on past values of X. Thus, a causal system must have memory, but the converse is not true. The system (3.2) is causal, while the system (3.7) is not. One of the major goals of modern econometrics is to discover causal systems.

Deterministic

If the relationship between inputs and outputs is immune from chance influences, it is deterministic. Systems (3.1)-(3.7) are all deterministic. If a random error enters a system, the system becomes stochastic.

Time Invariance

If the relationship between inputs and outputs does not depend explicitly on time, the system is time invariant. Systems (3.1)-(3.7) are all time invariant. An example of a time variant system is

$$y(t) = tx(t) \tag{3.8}$$

Thus, time invariant systems have constant coefficients, whereas systems with variable coefficients are time variant.

Stability

Consider an equilibrium of system (3.5), that is, a P^* such that

$$0 = \frac{dP}{dt} = F(P^*) \tag{3.9}$$

This system is <u>stable</u> if for an initial value P(0) in the neighborhood of P^*, P(t) approaches P^* over time. If the system approaches P^* for any initial P(0), the system (3.5) is <u>globally stable</u>. In the system literature, such a system is sometimes called <u>equifinal</u>. Where the system finally ends up does not depend on where it starts.

Linearity

A system is linear if F is linear in its argument. With the exception of (3.5), all systems considered so far have been linear. Indeed, the vast majority of applications of systems in economics are linear.

Controllability

Consider the system

$$\frac{dX}{dt} = F(X, U) \tag{3.10}$$

where X denotes the state of the system and U, the control being applied to the system. The output is the rate of change of the state of the system. System (3.10) is controllable if for any initial time t_0 and any two states $\underline{X}$ and X, there exists a finite time T and control U such that the system reaches X by time T starting from $\underline{X}$ at t_0. In a controllable system, the question of optimization is well posed.

With these nine major characteristics of systems in mind, it is time to turn to some applications of them in economics.

THE VON NEUMANN SYSTEM

One of the first and still among the most important examples of systems theory in economics is von Neumann's system.

Published over 50 years ago in German as "On an Economic Equation System and a Generalization of Brouwer's Fixedpoint Theorem," it appeared in an English translation in 1945. From a systems point of view, it represents a model of production as a discrete, deterministic, time invariant system with memory. This section outlines the economic meaning of the von Neumann system.

The simplest version of the von Neumann system which we will discuss here has two inputs and two outputs. Denote by

$$Y = \begin{bmatrix} y_1 \\ y_2 \end{bmatrix}$$

the vector of outputs and

$$X = \begin{bmatrix} x_1 \\ x_2 \end{bmatrix}$$

the vector of inputs. Let X_{ij} be the amount of input i allocated to the production of output j. The production function F_j for output j exhibits fixed proportions:

$$F_j = \min_i (k_{ij} x_{ij}) \tag{3.11}$$

where $k_{ij} > 0$ are fixed coefficients. A feasible allocation of resources satisfies the condition

$$\sum_{j=1}^{2} x_{ij} \leqq x_i \qquad \text{for all } i \tag{3.12}$$

The generalization from two to any number of inputs and outputs is immediate.

The feasible resource allocations constitute the frame of an Edgeworth box. The efficient resource allocations are identified within that frame. For instance, suppose that $x_1 = x_2 = 1$ and the fixed coefficients are $k_{11} = 3$, $k_{12} = 3$, $k_{21} = 4$, $k_{22} = 2$. Then the production functions satisfy

$$\begin{bmatrix} y_1 \\ y_2 \end{bmatrix} = \begin{bmatrix} \min(3x_{11}, 4x_{21}) \\ \min(3x_{12}, 2x_{22}) \end{bmatrix} \tag{3.13}$$

The efficient resource allocations for this system are depicted in Figure 3.1. Notice that the set of efficient allocations is not a line but rather a larger set, darkened in the figure. These multiple efficient allocations, corresponding to a given level of production, arise from the nonsubstitutibility within the production relations (3.13).

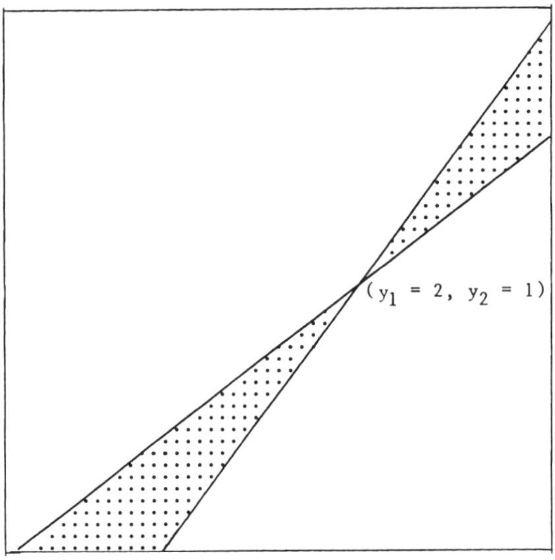

FIG. 3.1. Efficient resource allocations.

The system is closed by assuming that this period's outputs become next period's inputs:

$$X(t+1) = Y(t) \tag{3.14}$$

Concerning this assumption, von Neumann (1945) says, "Consumption of goods takes place only through the processes of production which include necessities of life consumed by workers and employees. . . . It is obvious to what kind of theoretical models the above assumptions correspond." Indeed, the closed version of the system has close affinities with Marx's notions of simple and expanded reproduction in volume 2 of *Capital* (1967, first published in 1885).

Several economic issues arise in the study of this model. First is the issue of *reproducibility*, that is, whether the system can at least sustain levels of output over time. The condition for reproducibility is that the inequality (3.15) holds for all time t:

$$Y(t+1) \geq Y(t) \tag{3.15}$$

Notice that the system (3.13) is reproducible. To show this, it suffices to exhibit a feasible allocation and corresponding output vector satisfying (3.15). Consider the feasible allocation of resources $x_{11} = 2/3$, $x_{21} = 1/2$, $x_{12} = 1/3$, $x_{22} = 1/2$. The corresponding output vector is $y_1 = 1$, $y_2 = 2$. Using the same resource allocation in the next period (there will be 1 unit of resource 2 left over) will reproduce the output vector y_1

= 1, y_2 = 2. By time invariance, the relation (3.14) holds for any time t.

Reproducibility is a precondition for expansion and growth of the economy. One can ask of a reproducible von Neumann system, what is the largest rate of growth of which it is capable, while at the same time maintaining constant proportions among its various outputs? Indeed, the major result of von Neumann (1945) is to prove the existence of such a maximal balanced growth rate. We will omit a demonstration of this result here, and instead, illustrate it for the system (3.13). Begin with $y_1(t-1) = y_2(t-1) = 1$. Next, compute the largest possible $y_1(t) = y_2(t) > 1$ satisfying the resource constraint. The result will be the maximal balanced growth rate for one period. By time invariance, this is the maximal rate of growth over any longer period.

To perform this computation, the first step is to compute the production possibilities corresponding to the efficient allocations. The result of this calculation is portrayed in Figure 3.2. The kink in the production possibility locus corresponds to the unique efficient allocation where both resource constraints are binding. To the right of the kink, only the resource 1 constraint is binding; to the left, only the resource 2 constraint. The balanced expansion path is the line from the origin passing through (1, 1). The distance from (1, 1) to the production possibility locus is the growth rate for the economy.

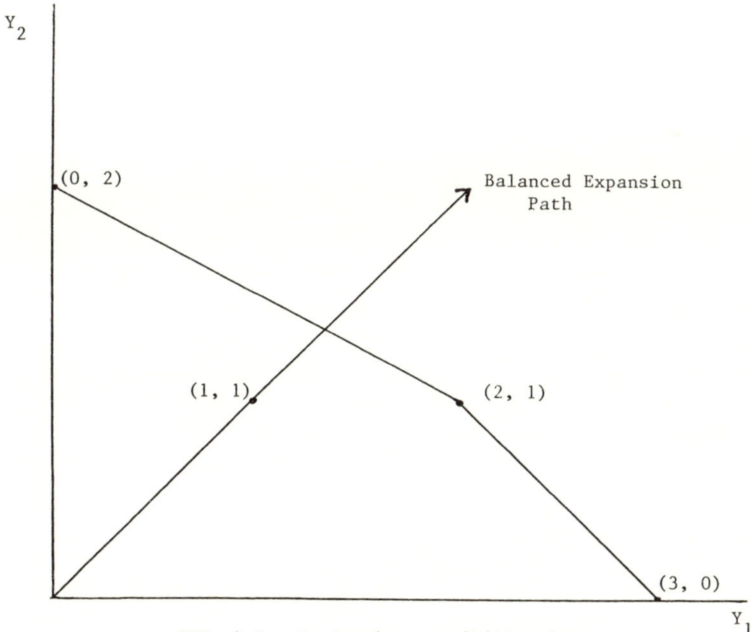

FIG. 3.2. Production possibility locus.

The solution here is $y_1 = y_2 = 4/3$, which is achieved by (among others) the resource allocation $x_{11} = 1/2$, $x_{21} = 1/3$, $x_{12} = 1/2$, $x_{22} = 2/3$. The maximal balanced growth rate of this system is 33 1/3%.

The von Neumann system displays a remarkable duality between growth rates and interest rates. The maximal balanced growth rate is equal to the minimum interest rate consistent with zero profits on the production of any good. For the system (3.13) this means a real rate of interest of 33 1/3%, which rate would be lower if the system were less expansive. It follows that non-reproducible systems will give rise to negative real interest rates when profits are zero. The von Neumann system has had an enormous influence on economic theory. The vast literature devoted to its generalization and extensions (e.g., turnpike theory) is witness to the fecundity of systems theory in this branch of economics.

STABILITY OF A SYSTEM

An important concept in systems theory is stability (equifinality). Stability is important principally in forecasting the evolution of a system: it allows one to pinpoint where a system is headed, without having to know exactly where the system is at present. This section will focus on the notion of stability due to Liapunov.

Consider the continuous dynamic system

$$\frac{dX}{dt} = F(X, t) \tag{3.16}$$

an equilibrium of which, X^*, satisfies

$$\frac{dX}{dt} = 0 = F(X^*, t) \tag{3.17}$$

The system (3.16) is stable in the sense of initial Liapunov if for all time t_0 and positive ε, there exists a δ, such that if $X(t_0)$ is in a δ neighborhood of X^*, then $X(t)$ is in an ε neighborhood of X^* for all t greater than t_0. Intuitively, this means that a stable system approaches an equilibrium when it is "close enough" in the first place. To characterize the stability concept inherent in this definition, it is useful to define a real-valued function $V(X, t)$ satisfying the conditions

$$V(X^*, t) = 0 \tag{3.18}$$

$$V(X, t) > 0 \quad \text{otherwise}$$

and that V be bounded above and below by continuous, nondecreasing monotonic functions increasing indefinitely in their argument (the distance between X and X^*). Such a function V is called a Liapunov function for the system (3.16). Thus, to say that the Liapunov function takes a value of zero means the system is at equilibrium. Differentiable V provides a very useful characterization of stable systems, as shown by Faurre and Depeyrot 1977, Theorem 5.1. If there exists a Liapunov function for the system (3.16) whose derivative is nonpositive for all (X, t), then the system is stable.

To illustrate the role this theorem plays in economic theory, we will address some issues in price dynamics. (For a more thorough discussion, see Arrow and Hahn 1971, Chapters 11-12.) Recall the system (3.5), according to which market prices P obey

$$\frac{dP}{dt} = F(P)$$

In fact, system (3.5) expresses the law of supply and demand. Suppose there are n markets. If there is excess demand in market i, $F_i(P) > 0$, and the price in that market, P_i, should rise.

An equilibrium of the system P^* is a price vector where all markets clear. The reason time does not enter explicitly in the dynamics is that the analysis assumes recontracting: no contract is final until all markets clear. The question immediately arises whether the law of supply and demand is stable; i.e., will the invisible hand lead prices to equilibrium?

To answer this question, we construct a Liapunov function for the system. Consider the function V(P) given by

$$V(P) = \sum_{i=1}^{n} (P_i - P_i^*)^2 \qquad (3.19)$$

This clearly satisfies (3.18) and the boundedness conditions (use 1/2 V and 2 V as bounding functions). Therefore, (3.19) is a Liapunov function for the market system. To be able to use the stability result, one has to be able to establish the nonpositive sign of the derivative of V:

$$\frac{dV}{dP} = 2 \Sigma (P_i - P_i^*) \frac{dP_i}{dt} \qquad (3.20)$$

$$= 2 \Sigma (P_i - P_i^*) F_i(P)$$

This requires a substantive economic hypothesis, namely, that the economy as a whole obeys the weak axiom of revealed preference. The economy satisfies the weak axiom of revealed preference if for all P

$$\Sigma P^* F(P) > 0 \qquad (3.21)$$

Now we can calculate the derivative of the Liapunov function,

(3.20). By Walras's Law, $\sum_{i=1}^{n} P_i F_i(P) = 0$; therefore, (3.20) becomes

$$\frac{dV}{dP} = -2 \Sigma P_i^* F_i(P) < 0 \tag{3.22}$$

the inequality following from (3.21). Since the Liapunov function has a negative derivative, the system is stable.

The hypothesis (3.21) is quite restrictive, and in fact, stability of supply-demand systems like (3.5) can be proved under more general conditions. However, this usually requires a Liapunov function different from (3.19). The interested reader should consult Arrow and Hahn's excellent treatment for details.

There have been numerous applications of Liapunov's theorem in economics, both micro- and macroeconomics. It is a remarkable fact that substantial progress in this area has depended so crucially on system theoretic results.

CONTROLLING A SYSTEM

Often in economics, interest focuses not merely on describing a system, but on controlling it. Indeed, this is the foremost concern of policy analysis. This section of the paper will consider the issues surrounding the control of a system.

Begin with the following linear version of system (3.10):

$$\frac{dX}{dt} = FX + GU \tag{3.23}$$

where X is an n-vector describing the state of the system, U is an n-vector of controls, and the matrices X and G are n-dimensional. System (3.23) might describe a business cycle for example, with components of X relating to income, employment, prices, and money, and components of U relating to various monetary and fiscal policy measures. Since F and G are constant matrices, the system (3.23) is time invariant.

The system (3.23) is <u>controllable</u> at time t_0 if, for a finite time T and pair of states $\underline{X}$ and $\bar{X}$, there exists a control U satisfying (3.23) and the endpoint constraints $X(t_0) = \underline{X}$ and $X(T) = \bar{X}$. A system is <u>completely controllable</u> if it is controllable for every time t_0. A sufficient condition for the complete controllability of the system (3.23) is given by the following theorem (Faurre and Depeyrot 1977, Theorem 4.2.2): System (3.23) is completely controllable if and only if

$$\text{rank } [G] = \text{rank } [FG] = \ldots \text{rank } [F^{n-1}G] = n \tag{3.24}$$

To illustrate this theorem, consider the following scalar version of (3.23):

$$\frac{dx}{dt} = \alpha + (\lambda - 1)x + \beta m \tag{3.25}$$

where x is national income, the state variable, and m is money, the control variable. The test for controllability (3.24) boils down to rank $[\beta] = 1$, that is, that β is non-zero. As long as the system (3.25) meets this condition, the policymaker can drive income to any desired level in finite time. Naturally, testing for complete controllability in a larger system is more involved.

Even so simple a system as (3.25) can make an important point about complete controllability. Suppose that (3.25) is amended to reflect the Lucas (1973) supply mechanism

$$\frac{dx}{dt} = \alpha + (\lambda - 1)x + \beta(m - E_{t-1}m) \tag{3.25$'$}$$

where $E_{t-1}m$ reflects the public's expectation of monetary policy prior to the policymaker's actual decision. Complete controllability of the system (3.25)' now involves two tests; first, that $B \neq 0$ and, second, that $m \neq E_{t-1}m$. This last means that for the system to be completely controllable, the public must be systematically mistaken in its expectations of monetary policy. If on the contrary, the public has rational expectations ($E_{t-1}m = m$), the system is not completely controllable. Thus, the result of Sargent and Wallace (1976) has a natural expression in systems theory. For the vector system (3.23)'

$$\frac{dX}{dt} = FX + G(U - E_{t-1}U) \tag{3.23$'$}$$

the Sargent and Wallace result generalizes as follows. As before, the rank condition (3.24) must be met. Furthermore, the <u>systematic deception</u> condition

$$U \neq E_{t-1}U \tag{3.26}$$

must also be met. Then the system (3.23)' is completely controllable.

The Sargent and Wallace result was originally stated for stochastic systems. We sketch the appropriate extension here. Let Z be a random error vector with mean zero in the system (3.23):

$$\frac{dX}{dt} = FX + GU + Z \tag{3.27}$$

Define the system Z to be <u>mean controllable</u> at time t_0 if for a finite time T and any pair of states $\underline{X}$, $\bar{X}$, there exists a control U satisfying (3.23) and the endpoint constraints $X(t_0) = \underline{X}$ and $E[X(T)] = \bar{X}$. The system is completely mean controllable if it is mean controllable for every time t_0. The rank test suffices for complete mean controllability as well. Moreover, for the system (3.27)' incorporating the Lucas supply mechanism

$$\frac{dX}{dt} = FX + G(U - E_{t-1}U) + Z \tag{3.27$'$}$$

conditions (3.24) and (3.26) make the system completely mean controllable.

If a system is completely controllable, then the question of the optimal control of the system is well posed. The branch of optimization theory dealing with systems has penetrated economics to a substantial degree (see Kamien and Schwartz 1981 and the references contained therein), and we touch upon it only briefly here.

Typically, control is costly to exercise. The government incurs costs when it conducts monetary policy, among them the transactions costs of trading bonds. Consider the following special version of (3.25)'

$$\frac{dx}{dt} = (\lambda - 1)x + m'' \qquad (3.25)''$$

corresponding to $\alpha = 0$ and $\beta = 1$. The objective of the control is to make income grow q% during the next year. Suppose that the costs associated with monetary policy are proportional to m^2 and not discounted. Then the optimal monetary policy is to

$$\text{minimize} \int_t^{t+1} m^2 \, dt$$

subject to (3.25)" and the constraint $x(t + 1) = (1 + q)x(t)$. The optimal control is characterized by the first order condition

$$\frac{dm}{dt} = (1 - \lambda)m \qquad (3.28)$$

Equation (3.28) implies that the optimal monetary policy follows Friedman's k% rule (Friedman 1969), where $k = 1 - \lambda$. Thus, optimal control theory can give a theoretical foundation to Friedman's recommended monetary policy. It can do much else besides. It has solved important problems in nearly every area of economics--natural resources, capital theory, labor economics, and portfolio theory, to name just a few. This versatility is another aspect of the relevance of systems theory to mathematical economics.

CAUSAL SYSTEMS

So far we have considered the role of systems theory in theoretical economics. Systems theory also has a role to play in empirical economics. This section will consider the role of causal systems in particular. In a deterministic causal system, past values of inputs determine present values of outputs. If one introduces a random error term into a deterministic causal system, a stochastic causal system results. Thus, if $e(t)$ denotes a random error term, the following version of (3.2) is a stochastic causal system:

$$y(t) = x(t-1) + e(t) \tag{3.2)'$$

In the system (3.2)', we continue to say that x causes y.

The most general definition of causation in the systems sense is due to Granger (1969). Let W denote the set of all information available up to time t-1. Let W - x denote all information except that contained in the time series x up to time t-1. Let $\sigma^2(y/W)$ denote the forecast error variance of y conditional on W. Then x causes y (in the sense of Granger) if

$$\sigma^2 \, [y(t)/W] < \sigma^2 \, [y(t)/W - x] \tag{3.29}$$

Intuitively, (3.29) says that adding the information contained in past values of x makes possible better forecasts of y.

Applying (3.29) to the system yields the following result. Suppose that x and e are covariance stationary processes with instantaneous variance σ_x^2 and σ_e^2 respectively. Then the variance of the forecast error of y(t) conditional on all information except x(t-1) is $\sigma_x^2 + \sigma_e^2$, while the forecast conditional on all information is only σ_e^2, clearly smaller.

There are several things to notice about this notion of causation in stochastic systems. First, the causation relation is relative to the universe of information W. Spurious causation could arise econometrically between two variables, in the event that both are being caused by a third variable which is being excluded by the investigator. Again, the causation relation need not be asymmetric. For instance, it is possible for x to cause y and y to cause x, as in the system

$$\begin{aligned} y(t) &= ax(t-1) + e_1(t) \\ x(t) &= by(t-1) + e_2(t) \end{aligned} \tag{3.30}$$

A system such as (3.30) is called a feedback system. Feedback is therefore tantamount to simultaneous causation.

To test for causality in the x causes y direction, a standard procedure is the following. First, estimate the lag equation

$$y(t) = \sum_{i=1}^{m} a(i)y(t-i) + \sum_{j=1}^{m} b(j)x(t-j) + e(t) \tag{3.31}$$

Then, perform an F-test on the hypothesis b(j) = 0 for all j. If the F value is large enough to reject the hypothesis, then some b(j) differs significantly from zero and x causes y. To check for feedback, one runs the converse test, reversing the roles of x and y in (3.31). For practical details, see Sims 1972.

Causality is a central notion in contemporary econometrics.

For one thing, it is an important ingredient in establishing exogeneity relationships, as the recent work of Engle et al. (1983) shows. For another thing, causality can often provide a new approach to testing more effectively contested economic theories. We will consider an instance of each of these possibilities in turn.

Suppose an investigator is modeling the income-money relationship. Suppose further that money in fact causes income but not the converse. Then it is a serious error to specify this relationship as (3.31) with y = money and x = income. Income cannot be treated as exogenous in the money equation if money causes income. This is precisely the thrust of Sims (1972), in particular of his empirical finding that money causes income but not the converse. Notice also that this last result lends credence to the Lucas supply function in discrete form:

$$y(t) = \alpha + \lambda y(t-1) + \beta[m(t) - E_{t-1}m(t)] + e(t) \qquad (3.32)$$

If the public's expectation of current money supply, $E_{t-1}m(t)$, itself depends on past money, then money will cause income in (3.30).

As a second example, consider the efficient markets hypothesis applied to the spot-forward price relationship. If the market for foreign exchange, say, is efficient, then this relationship should satisfy

$$s(t+1) = f(t) + e(t+1) \qquad (3.33)$$

where s(t) is the spot price next period, f(t) is the one-period-forward price, and e(t+1) is a random error with mean zero. In particular, it follows from (3.33) that E[s(t+1)] = f(t); the forward price predicts the future spot price. Now if the efficient markets hypothesis is true, then speculators or other price forecasters should not be able to forecast future spot prices more effectively by reacting to their previous errors. That is, past spot-forward deviations should not cause spot prices. Thus, in the equation

$$s(t+1) = a_1[s(t) - f(t-1)] + a_2[s(t-1) - f(t-2)] + e(t+1) \qquad (3.34)$$

the coefficients a_1 and a_2 should both be zero if the foreign exchange market is to be efficient. Hansen and Hodrick (1980) test equation (3.34) for various currencies, finding, for instance, that the market for German marks against English pounds was not efficient during the 1923-1924 German hyperinflation.

Just as in economic theory, systems theoretic concepts have proved to be of great value in econometrics. The role they play can only increase as more econometric relationships are viewed from the point of view of causality.

COMPARING SYSTEMS

The word "system" in economics is significantly ambiguous. Throughout this paper, a system has meant a certain mathematical relationship. However, system can also refer to the entire set of institutions which comprise the economy, hence, the classical dichotomy of economic systems into capitalist and socialist. This section will exploit the ambiguity, with the intention of showing how systems theory in the former sense helps compare economic systems in the latter sense.

The basic paper in this area is the contribution by Koopmans and Montias (1971), who were the first to apply a systems theory approach to this question. Let x denote the environment; s, the economic system; and p_s, the set of policies chosen within the system. Then taking (x, s, p_s) as a vector of inputs, one has the system

$$y = f(x, s, p_s) \tag{3.35}$$

where y denotes the outcome of the system. Equation (3.35) provides a general system description of an economic system.

One of the major objectives of the study of any economic system is to discover the relationship f. Another major objective is to compare various outcomes. To this end, let W denote a welfare comparison function, and suppose y_1 and y_2 are the outcomes of systems 1 and 2 respectively. Then system 1 performs better than system 2 if

$$W(y_1) > W(y_2) \tag{3.36}$$

If the outcome y is itself a vector, then W is often taken to be a weighted sum with outcome weights λ:

$$W(y) = \sum_{i=1}^{m} \lambda(i)y(i) \tag{3.37}$$

For example, inflation, unemployment, income, growth, and various other indicators of economic performance may enter the outcome vector y. This section will show how these ideas apply to some Soviet-American economic comparisons based on the work of Gardner and Strauss (1981).

One basis for comparing the Soviet and American economies is in terms of inflation. In light of Lenin's dictum that inflation corrodes the structure of capitalist society, such a comparison is especially ideologically compelling. In this light, the recent American experience has been far from encouraging: since 1967, the CPI has nearly tripled. Meanwhile, in the Soviet

Union, there has been hardly any inflation. For instance, the Soviet counterpart to the CPI, the index of state goods prices, went up from 138 in 1955 to 139 in 1975. There is a great temptation to say that the Soviet data is pure falsification and therefore to be ignored. If one resists this temptation long enough to delve more deeply into matters, however, one can arrive at a meaningful comparison. After all, prices in the American economic system reflect the forces of supply and demand. If prices do not reflect such forces in the Soviet system, then the stability of the price index may signal a qualitatively different outcome, viz. repressed inflation.

To argue this, one has to compare two possible regimes of the Soviet system, corresponding to equilibrium or repressed inflation in the state-controlled goods market. Let i be the level of inventories of state-controlled goods; y_1, the net material product; M, the quantity of money; W, the aggregate wages; and C, aggregate expenditure outside of state stores. If the Soviet system is in equilibrium, then these variables can be described by the following linear system with memory (see Gardner and Strauss 1981 for details):

$$\bar{i}(t+1) = .14\ [\bar{i}(t) + y_1(t)] \tag{3.38}$$

$$\bar{M}(t+1) = .21\ [\bar{M}(t) + W(t)] \tag{3.39}$$

The system (3.38)-(3.39) appears to best describe the Soviet economy during the Khrushchev era.

If the state-controlled goods market is in excess demand, with the price held artificially low to repress inflation, then the system description changes. It turns out that equation (3.38) still holds in this case, but that (3.39) must be replaced by

$$\bar{M}(t+1) = .84\ [\bar{M}(t) + W(t) - C(t)] \tag{3.39'}$$

The data strongly suggest that the latter system best describes the state-controlled goods market in the Brezhnev era. In the year 1975, for example, the repressed inflation appears to have led to about 40 billion rubles of excess demand, compared to total state goods market expenditures of 210 billion rubles. It is estimated that about 7 billion rubles of this excess demand took the form of forced substitution (purchase of goods on the black market, etc.). The rest went into forced savings. Savings account balances for this year were 91 billion rubles; over a third of this appears to have been forced.

Thus, the stability of the official price index may indeed reflect price stability in the Soviet economy. However, the basis for system comparison is not at all one-sided. Against the costs of inflation to the American economy, one must set the costs of repressed inflation in the Soviet economy. In this regard, systems theory leads to a much more "powerful" and useful comparison of these two systems than the superficial comparison of the two price indices might suggest.

CONCLUSION

This paper has surveyed applications of systems theory in several areas of economics--economic growth, systems stability, systems control, causal systems, and comparing whole economies. The ideas of systems theory are remarkable for their versatility and depth in contributing to economic understanding. Yet an air of paradox surrounds this contribution, for very few (if any) economics departments offer a course in systems theory. The situation is much like that of game theory, which has also had a remarkable impact on economics but which few departments teach. The moral is that field and department designations are mainly for the benefit of university administrations and hardly reflect the underlying unity of a science, especially when it is undergoing significant change. Today's graduate student in economics must know a nontrivial amount of systems theory, whether he has the benefit of a course in the subject or not.

Part of the spur to advance in any science is the infusion of new ideas from the outside. Economists have too often been prone to say, "It's all in Marshall," when--as in the case of systems theory--none of it is in Marshall. Systems theory is vital to research at the forefront of economics and promises to grow in importance in the years to come.

NOTES

1. For a useful introduction to systems theory, see Faurre and Depeyrot 1977.

REFERENCES

Arrow, K. J., and F. H. Hahn. 1971. *General Competitive Analysis*. San Francisco: Holden-Day.

Engle, R. F., D. F. Hendry, and J. F. Richard. 1983. "Exogeneity." *Econometrica* 51: 277-304.

Faurre, P., and M. Depeyrot. 1977. *Elements of System Theory*. New York: North-Holland.

Friedman, M. 1969. *The Optimum Quantity of Money, and Other Essays*. Chicago: Aldine.

Gardner, R., and J. Strauss. 1981. "Repressed Inflation in the Soviet Union." *European Economic Review* 16: 387-404.

Granger, C. W. J. 1969. "Investigating Causal Relations by Econometric Models and Cross-Spectral Methods." *Econometrica* 37: 424-438.

Hansen, L. P., and R. J. Hodrick. 1980. "Forward Exchange Rates as Optimal Predictors of Future Spot Rates: An Econometric Analysis." *Journal of Political Economy* 88: 829-853.

Kamien, M., and N. Schwartz. 1981. *Dynamic Optimization*. New York: North-Holland.

Koopmans, T. C., and J. M. Montias. 1971. "On the Comparison of Economic Systems." In A. Eckstein, ed., *Comparison of Economic Systems: Theoretical and Methodological Approaches*. Berkeley: University of California Press.

Lucas, R. 1973. "Some International Evidence on Output-Inflation Tradeoffs." *American Economic Review* 63: 326-334.

Marx, K. 1967. *Capital*. Volume II. New York: International Publishers. (First published in 1885.)

Sargent, T. J., and N. Wallace. 1976. "Rational Expectations and the Theory of Economic Policy." *Journal of Monetary Economics* 2: 199-213.

Sims, C. 1972. "Money, Income, and Causality." *American Economic Review* 62: 540-552.

von Neumann, J. 1945. "A Model of General Economic Equilibrium." *Review of Economic Studies* 13: 1-9.

4

The Concept of Variety in Systems Behavior: Applications to Behavior Settings, Product-differentiation, and Representative Firms

JATI K. SENGUPTA

INTRODUCTION

Since its inception, economics has been a part of behavioral science and is also an evolutionary science. Yet its tools have been very limited when it has had to analyze social behavior and even more so when it has had to explain why the same innovation succeeded in one culture while failing in another.

The economist acts here much like the manager of a business enterprise. He is certainly aware that social dynamics are as important for market demand as for community interaction; yet he limits his expertise to forecasting market demand and perhaps simulating a variety of market scenarios. No theory of social dynamics has filtered into most economists' concept of management and managerial efficiency.

In addition to Boulding's work, there are two exceptions to this pattern. One is the recent theory of comparative evaluation of alternative managerial styles, e.g., Japanese vs. American styles. Customary and somewhat popular discussions here often refer to sociological and cultural factors behind the enterprise system as a whole. However, what seems to be lacking is a set of basic postulates forming the core of a systematic theory which can generate testable hypotheses.

The second exception is offered by the economist's dissatisfaction with the so-called mechanistic theories of economic development which run in terms of neoclassical growth models defined in difference-differential equations. These theories smack of cause-effect relationships; e.g., a given dose of investment must lead to a certain level of output and income, except perhaps for some random error which can be neglected for all practical purposes. By tinkering with random errors as a catchall term, the delusion is created that the cause-effect or input-output relations are changed from technological to behavioral responses. The conjuncture, a term used by Alfred Marshall to describe the overall socioeconomic framework, is left to hang by its bootstraps either in the catchall term or in the minds of noneconomists.

It is clear that some soul searching is called for. The economist has to evaluate his concepts and tools and ask why his theory has not delved deep into social behavior to turn itself into a viable social theory. It is true that in several specific areas economic theory has extended its market-oriented boundaries, e.g., human capital theory, social indicators, theory of search, and public goods. Also, the classical notions of equilibrium have been seriously questioned in recent developments of economic theory; so has the notion that the process of information transfer is either automatic or costless.

These developments, however, are fundamentally based on the <u>economic method</u>, which for our purpose may be taken to comprise three aspects: a market system, a choice mechanism, and a set of constraints. While the market system with its prices allows variables to be observed, measured, and traded currently and over the future, the choice mechanism, with the relevant institutional constraints, brings in the optimization objectives of the economic agents, which may or may not always be mutually compatible.

This economic method may still be applicable, at least in part, to the resource allocation decisions of nonprofit agencies such as schools, hospitals, and other public units involved in production of goods and services. Queueing and waiting line models in operations research have been very successful in developing viable economic models in this area, based on implicit optimization criteria such as service characteristics. Also, cybernetic systems have developed probabilistic error criteria.

Assume, however, a framework in which there are no markets, no observable prices, and it is not known if there are any optimization objectives implicit in the agents' behavior. There may be constraints due to the environment, although these may not be clearly known. It is apparent that this state of the world is very germane to the description of the natural distribution of species in the ecological environment. In this environment, individual species form groups and clusters, they interact and compete, and the evolution dynamics display characteristics of diversity and branching, which are sometimes analyzed by mathematical models known as "bifurcation phenomena in nonlinear systems."

It is true that the natural selection principle and the maximum entropy distribution are sometimes used as choice mechanisms to postulate the growth and survival of certain species against others. These choice mechanisms are, however, partitioning devices for classification. They may also be viewed as methods for delimiting the overall problem of describing the ecological pattern.

Two features of this ecological pattern have been striking: one is that of diversity and the other that of interacting phenomena in evolutionary dynamics. Diversity is a form of variety having many facets and multivariate features, not all of which have been fully explored even today. Interaction in growth or decline among species, clusters, or habitats provides both a stabilizing and a destabilizing force depending on specific situations. Analysis of such situations thus provides an important line of inquiry, which has been exploited in part by the statistical theories of stochastic processes involving contagious distributions and mixtures of dissimilar components.

Constraints in the natural environment take the forms of truncation and rigidity. The former occurs when the probability distribution of a certain species, for example, gets transformed over time due to barriers to propagation or other exogenous changes in the environment. It may also be due to conditioning variables which may alter the conditional distribution or growth of a species. Rigidity implies a lack of flexibility in the scope of choice, and in physical sciences flexibility is measured by the degree of freedom.

It is clear that variety in the sense of diversity is reduced by rigidity, since the degree of freedom is lowered by constraints. Thus Ashby (1958) defines a constraint as a relation between two sets which occurs when the variety that exists under one condition is less than the variety that exists under another. For example, the variety in the human sexes (measured by the logarithm to the base 2 of the number of distinct elements) is 1 bit, but if a certain school admits only boys, the variety in the sexes within the school is zero. Since zero is less than unity, a constraint exists.

This notion of variety can of course be generalized to include vectors of measurements, e.g., vectors of characteristics or attributes, and then the constraints appear to reduce the feasibility space defined by the vector points. In the limit, some constraints may reduce the variety to zero, as the shadow costs associated with the constraints become too high. This has led Boulding (1981) to conjecture that there is indeed an optimum degree of variety in ecological patterns, and those species which have stood the test of time and have therefore displayed more efficiency are precisely those displaying an optimal degree of variety in a statistical sense.

We have described here the basic elementary steps required for characterizing an eco-behavioral system, which combines the ecological in the sense of nonmarket-oriented behavior and the behavioral in the sense of market-oriented responses. Clusters or genotypes replace the notion of markets. Variety displays the choice mechanism through mutual interaction and spatial competition over inputs, outputs, and exchange of information. Finally, constraints impose adaptation in behavior, either through learning or by reducing the variety of behavior. Learning is worthwhile when the environment shows constraints. It is also gainful when there is uncertainty and risk in the information transfer process.

This paper has two main objectives: (1) to emphasize and illustrate some basic elements of a general theory of behavior settings in which variety occupies a central place and (2) to point out some key economic areas in which the concept of variety can be profitably explored and applied. The theory of behavior settings, originated by Roger Barker and his associates (1968, 1973), has been considerably extended by Karl Fox (1974) and his associates over the past nine years, particularly by Fox and Sengupta (1977), Fox (1983, 1984, 1985), and Sengupta (1978a, b, c; 1986). Since my comments on the Fox-Barker eco-behavioral system are reported elsewhere, we will not discuss them in any technical detail here. Instead, we will concentrate on some of the important implications of such a theory, which generalizes the economic basis of a social theory.

VARIETY IN BEHAVIOR SETTINGS

In the theory of behavior settings, the unit of behavior pattern of individuals in an organization is a behavior setting, which denotes one or more standing patterns of behavior with a habitat (location) where individuals participate in different forms under different organizational systems; e.g., a medical clinic in a community is a behavior setting with a primary health habitat, a retail neighborhood store is a behavior setting with a trade habitat. It is clear that the concept of a behavior setting is more general than the concept of an activity used in activity analysis, pioneered by von Neumann's contributions.

Participation in a behavior setting involves, of course, some allocation of time and resources for every participant, and in purely job-related behavior settings such time allocations may be given an optimal interpretation, as Fox (1974) has done in his extension of Barker's original theory. But even in job-related settings, there exist extra-economic and extra-individual consequences of participation: variety and richness as outcomes of participation (e.g., job satisfaction), erosion or innovation of behavior settings (analogous to the disappearance of old goods and services to accommodate new ones in the consumption basket), and the quality of participation in a setting measured by the hierarchy of performance zones (e.g., in settings such as fourth grade classes the teachers are in the leadership zones of performance).

The participation in a behavior setting, its quality and intensity, are greatly affected, if not also conditioned, by two forces. One is the existence of different authority systems such as private enterprises, government agencies, and religious institutions with their respective rules of prescribed behavior.

The second is the signalling and communication mechanism for information transfer. Both affect and modify the intensity and quality of participation in a specific behavior setting.

For the economist, the most convenient authority system is of course that of private enterprises, where the market provides a set of signalling devices mostly through prices and the rules of behavior are laid down by the state of competition, the optimizing objectives of the participants, and the intensity of search for relevant information. It is only very recently that economists have begun to reexamine the whole theory of competitive equilibrium and its efficiency with respect to informational messages: the way they are formed, transmitted through decentralized decisions, and hopefully guide the various agents to convergence. For other authority systems, in default of observable prices, it is clear that the equilibrium and efficiency calculus of the competitive equilibrium model have to be considerably modified, if not rejected altogether.

The second major component in the theory of behavior settings is its emphasis on the cluster of settings called a genotype, which comprises settings with almost identical coded programs (for example, several grocery stores or several elementary school classes). The genotype concept thus indicates aggregation as a characteristic of the total behavior of a community in terms of the totality of interactions of individuals with their community environment which result in a given spatial and temporal distribution of settings.

The degree of behavior setting similarity for establishing a genotype has been defined by Barker broadly in terms of similarity of standing patterns and of participation in behavior settings (e.g., two school classes or two retail stores specializing in similar merchandise). To any economist familiar with the problem of applying Leontief-type input-output models to real life data, the criterion of similarity of functions as a basis for grouping industries into sectors seems very familiar; one must remember, however, that the genotype concept should apply not only to private enterprises but to other authority systems as well.

Genotypes or clusters may of course be aggregated at higher levels to comprise, for example, a supergenotype, just as a many-player game may be aggregated to a supergame involving two players with aggregated strategies. Suppose the intensity of participation in a behavior setting is measured by occupancy hours per person (i.e., time use) and the totality of behavior settings in a town or community is classified into N clusters or behavior setting aggregates by the following statistical principle of classification: the basis of stratification is such that the variability of occupancy hours within a cluster is minimized, while at the same time maximizing the variability between clusters. Any such classification based purely on the statistical scatter may be called an optimal clustering. The number of clusters or supergenotypes in a town or an industrial sector and the extent of variability in occupancy hours between and within clusters would thus provide a very powerful measure of habitat variety, i.e., a measure of the diversity of behavior resources and capacities and the resultant behavioral output.

Indeed, Barker used the number of genotypes in a community as a measure of its habitat variety and attempted dynamic comparisons of two communities (e.g., Midwest, Kansas, and Yoredale, Yorkshire) as they evolved from 1954-1955 to 1963-1964 and simultaneous comparisons of several high schools in northeast Kansas, some small and others big. The first type of comparison showed, for instance, how increasing urbanization has affected community life in terms of the primary habitats of health, education, recreation, social contact, and other action patterns. The second comparison measured the impact of school-size increase on the number and variety of genotypes or clusters of behavior settings, their variability of occupancy hours between and within groups.

The total number and kinds of athletic behavior settings were found to increase as the school size became larger, but some of the invisible costs had been almost ignored. For example, in spite of the greater number and variety of educational behavior settings in the large schools, the available evidence indicates that (as was true with the athletic and other extracurricular behavior settings) the large schools' students participated in fewer classes and varieties of classes _per student_ than did the small schools' students. The problem of specialization and school size was further investigated in the case of a single subject matter area, music, and it was found by complete enumeration that musical education and experience were more widely distributed among the small schools' than among the large schools' students. It is clear that if versatility of experience is preferred over opportunity for specialization, a smaller school is better than a larger one; if specialization is desired, the larger school is the better.

Another component of the theory of behavior settings, emphasized and extended by Karl Fox and his associates, is that the participation in various behavior settings can be decomposed into suitable inputs (behavior capacities) and suitable outputs (intrinsic and extrinsic rewards). This has two major implications for a dynamic theory. First, it leads to a concept of "total income," or "full income," defined as the product of a person's average return to his behavioral capacity utilized and his effective available hours per year. Some of the returns are nonmonetary and not market related. This provides a firm basis for generalizing the concept of national income into a more meaningful social indicator index.

The second implication is that an individual's time allocation model leads to a generalized formulation by adding specific life-style and human resource vectors for each member of an exhaustive set of population subgroups to a stationary demographic model. Changes in specific resource vectors may then be interpreted as generalized human capital transactions; these transactions may be due to the transition, for example, of a vector of individuals belonging to h life-style categories from one state to another at two consecutive ages i and i+1.

An important way to generalize the theory of behavior settings is to develop empirical tests on the pattern of behavior settings, its clusters and interrelations. To fix ideas, let x_{ijk} denote the time spent by individual i in setting j in an authority system k, where $i \varepsilon I$, $j \varepsilon J$, $k \varepsilon K$, and $I = \{1, 2, \ldots, m\}$, $J = \{1, 2, \ldots, n\}$, $K = \{1, 2, \ldots, r\}$. Time, or occupancy hours, is used only for illustrative purposes, although a more general concept of numeraire may have to be devised. Denote the subtotals $\sum_{i \varepsilon I} x_{ijk}$, $\sum_{j \varepsilon J} x_{ijk}$, $\sum_{k \varepsilon K} x_{ijk}$ by $x_{\bullet jk}$, $x_{i \bullet k}$, $x_{ij \bullet}$ respectively. Another level of aggregation may generate statistics such as $x_{\bullet\bullet k}$, $x_{i \bullet\bullet}$, and $x_{\bullet j \bullet}$ and their probability distributions. The task of a general theory is to establish, on the basis of the observed scatter $\{x_{ijk}\}$, whether there is a systematic pattern of variations measured by the aggregate level statistics, e.g., $x_{\bullet jk}$ and $x_{\bullet j \bullet}$. The genotypes of behavior settings in the Fox-Barker system do indeed postulate such systematic variations in communities, which can be empirically tested, analyzed, and improved upon. Three types of tests may be proposed for constructing a general theory along this line.

The first is a structural test whereby the linkages of genotypes of behavior settings are analyzed for similarity or dissimilarity. Does one cluster of behavior settings have a specified degree of interdependence (or independence) with other clusters? If the interdependence between clusters is very strong, does it imply an overall eco-behavioral system that is stable in some sense?

The second is a performance test, when input and output measures can be associated with the data $\{x_{ijk}\}$ on behavior settings. Thus, behavior settings are like activities through which input and output vectors can be defined, as is done in von Neumann's growth model. A given authority system at two points of time may thus be compared from these input-output vectors. Note that a set of market prices is not required.

The third is a stability test on the distribution of behavior settings, which shows the pattern of evolution of a community as a transition from one set of habitats to another. This aspect has been strongly emphasized by ecologists and demographers as a mechanism of adjustment with environments having both positive and negative feedback effects on the community.

The economic model is most suited to the performance test, when input costs and output values may be associated with behavior settings. Thus, one could usefully compare the relative efficiencies, e.g., of elementary schools using surrogate variables for inputs and outputs which are functions of participation in behavior settings (measured by occupancy hours, for example).

Thus, let y, z be vectors of inputs and outputs of school s which one can observe. There are S schools in the system. Let u and v be the vectors of imputed prices of inputs and outputs, so that we have for school s = 1, 2, ..., S the output-input ratio h_s defined by

$$h_s = v'z_s/u'y_s \tag{4.1}$$

where prime denotes transpose. School $s_0 \varepsilon S$ is then efficient relative to other schools in S if the maximum value of h_{s_0} denoted by $h^*_{s_0}$ is unity in the following optimization problem:

$$\underset{\{v,\, u\}}{\text{maximize}}\ h_{s_0} = v'z_{s_0}/u'y \tag{4.2}$$

$$\text{subject to} \quad 0 \leqslant h_s \leqslant 1, \quad u \geqslant 0, \quad v \geqslant 0$$

$$s = 1, 2, \ldots, s_0, s_0+1, \ldots, S$$

If at the optimal "prices" (v^*, u^*), the ratio $h^*_{s_0}$ is less than unity, we have relative inefficiency. This measure of relative efficiency, originally proposed by Charnes, Cooper, and Rhodes (1978), is closely related to Pareto efficiency in economics and can be considerably improved upon if there are competitive markets for inputs and outputs. Thus, the imputed optimal prices v^*, u^* are surrogate prices useful for relative ranking; however, they are not unique. If against data variations in $\{z_s, y_s\}$ these prices were stable in the sense that the relative efficiency ranking remained invariant, then they would characterize the pattern of behavior setting clusters, be it schools, medical clinics, or retail stores.

The structural test for behavior setting clusters depends on multivariate measures of similarity and dissimilarity. Two types of measures may be readily suggested. One is based on the concept of a "distance" between the time-allocation matrices $\{x_{\cdot jk}\}$ for any pair of communities and the other on the affinity of probability distributions $p(x_{\cdot jk})$ generating these matrices. For example, assume that k is fixed (i.e., the authority hierarchy is fixed) and we have the vector $X_k = \{x_{\cdot j}\}$ and its associated probability $P_k = p(x_{\cdot j})$ for the behavior settings related to k. The distance between two vectors may then be measured by the Euclidean metric or, if the multivariate distribution of the vectors is approximately normal with means M_k and variances V_k, by the D^2-statistic

$$D^2_{12} = (M_1 - M_2)'(V_1 + V_2)^{-1}(M_1 - M_2) \tag{4.3}$$

For general cases, the maximum entropy distributions may

also be compared for affinity and diversity. For any two similar (dissimilar) communities, the value of D_{12}^2 will be very small (large). However, D_{12}^2 is a scalar measure and, as such, it has all the limitations of combining similarity or dissimilarity in the means M_k and the variances V_k. As in ecological diversity studies, the distance measure D_{12}^2 or its generalized equivalents may be very profitably used in the following socioeconomic situations: (a) comparison of the management hierarchies in two communities in a given culture, (b) the causes and consequences of dissimilarity in two communities unequally affected by a process of industrialization in a less developed country, and (c) the similarity in the pattern of migration across social classes and occupation categories in two communities.

The stability test, emphasizing the transition from one pattern of distribution of behavior setting genotypes to another over time, helps us to understand the stochastic dimension of change. For this, the most suitable tool is the theory of stochastic processes, particularly multiple stochastic processes. Some examples will be helpful in describing this test.

First, how does one explain the introduction of a new technology, a new set of goods, or a new set of behavior settings? How important are the linkage effects between existing activities and new ones?

Second, in the ecological evolution of species and their distribution over diverse habitats, the impact of truncation and conditioning of one distribution by another is very significant, due to the encroachment of human civilizations and their increased technological knowledge for exploiting natural resources.

Are there similar phenomena in the socioeconomic process of development? Historically, there are plenty of examples to show that international aid did not help the development process in many underdeveloped countries, and there is very little economic theory to explain the phenomena. If we classify community members into "adopters" of new technology and "nonadopters," then is it possible from observing the behavior pattern of adopters (e.g., buyers of a new good) and nonadopters (e.g., nonbuyers of a new good) to predict whether the new technology will succeed?

Third, how can one analyze the impact of age, education, and other socioeconomic characteristics on the transition from one pattern of behavior setting clusters to another? If all behavior setting clusters could be translated into output-value measures, as e.g., by Karl Fox's concept of full social income, then this characterization could be empirically implemented. In default, we have to analyze the dimension of change in terms of transition from one state to another.

An interesting example occurs in the theory of economic development, when market and nonmarket activities interact. Using the framework of an open-static Leontief-type input-output model, one could write the primal problem as

$$\underset{\{x,\ y\}}{\text{minimize}} \quad C = w'x + r'y \tag{4.4}$$

$$\text{subject to} \quad Ax + Ny \geq d_x + d_y$$

$$x \geq 0, \qquad y \geq 0$$

where x and y are output vectors, with x as economic or market determined and y determined by the time-allocation in behavior setting clusters. A and N are input-output matrices; d_x, d_y are the demands to be satisfied; and w, r are the vectors of costs associated with x and y. There is a certain degree of jointness in the two outputs x and y, which is of course ignored in (4.4).

The dual problem associated with (4.4) is

$$\text{maximize } I = p'(d_x + d_y) \tag{4.5}$$

$$\text{subject to} \quad p'A \leq w', \qquad p'N \leq r', \qquad p \geq 0$$

where p is the vector of shadow prices associated with the first inequality of (4.4). The typical economic approach is to either ignore the vector y of nonmarket outputs or to subsume it in the definition of market-determined outputs x and then determine an optimal price vector p^* at which the national income equilibrium

$$w'x^* = p^{*\prime}d_x$$

holds. It is clear that there occurs a specification bias, an over- or understatement, if the relation between x and y is not built into the framework.

A similar formulation for the dynamic framework, in line with von Neumann's model, would be as follows:

$$\text{maximize } \lambda \tag{4.6}$$

$$\text{subject to} \quad x(t+1) + \delta\, y(t+1) \geq \lambda\left[A\, x(t) + N\, y(t)\right]$$

$$x(t),\ y(t),\ \lambda \geq 0$$

where δ is a diagonal matrix representing trade-off rates for the two outputs, the one determined by markets and the other by behavior setting clusters. If the two outputs were completely separable, one could write the problem as

$$\text{maximize } \lambda + \mu \tag{4.7}$$

$$\text{subject to} \quad x(t+1) \geq \lambda\, A\, x(t), \qquad y(t+1) \geq \mu\, Ny(t)$$

$$x(t),\ y(t),\ \lambda,\ \mu \geq 0$$

The difference in optimal values of the objective function in the two models (4.6) and (4.7) provides a measure of variety in the sense of diversity. The process of economic development may then be viewed as a problem of mixing the two dimensions of an overall output, where one responds to market prices and the other to extrinsic rewards; one may be stable and competitive in a market-based economy, the other need not be stable and competitive in an eco-behavioral system.

VARIETY AND COMPETITION

The concept of variety has many dimensions. In statistics, the dispersion or variance is often used as a measure of variety in the scatter of points; in ecology, it is used as a measure of diversity to indicate the degree of crowding or concentration of species in habitats; in communications theory, it is related to entropy or information so that maximum entropy distributions characterize in some sense maximum variety.

In economics, there are two key areas where the concept is applied. One is product-differentiation, where creating product diversity is a strategy followed under monopolistic competition to insulate a seller from a certain minimal segment of the market. This may also arise in spatial and temporal markets, where costs of transportation or of finance may affect the product dimensions to a certain degree. It has been argued in the economic literature that product-differentiation and the related advertising strategies are the expected behavior for producers who are averse to risks of fluctuations in sales and profits. These risks are present even in competitive markets if either of the following holds: (1) information about products and markets is not freely and costlessly available or (2) the futures market for every good or contingent claim is not available in a competitive framework. Thus, incomplete information, subjectively or objectively held, leads to product diversification, and this may be carried to greater lengths where the proportion of fixed costs is very high.

A clear-cut example of diversification is evidenced in optimal portfolio choices based on the mean-variance analysis. Product-differentiation under monopolistic competition has, however, one basic difference from diversification in portfolio investment--i.e., product-differentiation is designed to emphasize the return aspect rather than the costs, whereas it is the cost of diversification that is minimized by minimizing the variance of return in a portfolio model.

Since the allocation of investment in a portfolio of securities is very similar to the allocation of time to alternative behavior settings under a given authority structure, one fruitful approach would be to reformulate the portfolio model by incorporating some specific measures of diversity. If x_j is the allocation proportion for security j = 1, 2, ..., n, the mean-variance model minimizes the total variance $\sigma^2 = \sum_{i=j}^{n} \sum_{j=1}^{n} x_i v_{ij} x_j$

subject to an expected return condition $\sum_{j=1}^{n} m_j x_j = c$ and a normalization condition $\sum_{j=1}^{n} x_j = 1$, where the positive scalar c has to be preassigned. If the x_j's are nonnegative and add up to one, they can be interpreted as probabilities; hence, a measure of diversity

$$d = 1 - \sum_{j=1}^{n} x_j^2 \qquad (4.8)$$

often used in ecology and market research may be used to replace the two constraints of the above portfolio model.

The term Σx_j^2 measures a degree of concentration, since it indicates the probability that any two securities selected at random will belong to the same portfolio. In the theory of behavior setting clusters, it will indicate the probability that any two settings selected at random will belong to the same genotype. On using a Lagrange multiplier λ for the diversity constraint (4.8), total variance σ^2 may now be maximized or minimized.

In the first case we select the maximum eigenvalue λ^* and the associated eigenvector x^*, whereas the minimum λ_* and x_* are selected for the minimum variance case

$$(V - \lambda I)x = 0, \qquad V = v_{ij}$$

The spectrum of eigenvalues $\lambda_1, \lambda_2, \ldots, \lambda_n$ and the associated eigenvectors thus provides a range of variations or spread. Variety in this context may be seen as a spectrum of eigenvalues and their associated eigenvectors. It may have a cost or return implication depending on the specific cases of application.

The second concept which is related to variety is that of a representative firm, first used by Alfred Marshall to describe the interdependence between a firm and the industry of which it is a part. A representative firm represents conditions typical to the industry, e.g., cost and demand conditions, in particular entry and exit conditions and the industry's ability to adapt to exogenous changes in the overall economy. Marshall emphasized the evolutionary characteristics of the representative firm, its survival value under conditions of long-run changes. It is somewhat surprising that this concept has never been explored in microtheory or its empirical applications, although it is implicitly used all the time in imperfect competition theory. For example, in the theory of Cournot reaction curves, equilibrium solutions are defined by the condition that each firm's strategy is consistent with all the others in the industry and hence with the representative firm.

The concept of representative firm is useful in the theory

of behavior settings as a representative cluster, in terms of which all other individual clusters may be compared and contrasted. Three aspects of this concept are particularly important and they may be most easily illustrated in terms of microeconomic theory as follows:

First, the market and cost conditions facing a representative firm provide a benchmark or reference through which an individual firm may analyze its response to risks of fluctuations in the external market. In the language of portfolio theory in finance, the market portfolio under conditions of efficient capital markets provides the benchmark through which individual investors may adjust their own portfolios. Staying too far from the market portfolio may not be profitable, unless some inside information is available.

For a competitive firm with a quadratic cost function facing instability of prices, the impact of market fluctuations on profit may be easily evaluated as Nelson (1961) has shown. Let $\pi^*(p)$ be the profit if output x^* is produced and actual price is p, and let $\pi^{**}(p)$ be the profit which could have been achieved had price p been perfectly predicted and x^{**}, the best output for price p, been produced. Then it can be proved that

$$\pi^{**}(p) - \pi^*(p) = (2s)^{-1}(p - \bar{p})^2 \tag{4.9}$$

where $\bar{p}$ is the expected price in the market and s is the slope of the marginal cost curve of the individual firm. Taking expectations of both sides of (4.9) and making the rationality postulate due to Muth (1961):

$$Ep = \bar{p} \tag{4.10}$$

we obtain

$$E(\pi^{**} - \pi^*) = (2s)^{-1}\,\sigma_p^2 \tag{4.11}$$

where σ_p^2 is the variance of price computed under the rational expectations assumption (4.10) and E is expectation.

Thus, if variance of price is taken as a surrogate measure of variety, the competitive firm would make an effort to achieve variety only if a mechanism for forecasting could be developed and used. In default of this mechanism, the left-hand side of (4.11) indicates an expected loss in profits and the firm would attempt to reduce it by introducing brand differentiation, whereby the range of variation of p around $\bar{p}$ would be reduced. Thus, price variance due to incomplete information and risk may be partly a result of product diversity and partly a cause of, or reason for generating, product diversity.

A second aspect of the representative firm concept arises in the Cournot-Nash theory of reaction curves in monopolistic competition under demand uncertainty, when it may be profitable to follow mixed strategies in terms of random outputs and prices (see Sengupta 1978d). Here again, the lack of complete information to the players may lead to expected losses of profits, which would now be functions of subjectively held probability distributions of others' strategies, and the rational expectations postulate (4.10) may not hold. Choice of mixed strategies as opposed to pure ones implies more diversity, hence, more variety.

The third aspect refers to the survival characteristics of the representative firm, often emphasized in dynamic models of firm growth. Since the latter involves in some sense an optimal expansion of capacity for the future, which has various uncertainties, the strategy or strategies which are robust or flexible become important. In corporate planning, emphasis is very often laid on following such strategies, which are in many ways opposed to strictly profit-maximizing policies that assume the future state of the world is known.

These three aspects illustrate, in my opinion, the need for developing a dynamic theory of behavior settings which is applicable to both the market and the nonmarket features of eco-behavioral systems. Some beginnings have been made in Sengupta 1978a, b, c; 1986. It is my view that this theory would have significant payoffs in several fields of economics, e.g., national income accounting, nonprice elements of competition, and the basis for formation of coalitions and behavior setting clusters.

REFERENCES

Ashby, W. R. 1958. _An Introduction to Cybernetics_. London: Chapman and Hall.

Barker, R. G. 1968. _Ecological Psychology: Concepts and Methods for Studying the Environment of Human Behavior_. Stanford, CA: Stanford University Press.

Barker, R. G., and P. Schoggen. 1973. _Qualities of Community Life_. San Francisco: Jossey-Bass Publishers.

Boulding, K. E. 1981. _Evolutionary Economics_. London: Sage Publications.

Charnes, A., W. W. Cooper, and E. Rhodes. 1978. "Measuring the Efficiency of Decision-making Units." _European Journal of Operations Research_ 29: 833-842.

Fox, K. A., 1974. _Social Indicators and Social Theory: Elements of an Operational System_. New York: Wiley.

______. 1983. "The Eco-Behavioral View of Human Societies and Its Implications for Systems Science." _International Journal of Systems Science_ 14: 895-914.

______. 1984. "Behavior Settings and Eco-Behavioral Science: A New Arena for Mathematical Social Science Permitting a

Richer and More Coherent View of Human Activities in Social Systems:
Part I, Concepts, Measurements, and Linkages to Economic Data Systems, Time-Allocation Matrices, and Social System Accounts." *Mathematical Social Sciences* 7: 117-138.
Part II, Relationships to Established Disciplines and Needs for Mathematical Development." *Mathematical Social Sciences* 7: 139-165.

______. 1985. *Social System Accounts: Linking Social and Economic Indicators through Tangible Behavior Settings*. Dordrecht and Boston: D. Reidel.

Fox, K. A., and J. K. Sengupta. September 1977. "Models of Behavior Settings: Elements of Operational Theory for Socio-Economic Systems." Unpublished Paper.

Muth, J. R. 1961. "Rational Expectations and the Theory of Price Movements." *Econometrica* 24: 315-335.

Nelson, R. R. 1961. "Uncertainty, Prediction and Competitive Equilibrium." *Quarterly Journal of Economics* 75: 41-62.

Sengupta, J. K. September 1978a. "A Theory of Allocation of Behavior Capacity in a Community." Mimeographed Paper.

______. September 1978b. "Structure, Stability and Efficiency of the Distribution of Behavior Capacity in a Community." Mimeographed Paper.

______. October 1978c. "A Dynamic Theory of Behavior Settings in a Small Community." Mimeographed Paper.

______. 1978d. "Noncooperative Equilibria in Monopolistic Competition Under Uncertainty." *Zeitschrift fur Nationalokonomie* 38: 193-208.

______. 1986. "Modeling Eco-Behavioral Systems." *Mathematical Social Sciences* 11: 1-31.

PART 2

Applications

5

Holistic Modeling of Multidisciplinary Subject Matter and Problem Domains

GLENN L. JOHNSON

Two recent contributions to economic literature have expressed substantial dissatisfaction with research methods currently held in high regard by economists as well as with the main body of neoclassical theory which undergirds so much of our empirical work. Donald M. McCloskey's (1983) article in the *Journal of Economic Literature* entitled "The Rhetoric of Economics" contests the "modernism" of research methods employed by economists. Further, Israel M. Kirzner has a chapter entitled "The 'Austrian' Perspective" in *The Crisis in Economic Theory* (Bell and Kristol 1981) which complements the McCloskey article by criticizing the use of neoclassical economic theory. McCloskey deplores the methods of the economic research establishment. Kirzner, while not rejecting the use of neoclassical economic theory, points out its neglect of structural dynamics and, hence, the need for a complete restructuring of neoclassical theory. He regrets the failure of the economic research establishment to get on with the restructuring.

In the first section of this chapter, we briefly examine the McCloskey and Kirzner arguments. In the second, we examine problem-solving and subject matter research done by agricultural economists, and we distinguish such research from much less holistic disciplinary research designed to improve the discipline

---

Though this chapter has benefited greatly from the reviews and criticisms of James Bonnen, Lester Manderscheid, Michel Petit, William Rockwell, David Schweikhardt, Vernon Sorenson, and Stan Thompson, the author, of course, remains solely responsible for its contents.

of economics. In the third section, we demonstrate that agricultural economists doing research, consulting, and advising work have repeatedly encountered the difficulties stressed by McCloskey and Kirzner. In the fourth, we consider trends towards holism in modeling problem and subject matter domains relevant for agricultural development. We find that agricultural economists researching practical problems (which are generally multidisciplinary) and multidisciplinary subjects have made some progress in meeting the criticisms of McCloskey and Kirzner. Finally, in the fifth section, we lay out essential characteristics of models of problem and subject matter domains, reflect on the evaluation of such models, and propose a compromise with McCloskey.

McCLOSKEY'S CASE AGAINST MODERNISM AND KIRZNER'S CRITICISMS OF NEOCLASSICAL THEORY

What McCloskey (1983) has to say about modernism is obviously applicable and important, though not always entirely convincing. McCloskey characterizes "modernist" methods in economics as (1) having prediction as their goal, (2) holding that only the accuracy of theory's predictions make a difference, (3) being posited on the belief that observability requires reproducible experiments (and presumably the possibility of repeated observations on uncontrolled phenomena), (4) holding that proving a theory false requires that its experimental (and observational) implications be false, (5) holding that observations which depend upon interpretation are unscientific, (6) holding that knowledge not expressible in numbers is inadequate, (7) accepting that theories are _discoverable_ through metaphysics, esthetics, and introspection but that they are _not so justifiable_ (verifiable), (8) distinguishing the scientific from the nonscientific by identifying the former with positive and the latter with normative knowledge, which is to posit that science is not concerned with values, and (9) holding that scientific explanation is derived from laws. After so characterizing modernism in economics, McCloskey argues that modernism is obsolete in philosophy in large part because the logically positivistic premises underlying modernism are now rejected by many philosophers.

In this latter respect, his arguments are similar to those found in _The Legacy of Logical Positivism_ (Achinstein and Barker 1969; Shapere 1969, pp. 115-160). Logical positivism in that book is found to be inadequate because it (1) rejects the possibility of objective normative knowledge and (2) uncritically accepts an "air-tight" distinction between abstract (analytical) and primitive undefined terms (experiential knowledge) which can no longer be maintained in philosophic circles (Scriven 1969, pp. 197, 199f). McCloskey further argues in an important but not completely convincing manner that Karl Popper's ideas (1959) about falsification are not cogent, that prediction is impossible (he should state "not always possible") in economics, and that modernism is, in fact, impossible and therefore not really used (he should state "not universally used") by economists. Still further, following Feyerabend (1978), McCloskey argues that even the so-called hard sciences do not always follow the modernistic methods of the logical positivists.

In looking at what economists do, McCloskey finds that they often follow unorthodox (he means nonmodernist) approaches (or rhetorics, in his terms) which, while often effective, would not be generally accepted and endorsed by the research establishment of economists if made explicit. He pleads that we give the literary rhetoric of economics a recognized honorable position among our accepted methods. He argues that the models of economics are often metaphoric and that metaphors may be fundamental, not merely ornamental. Still further, he argues that mathematical models are also metaphorical and therefore a part, but not all, of what he calls the rhetoric of economics. McCloskey points out that there are several alternatives to modernism which are also rational and that to abandon modernism is not to let the "barbarians (irrationalists) through the gates." He believes that more acceptance of and more respectability for the various unofficial rhetorics of economics would improve our writing, our teaching, our relationship with other disciplines, and produce a better "science of economics" as well as better dispositions on our own parts.

Kirzner deplores the omissions of neoclassical theory without attempting to destroy it; however, he holds that neoclassical theory must be thoroughly reconstructed because it (1) overemphasizes equilibrium conditions; (2) fails, in treating market competition, to include competition in the development of new technologies, institutions, and people; (3) ignores what agricultural economists might call the economics of managerial processes (information processes and systems); (4) is unduly simplistic in aggregating the welfares of individuals; and (5) ignores the need to plan the social coordination of participants in the market. Kirzner recognizes that many people working in the neoclassical tradition attempt to overcome these flaws and omissions on a piecemeal basis but regrets that they fail to recognize the unity (holism) of the economic theory needed. He sees a need for a theory which will transcend the mechanics of neoclassical economics. Overall, Kirzner's view is quite consistent with that of McCloskey, who also wants us to move away from the mechanical formulation of the modernists to a more literary approach to deal with the structural dynamics of societies and economies--with a structural dynamics in which markets, in their broadest sense, originate technological, institutional, and human change as well as react to such changes occurring outside of even such broadly conceived markets.

It was indicated above that McCloskey's arguments are important but not entirely convincing. For this chapter, their importance lies in the room which they establish for nonmodernist approaches. This "breathing space" can be established and used without unreserved acceptance of McCloskey's arguments that (1) prediction is impossible in economics and (2) modernism is impossible and is not used in economics. This chapter (1) seeks balance in the use of both modernist and nonmodernist methods and (2) accepts Kirzner's position that our task is to add onto rather than to entirely reject and replace neoclassical theory (Johnson 1972).

HOLISM AND THE RESPONSIBILITIES OF AGRICULTURAL ECONOMISTS

Collectively, agricultural economists are assigned and/or accept responsibility for doing problem-solving (PS), subject matter (SM), and disciplinary (DISC) research and other related work. Holism treats systems as wholes which cannot be subdivided without loss of essential components. Solutions to problems require simultaneous attention to all variables defining a problem and necessary for its solution. Omission of any of these variables precludes reaching a solution. Problem solving is therefore holistic. In turn, subject matter work (as it will be defined later) is less holistic than problem solving. Both are multidisciplinary and, hence, more holistic than disciplinary research in that they deal with the several different disciplinary dimensions of practical problems with a focus on solutions. Disciplinary work, on the other hand, is reductionist, the opposite of holistic. Economists as disciplinarians subdivide their discipline and its ancillary "tool-providing disciplines" (such as mathematics, statistics, history, philosophy, psychology) to answer subdisciplinary questions important for economics, even if of no obvious and immediate interest to the problem solvers of the real world. Each of these three kinds of research and related work are considered in more detail in this section. A fuller treatment is given in Johnson 1986b.

Agricultural economists sometimes participate in PS research and other efforts designed to find solutions to problems faced by specific decision makers. Typically they do such work as members of or as consultants to agricultural experiment station staffs; governmental and parastatal organizations such as the World Bank, USAID, marketing boards, commissions, certain parts of the USDA; and when working as consultants, advisors, and extension agents for private industry (mainly agribusinesses, including farm firms). As most PS efforts are multidisciplinary, economists typically serve as contributing members of a multidisciplinary team.

Agricultural economists also contribute to multidisciplinary SM research and other efforts. Like PS efforts, SM efforts involve contributions from disciplines other than economics and from other multidisciplinary or institute-like departments in colleges of agriculture. Among the many important multidisciplinary subject matter areas studied by agricultural economists are integrated pest management, environmental quality, poverty, food contamination, agricultural development, agro-ethics, and the exhaustion of fossil fuels.

Agricultural economists, as such, are not really expected to do a great deal to improve the discipline of economics. Nonetheless, they often find it necessary to do relevant (DISC) research in economics to remedy certain shortcomings of economics in order to meet their PS and SM research and related responsibilities. This DISC research includes work in such ancillary "tool" disciplines for economists as mathematics, statistics, philosophy, history, and even psychology and sociology. When these disciplines provide tools for economics, they simply support and facilitate DISC research in economics.

The models for PS research have to be holistic in the sense of modeling important different disciplinary dimensions of the entire problem. Problems are defined and solved on the basis of knowledge of both values and other characteristics of conditions, situations, and things in the world. As a result, problem-solving models often involve (1) the hard science disciplines, (2) the humanities and social sciences, and (3) one or more of the decision disciplines and subjects (such as economics, engineering, architecture, medicine, dentistry, and military science) which deal with the decision rules for translating positive and normative (about values or goodness and badness) knowledge (Moore 1956) into prescriptions to solve problems.

PS models are more holistic than SM models. SM models, in turn, are more holistic than DISC models, which by definition are reductionist as they focus on a discipline or part of a discipline rather than a multidisciplinary problem or subject of importance in solving a set of problems. Accordingly, the models used in doing the three kinds of research reflect these different degrees of holism.

In addition to their numerous disciplinary dimensions, PS and SM models may have time, spatial, demographic, probabilistic, and other dimensions which contribute to their holism. Almost all PS models have a crucial time dimension; so do many SM models. DISC models may or may not have these dimensions depending on how dynamic they are (Samuelson 1947, pp. 311-17). Similarly, PS, SM, and DISC models may or may not have the probabilistic dimensions which generate Kirzner's concern with imperfect knowledge, information, and learning.

DIFFICULTIES WITH MODERNISM AND ECONOMIC THEORY ENCOUNTERED BY AGRICULTURAL ECONOMISTS

Many experiences of agricultural economists illustrate the importance and relevance of much of what McCloskey and Kirzner have to say. In this section we briefly examine a selection of these experiences including (1) the incorporation of production economics into farm management, (2) research on managerial processes by students of farm management, (3) industrial organization research of agricultural economists, (4) attempts to keep farm management relevant, (5) Schultz's studies of human development, (6) studies of induced institutional and technological change, (7) institutional research of agricultural economists, (8) earlier studies of U.S. agriculture by Black and his associates and by Cromarty, and (9) various agricultural development studies abroad. As the modeling work of agricultural development researchers abroad is particularly relevant to the title of this chapter, special emphasis is placed on them at the end of this section before proceeding to a consideration of holistic modeling of SM and PS domains in the fourth section.

The Introduction of Production Economics into Farm Management

Following World War II, a number of young agricultural economists interested both in production economics and farm management attempted to "modernize" farm management in the McCloskey sense by adding production economics to it (Johnson 1957). While this effort added the beneficial power of static neoclassical economics to farm management, a heavy price was paid as farm management was made less holistic by specializing on but one part of neoclassical economics--production economics (Johnson 1969). Earlier farm management workers, who were not modernist, had given much more attention to technological advance, the human factor (management and skills), and institutions than to the equilibria of static production economics. It should be remembered that most departments of rural sociology originated in the desire of farm management department administrators for a sociologist to handle the institutional dimensions of farm management. Also, close contacts had been maintained with the technical agriculturalists who generate technological change. By contrast and as T. W. Schultz (1958) pointed out, the production economists working in farm management were more interested in optimization (given technology, institutions, and people) than in the origin and effects of technological, institutional, and human change. The relevance of Schultz's criticism is particularly apparent for the 15-year period, 1956-1971, when U.S. agricultural output almost doubled as a result of new technology, improved human performance, and institutional change, while production economics researchers in farm management concentrated on disciplinary production function analyses and linear programs to define static optima while ignoring the dynamics of the disequilibria being generated by the tremendous structural changes then taking place. Production economics was added at the expense of (1) eliminating much that was useful and (2) failing to add much that was needed, both of which were beyond modernism. Clearly, the introduction of static economics as part of a trend towards modernism was done at an undue and unnecessary cost.

Managerial Processes

Both the earlier farm management researchers and some of the static production economists introducing themselves into farm management after World War II tended to ignore imperfect knowledge, managerial processes, and learning. Before the war, T. W. Schultz (1939) had drawn on Frank Knight (1921) to call this shortcoming to the attention of both static production economists and farm management scholars. The importance of this shortcoming became apparent to some but not all of the production economists working in farm management after World War II. As a result, some of the production economists as well as some of the more traditionally oriented farm management workers devoted specific attention to managerial processes (Johnson and Haver 1953), including the economics of learning. The empirical research on managerial processes which followed was not modernist in the McCloskey sense. Moreover, it met Kirzner's later call (1981, pp. 117f) for more attention to information systems--to managerial processes including the economics of managerial systems and the role of learning in a firm's information, decision-making, and action-taking system. The models of the managerial process which were developed were (1) rhetorical, in the McCloskey sense, and (2) in accordance with Kirzner's desires, extended static neoclassical economics without destroying it (Johnson et al. 1961).

Industrial Organization Research

The industrial organization approach has been used by a substantial number of agricultural economists in the analysis of the structure of and structural change in agricultural subsectors. The structures and structural changes investigated have had to do with institutions and technology commonly assumed fixed in static neoclassical theory (Knight 1921, p. 33). In dealing with such changes, industrial organization analysts often violate a high proportion of the tenets of modernism listed by McCloskey and summarized at the beginning of this chapter. Also, they have often extended theory beyond neoclassical static market economics. Substantial practical contributions have been made to our knowledge of agribusiness subsectors (Cook et al. 1978).

Keeping Farm Management Relevant

Not all farm management researchers became modernistic in the post-World War II era, and this was fortunate. Among farm management researchers not specializing in production economics were those concerned with (1) taxation, social security, workers compensation, price supports, and other institutional changes important in managing farms; (2) the technological changes then being rapidly spawned in the public and private sectors; and (3) the household, as well as the firm, end of farming. Some were interested in the implications of institutional changes and others in the implications of existing institutions for farmers. These farm management workers found it more important for farmers to make gross adjustments to institutional changes and technological advances than to make fine mathematical adjustments to equate marginal factor costs with marginal value products under the unrealistic assumption that institutions and technology were unchanging. Also, some very useful farm management research and extension work was done by those attempting to more fully understand and improve farm/home interrelationships (Johnson 1982a).

The work on farm/home interrelationships first developed among traditional farm management workers in the Balanced Farming Program at the University of Missouri (Bradford and Johnson 1953; Hagan 1963). In turn, that approach spread to mid-southern states including Kentucky, where it became known as the Farm and Home Development Program. Later, the Office of the Cooperative State Extension Services in the USDA promoted a nationwide farm and home development extension program. Eventually there was a nonmodernist intellectual melding of ideas from farm and home development workers with those emerging from the study of managerial processes described above. Significantly, the work of traditional farm managers on institutional change and on farm/home development was not modernist in nature and went beyond the inadequate static assumption of neoclassical theory (Bradford and Johnson 1953; Johnson et al. 1961).

Schultz's Studies of Human Development (Capital)

Schultz's work on the formation of human capital goes beyond the rather narrowly conceived markets of static neoclassical economics, which assumes populations and skills fixed, to explore more broadly conceived markets for human capital. Schultz was concerned first with changes in the productivity of U.S. agriculture and later with changes in the productivity of entire economies as a result of investments in human capital. His training in institutional economics at the University of Wisconsin probably contributed to his willingness to strike out beyond the bounds of traditionally conceived static economic markets into the structural dynamics of human capital formation. Though Schultz's Chicago environment may have kept him from going beyond markets (broadly defined) into changes in the productive capacity of human beings which originate outside such markets, he did break away from the narrow neoclassical concept of markets which Kirzner finds confining to produce research outstanding enough to earn a Nobel Prize.

It is informative and important to note that while Schultz did not allow himself to be dominated by modernism, his total research program involved modernist efforts by such colleagues and students as Gary Becker, Finis Welch, and Albert Rees. In this respect, Schultz exploited the strengths of modernism without allowing himself to be constrained by either its limitations or the limitations of a purely nonmodernist approach.

Studies of Induced Institutional and Technological Change

Vernon Ruttan, along with others, has considered the theory of induced technological and institutional changes in markets conceived more broadly than is typical among many others using neoclassical theory; had not this been true, his work would not have been noteworthy (Binswanger and Ruttan 1978). However, Ruttan did not go beyond such more broadly conceived markets to consider the technological and institutional changes which occur independently of either monetary or nonmonetary incentives and costs. Nonetheless, the usefulness of his conceptualization and analyses indicate the advantages of (1) bending neoclassical theory in directions suggested by Kirzner while (2) not being constrained by modernism.

Institutional Economics and Agricultural Economics

John R. Commons developed institutional economics, which, in turn, motivated a large number of agricultural economists to examine the structural dynamics of institutional change. His consideration of institutional change went beyond the more broadly conceived markets of T. W. Schultz, Vernon Ruttan, and others to explore institutional changes, whether or not motivated by gain. Such agricultural economists as Kenneth Parsons, Erven Long, Leonard Salter, John Timmons, Rainer Schickele, and more recently, Allan Randall and Allan Schmid have sought to understand the origins of institutional change and of existing institutions both within and beyond broadly conceived markets. For the most part, McCloskey should be happy with their avoidance of modernism while Kirzner should be happy with their views, except when they occasionally over-reject neoclassical economics. These investigators have demonstrated commendable productivity and in doing so have substantiated the views of McCloskey and Kirzner; yet, one cannot help but think that these institutionalists might have done better by joining Schultz in exploiting the strengths of modernism while avoiding its constraints.

Studies of U.S. Agriculture

Two early projective and nonmodernist studies were conducted by John D. Black of Harvard University. Ronald Mighell (Mighell and Black 1951) of the U.S. Department of Agriculture cooperated in the study of the dairy industry of the Lakes States. The second study with James Bonnen was of the U.S. agricultural economy (Black and Bonnen 1956).

The Black-Mighell Lakes States dairy study utilized budgets to determine the consequences through time of the changes then occurring in the Lakes States dairy industry. Their budget analyses tended to maximize returns, taking into account technical change, ability to finance, price changes, and institutional change. However, Mighell and Black did not assume that enough was always known about the future for dairy farmers to maximize their net returns in a precise manner. Black and Mighell predicted farmers' responses to such changes well enough to raise questions about McCloskey's assertion that prediction is impossible in economics. These responses were aggregated somewhat informally into regional estimates.

The Black and Bonnen effort was more macro but still retained a substantial micro base. It attempted to project and understand the consequences of various technical and institutional changes for U.S. agricultural output. Generally speaking, exclusive emphasis was not placed on maximization. However, the Black-Bonnen study did utilize the optima of neoclassical economics, even if it was not dominated by them.

These two studies, whose director instinctively avoided the constraints of modernism, were quite accurate and acceptable. Black spent considerable time investigating constraints and changes in technology and institutions before resorting to budgeting, other maximizing techniques, or even using supply and demand functions which presume maximizing behavior. Consequently, Black more successfully avoided premature maximization than others who spent less time on such activities before turning to the optimizing techniques of economics. Static neoclassical equilibria theory was used without being confined by it. A wide range of multidisciplinary information from different disciplines was advantageously used.

In sharp contrast to the Black-Mighell and Black-Bonnen studies was the modernist doctoral study of the U.S. agricultural sector by Cromarty (1957). That study was designed to contribute to the development of the Klein-Goldberger model of the economy of the United States. It utilized a system of equilibrium equations and econometric techniques which presumed optimizing behavior to estimate the parameters of systems of simultaneous equations. The model was operated through time to simulate the operation of the U.S. agricultural economy. The Cromarty effort was not as accurate as the earlier, less modernistic Black-Bonnen study. This should not be surprising. The Black-Bonnen effort drew on (1) a great deal of multidisciplinary information not contained in the time series data to which Cromarty confined himself and (2) logic from disciplines other than economics, while Cromarty, on the other hand, devoted inadequate attention to the disciplines concerned with changes in technology, the human factor, and institutions.

Studies of Agricultural Development Abroad

After the Point Four Program was established by President Truman in 1950, U.S. agricultural economists became increasingly involved in agricultural development studies abroad. In a very real sense this was an extension of the domestic development work agricultural economists had long been doing in European, Oceanic, and American countries. At this point in time, econometrics (including linear programming) was coming to the fore. Highly competent neoclassical economists made numerous econometric and linear programming studies of agricultural sectors and subsectors, which would be characterized as modernist by

McCloskey (Fletcher et al. 1970; Thorbecke and Hall 1982; Day and Singh 1977). These and other modernist studies by persons such as Earl Heady at Iowa State, Sam Daynes working for AID in Colombia, and still others placed heavy emphasis on the operation of narrowly conceived markets. Few, if any, of these studies went beyond narrowly conceived markets to consider induced institutional, technological, and human change in more broadly defined markets, thus leaving the field open for the successes of Schultz, Ruttan, and others (see above).

As in the case of production economics and farm management, the use of modernistic, mechanical neoclassical models and analyses yielded net benefits in studying agricultural development. Such usage made agricultural development studies more rigorous theoretically, mathematically, and statistically. However, as in the case of farm management, the modernist emphasis reduced attention to the main sources of structural dynamics and agricultural development: technological change, institutional change, and human development. Growth in the quantity and quality of capital was less ignored than the other three prime movers for development probably because the growth of capital (particularly bio/physical) is generally perceived to fall within the rather narrow purview of modernist economics.

On the other hand, practitioners of agricultural development, as contrasted to the modernist economists and agricultural economists _researching_ development, have given substantial attention to technology transfer; the establishment of agricultural credit, market, and cooperative agencies; community (later, rural) development; institution building; family planning; nonformal education; agricultural extension; vocational agriculture; the creation of agricultural colleges and universities; agricultural research centers; and a host of other projects and programs having to do with improving technology, institutions, and people. These practitioners--agricultural economists serving as advisors and consultants; USDA, AID, and IBRD administrators and decision makers; legislators; program and project analysts; and so forth--were forced by practical exigencies to rise above and go beyond the confines of the narrow theories and specialized methods of economics and modernism which were inadequate for the tasks they had to perform.

Towards Holism in Modeling Problem-solving and Subject Matter Domains Relevant for Agricultural Development

The previous section discussed difficulties with modernism and neoclassical theory encountered by U.S. agricultural economists in several types of applied research. The latter part of that section in particular provided the background for this one by highlighting the difficulties encountered by agricultural economists doing modernist studies with concentration on neoclassical economics while being expected to deal realistically with the multidisciplinary dimensions of problematic and subject matter domains relevant for agricultural development. These difficulties were encountered long before McCloskey identified the problems associated with modernism and long before Kirzner wrote his specific chapter on "The 'Austrian' Perspective" in The Crisis in Economic Theory.

At this point some additional background is needed to indicate how the author of this chapter developed his point of view, which is presented in the following section on modeling problematic and subject matter domains. Because of its resultant personal content, the rest of this section and all of the next are written in the first person.

I was an active participant in the attempt to make farm management modernist (in McCloskey's sense) by introducing static neoclassical production economics into farm management (Johnson 1957). I also participated in the nonmodernistic attempt to study managerial processes following a dynamic approach which would likely now win the approval of Kirzner (Johnson et al. 1961). As Cromarty's major professor, I participated in his modernistic analysis. At one point I arranged for Cromarty and Bonnen to author a paper later published as a chapter in a book (1958). As the modernism I had built into Cromarty did not mix with the nonmodernistic approach Bonnen had acquired from John D. Black, their chapter consists of two fairly distinct papers.

It is of interest to note, in this connection, that John D. Black had been modernist earlier in his career, having produced the first textbook on agricultural production economics to lay the groundwork for the post-World War II "modernization" of farm management by production economists. Also, ironically, the 1939 Schultz article referred to earlier pointed out (in a way which Kirzner would now approve) that both the traditional farm managers and the modernist production economists (mainly John D. Black before World War II) were ignoring the managerial processes considered to be so important by Knight in his much earlier (1921) book Risk, Uncertainty and Profit.

I was also one of the persons who designed the Lakes States dairy adjustment study (NCR-4) in the 1950s and a member of NC-54 which conducted a major study of feed grain and livestock adjustments in the early 1960s (Colyer and Irwin 1967). During these latter experiences, I became painfully aware of the inadequacies of "modernism" at a time when McCloskey's critique was still two decades away.

By the time I began to work out an agreement with Resources for the Future (RFF) to analyze U.S. agricultural policies from 1917 to the early 1960s, I was so concerned about the shortcomings of modernism that I disavowed adherence to any particular quantitative technique or theoretical formulation; instead, I took an eclectic and nonmodernist stance. The agreement emphasized understanding the phenomena under examination rather than use of a particular disciplinary technique or theory. Because of my experiences with the Cromarty model and the dairy states and feed grain livestock models, the research done under the RFF grant made no pretense of developing a single modernist model capable of analyzing and tracking the developments and changes which occurred in U.S. agriculture during the 1917-1965 period. Instead, heavy reliance was placed on various nonmechanical, historical analyses of different parts of the period. Gladys Baker, agricultural historian in the USDA, played a prominent role in these analyses.

The historical analyses she helped conduct were supplemented by several other studies. Some but not all of these were econometric and modernistic, indicating that I would not have found all of McCloskey's arguments against modernism entirely convincing had they been before me at that time. I refer to studies by Leroy Quance, Bob Jones, Ed Rossmiller, Francis VanGigch, and others reported in _The Overproduction Trap_ (Johnson and Quance 1972). Specific attention was given to institutional, technological, and human changes as well as to changes in the quantity and quality of the biophysical capital base for American agriculture.

In another important period of my life as the director of the Economic Development Institute at the University of Nigeria, I also avoided modernism without completely rejecting it. I kept that institute separate from the economics department of the University of Nigeria so that it could draw on any combination of departments in the university having knowledge and expertise needed to carry out the different multidisciplinary problem-solving and subject matter research responsibilities the institute accepted. The policy of the institute became one of avoiding undue emphasis on economics to the preclusion of the other disciplines necessary to address the practical development problems and issues (subjects) important for Nigeria. As I now view it, it was unfortunate that a contractual obligation involving the University of Nigeria, USAID, and Michigan State University required that the institute be named the _Economic Development Institute_ (EDI) rather than, more appropriately, the _Development Institute_.

After the institute had been created and became operational, I was asked by the Agency for International Development (AID) to direct the work of the Consortium for the Study of Nigerian Rural Development (CSNRD) which was being established for the purpose of evaluating the agricultural program of the United States Agency for International Development in Lagos (USAID/Lagos), Nigeria. The Nigerian program then was AID's largest agricultural development country program, bigger even than its agricultural program for India.

At that time, I was instinctively aware of the difference between doing (1) academic research on disciplinary questions including applied economics and (2) problem-solving and subject matter research to assist public decision makers. I was asked by AID administrators in Washington to direct CSNRD since they knew from experience that I knew the difference between doing academic disciplinary research and doing research to assist governmental officials (such as themselves) in making decisions either by (1) working directly on one or more of their problems or (2) through developing bodies of information on subjects crucial to the decisions they had to make. They wanted (and I wanted to do) problem-solving and/or subject matter research relevant to the success or failure of the USAID/Lagos agricultural development programs and projects in Nigeria. This required attention to the entire agricultural sector of Nigeria and the role which USAID was playing vis-a-vis various Nigerian state and federal ministries and other bilateral and multinational donors. It was abundantly clear that the approach had to be multidisciplinary and that what McCloskey now calls a modernistic economic approach was obviously and patently infeasible. Specialization on economics and any one of its many quantitative techniques would have neglected the flux of political, religious, military, and human variables then both changing Nigeria and driving her into civil war.

At about this time (circa 1965), agricultural economists in the North Central region of the United States developed an interest in systems simulation. As director of CSNRD, I recognized the multidisciplinary, nonmodernist nature of the systems simulation approach and was attracted by its disciplinary philosophic and methodological eclecticism. It appeared that the general point of view which had been guiding the work of the CSNRD was reflected in the systems simulation approach. Consequently, a conference was held which was attended by a number of econometricians, Nigerian experts, and especially, systems simulation experts. The conclusion from that conference was that, indeed, the systems simulation approach was appropriate for studying Nigerian rural development, but unfortunately, the necessary software for modeling the several crucial dimensions of its domain was not yet available and would be too expensive and time consuming to develop within the monetary and time constraints faced by CSNRD.

Consequently, CSNRD researchers proceeded to study Nigerian rural development with an uncomputerized eclectic, nonmodernist, multidisciplinary mixture of techniques and approaches which made it possible for them to envision the consequences of three important alternative development programs for Nigeria. These programs dealt with institutional and technical change as well as human development. Economics was neither ignored nor permitted to dominate CSNRD's work. Modernistic linear programs and econometric analyses contributed but were not permitted to dominate the quantitative work done by CSNRD. Most of the work done in Nigeria was done with desk calculators and worksheets guided by knowledge of Nigeria's changing people, institutions, and technology possessed by several Nigerians working on the project along with several Americans having a total of over 60 years of working experience in Nigerian agriculture (Johnson et al. 1969).

John D. Black, T. W. Schultz, McCloskey, and Kirzner would have applauded.

Like Black's earlier work, CSNRD research results proved useful. USAID administrators in Lagos used them extensively and they played a prominent role in a Nigerian conference on the future of Nigerian agriculture which was held after the end of the Biafran difficulty. In this conference, the CSNRD report along with a nonmodernist FAO Study of Nigerian Agriculture provided the point of departure for Nigerian planning.

After CSNRD's work was completed, the question arose in AID/Washington as to whether it would have been much more economical to do CSNRD's research following a computerized system simulation approach. This led to an "exploratory" contract with Michigan State University to see if the analyses and projections developed by CSNRD could have been advantageously computerized in view of the software developments which had taken place since CSNRD's earlier decision not to use a computerized systems simulation approach.

Under this exploratory contract, a superior model and analysis was developed for an expenditure about one-tenth that for CSNRD. The 90 percent savings in cost was, of course, somewhat illusionary because three years of CSNRD research and hard work had revealed the important crucial components to be modeled. Nonetheless, the savings were impressive. Still more impressive was the reduced cost of carrying out analyses with the model. Actually, the computerized systems simulation model for Nigeria became usable just before the agricultural planning conference mentioned above took place. The paper and pencil, desk calculator model developed by CSNRD had been used at great expense to develop projections for three alternative agricultural development programs at three points in time (nine points in all) (Johnson et al. 1969). By contrast, the computerized general systems model was cheaply run for 17 alternative policies with results printed out year by year for as many years as the analysts felt they could safely let the computers run. In the final book on agricultural perspectives produced by Nigerians for Nigeria, there are 90 pages of data generated by S. O. Olayide, now Vice Chancellor of the University of Ibadan, using the general systems simulation model on Michigan State University (MSU) computers.

The two Nigerian studies--one computerized and the other not--provide the basis for concluding that computerization is not an essential characteristic of holistic, nonmodernist models and approaches. Computers merely facilitate computations. It is possible, however unfeasible and costly it may be in many instances, to do anything a computer can do without a computer. Closely related to this is the false conclusion that nonmodernist models and analysis of PS and SM domains are infeasible because they must be large and exceed the availability of necessary data. While useful models of PS and SM domains must model the whole of the relevant domain, the size of the model depends on the detail with which the domain is modeled and the size of the domain itself. Some problematic and subject matter domains simply cannot be modeled in enough detail with available resources and, hence, have to be left unmodeled. Specialized disciplinary (modernist) models of parts of such domains cannot be adequate.

USAID administrators in Nigeria drew heavily on results generated by the informal noncomputerized model of agriculture. However, they knew little about the later computerized model which was financed by AID/Washington, not USAID/Lagos. When the director of USAID/Lagos was transferred to Seoul, South Korea, his satisfaction with the noncomputerized Nigerian study prompted him to contract with MSU for a sector study of Korean agriculture. I also served as director of this study. As the time and money budgets for the Korean study were much more limited than for Nigeria, there was no possibility of doing an inefficient noncomputerized agricultural study of Korea similar to the one done for Nigeria. It was equally clear that the study had to retain the nonmodernist, eclectic, multidisciplinary nature of the original CSNRD study rather than becoming a mechanical study specialized on economics and classifiable by McCloskey as "modernist." Consequently, it was decided at the very beginning that the study would be computerized following a general systems simulation approach to (1) take advantage of the computational efficiency of computers without (2) being forced into "modernism."

During construction of the Korean model, it was often referred to as a PS model. After it was built and made operational, it became clear to Ministry of Agriculture and Forestry officials and the model's builders that it was really a SM model. It provided useful information on a multidisciplinary subject--South Korean agricultural development--but did not provide adequate information to solve any particular agricultural development problem. Consequently, MSU was asked to provide three or four problem solvers to work in the Ministry's Planning Bureau to help use the model along with other sources of information to solve specific development problems in close iterative interaction with decision makers in the offices of the Planning Bureau (Ministry of Agriculture) and Deputy Prime Minister who had overall charge of economic planning in South Korea.

GENERAL SYSTEMS SIMULATION MODELS OF PROBLEMATIC AND SUBJECT MATTER DOMAINS: IMPORTANT CHARACTERISTICS, THEIR EVALUATION, AND A NEEDED COMPROMISE WITH McCLOSKEY

As the Nigerian and Korean general systems simulation studies discussed above are specifically documented in a number of generally available reports (Johnson et al. 1971; Rossmiller 1978; Johnson 1976b; Korean Agricultural Sector Study 1977; Lee et al. 1982; Thorbecke and Hall 1982), they are not summarized here. Instead, this section first lists important characteristics of such models; second, presents some observations and conclusions about what is involved in evaluating them; and third, points out that the need is to avoid modernist dominance but not to eliminate modernism.

Important Characteristics of General Systems Simulation Models of PS and SM Domains

The experiences of agricultural economists summarized above and the related arguments of McCloskey, Kirzner, and others have several important implications for model building. The implications indicate that it is important for general systems simulation models of problematic and subject matter domains to possess certain characteristics which, collectively, define what is meant by a general systems simulation analysis (GSSA) model. These characteristics are listed below:

1. Such models must be multidisciplinary, as both specific problems and subjects are multidisciplinary.
2. While the mixes of institutional, technological, and behavioral (human) components required vary widely from problem to problem but less so from subject to subject, a high proportion of PS and SM models require components dealing with all three.
3. PS models are directly and SM models are indirectly (instrumentally) parts of problem-solving processes. Such models may be built for, with, or by the decision unit responsible for solving any particular problem. In any event, decision makers are to a greater or lesser degree a part of the process(es) of solving a problem or problems. Decision makers possess relevant positive and normative knowledge necessary for building such models. Further, they have more or less power to establish the decision rule (what is to be maximized) used and to include in or preclude various kinds of knowledge from the process. Consequently, interaction between decision makers and model builders or analysts is an important part of the process of building such analytical models.
4. The purpose in building a PS model is to solve a problem and the purpose in building an SM model is to analyze the domain of an important subject (issue). Such models are not built to improve (directly, at any rate) the discipline of economics or, for that matter, any other discipline, even though they may reveal the need for or suggest relevant disciplinary work. Optimal designs of PS and SM models often neglect details of economics in order to model more important details studied in other disciplines.
5. PS models necessarily contain a maximizing component to convert positive knowledge (not about values or goodness and badness) and normative knowledge (about values or goodness and badness) into prescriptive statements about what "ought to be

done" in order to solve the problem under investigation (Johnson 1982b).

6. All problem-solving and many subject matter models have components dealing with goodness and badness (Lewis 1955; Moore 1956; Johnson 1982b, 1984) and, hence, are normative.

7. Descriptive knowledge of goodness and badness as characteristics of conditions, situations, and things is required to be interpersonally valid (though, like positive knowledge, not necessarily agreed upon) if prescriptions are to solve a practical problem by damaging one or more persons in order to benefit others.

8. Because positive, normative, and prescriptive knowledge may be parts of SM models and because all three are necessary parts of PS models, PS and SM models and their builders are required to be philosophically eclectic enough to exploit the methods and approaches of at least the following philosophies without being constrained by the limitations that they impose on each other (Johnson 1976a, 1986a, 1986b): (1) logical positivism, (2) various normative philosophies, and (3) pragmatism.

9. Power distributions are an inherent component of decision rules so long as there is imperfect knowledge and lack of unanimity among relevant decision makers and affected persons.

10. Models of PS and SM domains typically have important time dimensions. This is true because solutions depend on consequences through time and problem solving is a time-consuming process. In addition to the need to model problem-solving processes and consequences through time, it should be recognized that modeling is itself a process which benefits from interactions among decision makers, affected persons, and model building analysts. The process of building a model must be iterative as it unavoidably involves false starts and delayed insights. Also, information neglected in initial formulations of the PS and SM models is creatable or discoverable through interaction; thus, modeling processes also seem to be inevitably iterative. <u>Iterative interaction</u> with decision makers and affected persons in building and using PS and SM models is highly important. Man/machine GSSA models sometimes make such iterative interactions a part of a model.

11. The iterations referred to above are likely to involve a number of steps in which the preconditions for optimization are established. Problem-solving GSSA models should either provide for these steps or be based on a determination that they are unnecessary. These preconditions for optimization include (1) attainment of a common denominator among the goods and bads involved, (2) interpersonal validity of the common denominator of values if it is to be used to reach non-Pareto optimal prescriptions to benefit some by harming others, (3) the existence of an optimum to find (second order condition for a maximum in the case

of a twice differentiable function), and (4) an agreed on definition of what constitutes a maximum to prescribe as a solution to a problem in the case of imperfect knowledge.

The Evaluation of General Systems Simulation Models of Problem and Subject Matter Domains

The position taken here is that such models have to be evaluated for what they are--PS and/or SM models--and not DISC models. While the criteria used in evaluating models are generally similar for all three kinds, there are important differences in their use. Both the criteria and the differences in their use should become contextually obvious to the reader who studies the following eight points:

1. PS and SM models are unavoidably multidisciplinary; hence, evaluative responsibility is not appropriately placed exclusively on peers in any one discipline.

2. When peers in a discipline are asked to evaluate that part of a PS or SM model involving their discipline, the evaluation of that part should be in terms of what the discipline should be expected to contribute to a balanced model or analysis of the domain of the problem or subject under consideration.

3. Decision makers and persons affected by their decisions are as relevant or more relevant than disciplinary peers for the evaluation of models of PS and SM domains. Their standards are substantially different from those of disciplinary peers as a result of their relationship to (1) the particular problem being addressed in the case of PS models or (2) one or more of the problems in the set of problems for which a SM model is relevant. These practical peers have a keen interest in the prescriptions produced by a PS model and in the usefulness of SM model results for purposes of reaching a prescription.

4. PS models necessarily include normative information and generate prescriptions. SM models often include normative information. Positive information is commonly contained in both. The pragmatic test of workability is often important for PS models. Thus, evaluators of general systems science simulation models should be philosophically eclectic enough to evaluate the positive, normative, and prescriptive knowledge and components of such models without succumbing to the constraints which different philosophies place on ability to evaluate different kinds of knowledge (Johnson and Zerby 1973, Ch. 11).

5. Disciplinary peers can be viewed as evaluating models on the basis of their coherence (internal logical consistency), correspondence (consistency with experience), and clarity (lack of ambiguity). Practical peers (decision makers and affected persons) tend to add the criterion of workability. It is appropriate that the four criteria just listed be used differently by decision makers and affected people evaluating PS and SM models

than by disciplinary peers evaluating disciplinary models. Decision makers and affected persons should ensure (1) that the supposedly PS models do not become inappropriately specialized DISC models incapable of handling important parts of the PS and SM domain under investigation but are, instead, (2) eclectic, somewhat nonmodernist multidisciplinary models of use in reaching prescriptions to solve a particular problem in the case of PS research or of helping solve a set of problems in the case of SM research.

6. In accordance with Popper's view on falsifiability (Popper 1959), it is easier to describe when acceptability is lost among real world decision makers and affected persons than it is to define acceptability itself. Acceptability is lost when PS efforts <u>fail</u> to (1) include a kind of information (both about values and that free of values) known by decision makers to be relevant for solving the problem at hand, (2) include the bodies of logic known by the decision maker to be relevant for solving the problem, (3) consider values (nonmonetary as well as monetary) known by the decision maker to be relevant, (4) justify the decision rule the model uses to process positive and normative information into prescriptions about what ought to be done, and (5) reject knowledge which flunks the tests of logic (coherence), experience (correspondence), unambiguity (clarity), and workability. Modernist studies therefore have difficulty in establishing acceptability among real world decision makers and affected persons because they tend to (a) be unduly specialized on economics and (b) ignore crucial knowledge about values. On the other hand, modernist components may be extremely useful in PS and SM models.

7. Acceptability is more easily attained for SM than for PS models. To be acceptable, the results of multidisciplinary SM investigations must be useful for solving problems in the set of problems faced by the sets of decision makers under consideration. SM models which fail the tests of logic (coherence), experience (correspondence), clarity (lack of ambiguity), and workability (relevance for solving problems in the set of problems for which relevance is claimed) lose credibility.

8. General systems simulation models of the type developed for Nigeria and Korea are often adversely evaluated by modernist general economists, agricultural economists, and econometricians for failing to be modernistic (Thorbecke and Hall 1982; Egbert 1978). These criticisms have tended to focus on the absence of the characteristics of modernism described by McCloskey. It is important to note that studies acceptable by decision makers and affected people are not likely to be entirely modernist. Modernist studies are not likely to be acceptable among practical decision makers wanting to use models either to solve problems directly or as a source of information useful in solving their problems. On the other hand, the requirements for acceptability among disciplinary peers are often easily met by fragmented

modernist models highly specialized by disciplines, philosophic orientation, and techniques.

CONCLUSIONS ABOUT BALANCE BETWEEN THE MODERNIST AND NONMODERNIST APPROACHES TO MODELING HOLISTIC PS AND SM DOMAINS

The arguments of McCloskey and Kirzner have been given very serious consideration in this chapter. The research experiences which have been examined herein support substantial parts of their arguments; however, the experiences do not support other parts, and we believe their arguments need to be modified as in the following conclusions:

1. We have clearly established the relevance of many of the McCloskey-Kirzner arguments. There is a substantial correspondence between iterative, interactive, general systems simulation analyses of PS and SM domains, on one hand, and what is advocated by McCloskey and Kirzner, on the other.

2. Yet, we failed at the beginning of this chapter to find certain of McCloskey's arguments entirely convincing. Our examination of case studies of PS and SM modeling efforts in agriculture has tended to emphasize rather than eliminate these lingering doubts. More specifically and for reasons given immediately below, we do not find McCloskey's rejection of Karl Popper's falsification principles to be convincing.

McCloskey's rejection is inconsistent with his own argument that observations based upon interpretation should be regarded as scientific. If one accepts McCloskey's argument, which the author of this chapter does, then all descriptive knowledge originates ultimately in the <u>interpretation</u> of sense impressions and logic, and Karl Popper's falsification principle seems essential to McCloskey's position. The necessity of interpreting experiences means that our concepts of the "real world" are necessarily unprovable because of doubts about "proper" interpretation. Falsification, however, remains possible. This is supported in point 6 of the last section which accepts the position that it is easier to indicate when acceptability of a model is lost than when it is attained.

It also seems that McCloskey overstates the matter when he asserts that prediction is impossible for economics. While perfect prediction (without the remotest possibility of the smallest conceivable error) is obviously impossible in economics as in all descriptive sciences, reasonably good predictions are made by some economists about the phenomena that economists study.

3. The output of modernist research has been found to provide useful components in models of PS and SM domains. This, in itself, makes it necessary for the nonmodernist modelers of such domains to be more tolerant of modernism than is McCloskey.

4. McCloskey tends, in the opinion of the author, to denigrate mathematical models unduly in his article. We have found numerous quantitative models which are nonmodernist in all essen-

tial respects other than their quantitative mathematical form. I believe that McCloskey unduly restricts mathematics to modernist work, thereby depriving nonmodernist analysts of the substantial benefits which come from mathematics regarded by some as the highest form of logic.

5. Kirzner has argued that much of neoclassical theory should be preserved but that it needs a thorough reconstruction to incorporate what this author calls the structural dynamics of institutional, technological, and human change. The modeling efforts of agricultural economists examined herein substantiate Kirzner's argument but the substantiation is not complete.

There is clear evidence that agricultural economists modeling PS and SM domains have had to extend and improvise theory to deal with institutional, technological, and human change. However, there is little indication of success in developing an economic theory so massive and so complete that the structural dynamics of society is entirely manageable within that theory.

There has been much evidence that agricultural economists have been able to add technological, institutional, and human development components on an ad hoc basis in a manner more or less adequate for purposes of modeling the domain of a particular problem or subject but virtually none that an overall general model has been or is being attained. When one reflects on the matter, it becomes clear that a theory (economic or not) involving institutional, technological, and human change and the accumulation of conventional capital would be so massive it would encompass within itself all existing academic disciplines. To this author, such a theory seems to be beyond the grasp of mere mortals.

6. It is concluded, therefore, that the specialized academic disciplines which study different aspects of technological, institutional, and human change will continue to find it advantageous to focus on specific phenomena, leaving to holistic modelers of PS and SM domains the task of cobbling together reasonable (for the purposes at hand) models of different specific multidisciplinary PS and SM domains.

7. Our investigation indicates that the need for general eclectic (holistic) models of PS and SM domains is not a need for computerization of models. Either holistic or reductionistic models can be computerized. Nor are general eclectic (holistic) models necessarily large. Both holistic and reductionistic models can be either small or large depending on the detail that is modeled.

REFERENCES

Achinstein, P., and S. F. Barker, eds. 1969. _The Legacy of Logical Positivism: Studies in the Philosophy of Science._ Baltimore, MD: The Johns Hopkins University Press.

Bell, Daniel, and Irving Kristol, eds. 1981. _The Crisis in_

Economic Theory. New York: Basic Books, Inc.

Binswanger, Hans P., and Vernon W. Ruttan, eds. 1978. Induced Innovation: Technology, Institutions and Development. Baltimore, MD: Johns Hopkins University Press.

Black, J. D., and J. T. Bonnen. 1956. "A Balanced United States Agriculture in 1965." Special Report 42. Washington, DC: National Planning Association.

Bradford, L. A., and G. L. Johnson. 1953. Farm Management Analysis. New York: Wiley.

Colyer, Dale, and George D. Irwin. 1967. Beef, Pork, and Feed Grains in the Cornbelt: Supply Response and Resource Adjustments. Research Bulletin 921. North Central Regional Research Publication No. 178. Columbia: Universlty of Missouri.

Cook, H. L., L. Blakley, R. Jacobson, R. Knutson, R. Milligan, and R. Strain. 1978. The Dairy Subsector of American Agriculture: Organization and Vertical Coordination. North Central Regional Research Publication 257.

Cromarty, William A. 1957. Economic Structure in American Agriculture. Unpublished Ph.D. Thesis. East Lansing: Michigan State University.

Cromarty, W. A., and J. T. Bonnen. 1958. "The Structure of Agriculture." In E. O. Heady, H. G. Diesslin, H. R. Jensen, and G. L. Johnson, eds., Agricultural Adjustment Problems in a Growing Economy. Ames: Iowa State College Press.

Day, Richard H., and Inderjit Singh. 1977. Economic Development as an Adaptive Process. Cambridge: Cambridge University Press.

Egbert, Alvin E. October 1978. "Agricultural Sector Planning Models: A Selected Summary and Critique." World Bank Staff Working Paper No. 297, Washington, DC: IBRD.

Feyerabend, Paul. 1978. Against Method. Great Britain: Redwood Burn Limited Trowbridge & Esher.

Fletcher, L. B., Eric Graber, W. C. Merrill, and Erik Thorbecke. 1970. Guatemala's Economic Development: The Role of Agriculture. Ames: Iowa State University Press.

Hagan, Albert R. 1963. Family Farm Adjustments to Meet the Impacts of Economic, Technological, and Sociological Changes on Central Missouri Farms. Unpublished Ph.D. Thesis. East Lansing: Michigan State University.

Johnson, G. L. 1957. "Agricultural Economics, Production Economics and the Field of Farm Management." Journal of Farm Economics 39: 441-450.

________. 1969. "Stress on Production Economics." In K. A. Fox and D. G. Johnson, eds., Readings in the Economics of Agriculture. Homewood, IL: Richard T. Irwin.

________. 1972. "Alternatives to the Neoclassical Theory of the Firm." American Journal of Agricultural Economics 54: 295-303.

________. 1976a. "Philosophical Foundations: Problems,

Knowledge and Solutions." European Review of Agricultural Economics 3: 207-234.

________. 1976b. "General Systems Simulation Analyses (GSSA) of the Nigerian and Korean Agricultural Sectors and Related Efforts." European Review of Agricultural Economics 3: 391-410.

________. April 1982a. "Small Farms in a Changing World." In Wendy J. Sheppard, ed., Proceedings of Kansas State University's 1981 Farming Systems Research Symposium--Small Farms in a Changing World: Prospects for the Eighties. Farming Systems Research Paper (2): 7-28, 63-69. Manhattan: Kansas State University.

________. 1982b. "Agro-Ethics: Extension, Research and Teaching." Southern Journal of Agricultural Economics 14: 1-10.

________. 1984. "Ethics and the Economics of Energy and Food Conversion Systems." In David Pimentel and C. W. Hall, eds., Food and Energy Resources. New York: Academic Press.

________. 1986a. "Philosophic Foundations of Agricultural Economics Thought." In Lee R. Martin, ed., A Survey of Agricultural Economics Literature, Volume 4. Minneapolis: University of Minnesota Press.

________. 1986b. Research Methodology for Economists. New York: Macmillan.

Johnson, G. L., and Cecil B. Haver. 1953. Decision-Making Principles in Farm Management. Kentucky Agricultural Experiment Station Bulletin 593. Lexington: University of Kentucky.

Johnson, G. L., and C. L. Quance. 1972. The Overproduction Trap in U.S. Agriculture. Baltimore, MD: Johns Hopkins University Press.

Johnson, G. L., and L. K. Zerby. 1973. What Economists Do About Values--Case Studies of Their Answers to Questions They Don't Dare Ask. East Lansing: Department of Agricultural Economics, Michigan State University.

Johnson, G. L., A. Halter, H. R. Jensen, and D. Thomas, eds. 1961. A Study of Managerial Processes of Midwestern Farmers. Ames: Iowa State University Press.

Johnson, G. L., O. J. Scoville, G. K. Dike, and C. K. Eicher. July 1969. Strategies and Recommendations for Nigerian Rural Development, 1969/1985. East Lansing: Consortium for the Study of Nigerian Rural Development, Department of Agricultural Economics, Michigan State University.

Johnson, G. L., et al. 1971. A Generalized Simulation Approach to Agricultural Sector Analysis with Special Reference to Nigeria. East Lansing: Department of Agricultural Economics, Michigan State University.

Kirzner, Israel M. 1981. "The 'Austrian' Perspective." In

Daniel Bell and Irving Kristol, eds., The Crisis in Economic Theory. New York: Basic Books, Inc.

Knight, Frank H. 1921. Risk, Uncertainty and Profit. Boston: Houghton Mifflin Co.

Korean Agricultural Sector Study. 1977. Korean Agricultural Sector Model Technical Documentation (A Packet). East Lansing: Department of Agricultural Economics, Michigan State University.

Lee, Jeung-Han, Dong-Min Kim, Michael H. Abkin, and Tom W. Carroll. 1982. "Structure and Application of the Korean Agricultural Sector Model." In Max R. Langham and Ralph H. Ketzlaff, eds., Agricultural Sector Analysis in Asia. New York: Agricultural Development Council.

Lewis, C. I. 1955. The Ground and Nature of the Right. New York: Columbia University Press.

McCloskey, Donald N. 1983. "The Rhetoric of Economics." Journal of Economic Literature 21: 481-517.

Mighell, Ronald L., and John D. Black. 1951. Interregional Competition in Agriculture with Special Reference to Dairy Farming in the Lake States and New England. Cambridge: Harvard University Press.

Moore, G. E. 1956. Principia Ethica. Cambridge, England: Cambridge University Press. (Originally published in 1903).

Popper, Karl. 1959. The Logic of Scientific Discovery. New York: Harper and Row.

Rossmiller, George E., ed. 1978. Agricultural Sector Planning: A General Systems Simulation Approach. East Lansing: Department of Agricultural Economics, Michigan State University.

Samuelson, Paul A. 1947. Foundations of Economic Analysis. Cambridge: Harvard University Press.

Schultz, T. W. 1939. "Theory of the Firm and Farm Management Research." Journal of Farm Economics 21: 570-586.

________. 1958. "Output-Input Relationships Revisited." Journal of Farm Economics 40: 924-932.

Scriven, Michael. 1969. "Logical Positivism and the Behavioral Sciences." In P. Achinstein and S. F. Barker, eds., The Legacy of Logical Positivism: Studies in the Philosophy of Science. Baltimore, MD: The Johns Hopkins University Press.

Shapere, Dudley. 1969. "Notes Toward a Post-Positivistic Interpretation of Science." In P. Achinstein and S. F. Barker, eds., The Legacy of Logical Positivism: Studies in the Philosophy of Science. Baltimore, MD: The Johns Hopkins University Press.

Thorbecke, E., and L. Hall, eds. 1982. Agricultural Sector Analysis and Models in Developing Countries. FAO Economic and Social Development Paper 5. Rome: Food and Agricultural Organization.

6

Systems Management, Repair, and Improvement: Systems Economics Applied to a Small, Constrained Poultry Farm

DON G. MILES

INTRODUCTION

Applied systems economists consciously attempt to help make people better off and aware of the consequences of decisions within and beyond their control. They also attempt to establish a useful framework for understanding how and anticipating when world and national events affect the lives of individuals and different groups of people. In addition, applied systems economists employ decision criteria for the management, repair, improvement, and practical optimization of constrained and unconstrained systems.

A look at managing a small, constrained poultry farm illustrates the systems management, repair, and improvement rationale of applied systems economics. Many of the concepts and principles outlined in this example are believed to apply to other larger constrained and unconstrained farm business and corporate systems. Modeling the complexities of large (including regional) socioeconomic-ecologic systems, mathematically maximizing net benefits and efficiently minimizing detriments to help make people better off in addition to taking account of factors within and beyond the ability of decision makers to control, has been addressed elsewhere.[1] The importance of materials, money, energy, information, and prices as a useful framework for understanding how and anticipating when world and national events affect the lives of individuals and different groups of people has also been addressed in an earlier work.[2] Thus, the focus of this chapter is limited to illustrating the systems management, repair, improvement, and optimization rationale of applied systems economics.

AN APPLICATION OF SYSTEMS ECONOMICS

Consider the example of a small poultry farm which operates to generate sufficient high quality large eggs, other outputs, and net benefits (including capital gains) that a satisfying way of life can be maintained for the owner and his or her employee/farm manager. Although it is recognized that an absentee owner supplies capital and information from other sources, only the actual farm is used as the systems boundary. The farm is the primary behavior setting for the resident manager. The operation is constrained because of an Australia-wide system of quotas which limits the number of laying hens on this farm to 10,000. It is small because of the very limited number of hens farmed and because of the small scale and range of other activities such as producing olives, fruit, pangola grass, and wood.

It is assumed that the manager possesses the knowledge and skills necessary to successfully operate, repair, improve, and construct subsystems on this extensively automated farm. If needed, replacement parts and additional skills can be purchased from the appropriate markets. Thus a malfunction can be "repaired" by identification of the problem rather than a detailed explanation of how to actually repair the automatic feeding subsystem, for example. The reader is also assumed to have no interest in wanting to know the actual farm layout, shed design, composition of rations, or the socioeconomic-ecologic setting within which this farm operates.

The key to the successful operation, early repair, and improvement of this system is the continual monitoring of the system's indicators. These indicators measure the performance of the system, subsystems, linkages, and so on. The key to constructing new systems, expanding the existing system, or comparing it to others is this system's structure. Both indicators and structure exist as parts of the operational whole. But the whole is not always improved by improving the performance or structure of a subsystem or component. The whole system may well be damaged by short-term maximization of egg production, minimization of feed input, or by considering a component such as (hours of) lighting in isolation from the rest of the system. Furthermore, the long-term survival of the whole farm is dependent upon the successful operation of the main subsystem--the shed, equipment, hens, and so on. The successful operation of the main subsystem also requires a system of management if any satisfactory levels of predictability and performance are to be maintained.

Operational System of Management

For this farm, a simplified, operational system of management which maintains the desired performance and predictability is: (A) continually assess system, subsystems, components, and socioeconomic-ecologic context; (B) monitor and generate feedforward (for owner, other employees, records, etc.); (C) buy and coordinate all nonpublic good inputs; (D) coordinate and organize all controllable throughputs, interactions, resources, etc.; (E) monitor and react to all significant uncontrolled inputs, throughputs, interactions, etc.; (F) adjust for attributes which affect system and for the system affecting the attributes; (G) repair faults, lags, malfunctions; (H) improve system, interactions, performance and not just parts; (I) maximize desired outputs within accepted constraints; (J) utilize by-products; (K) minimize undesirable outputs, detrimental shifts; (L) monitor outputs, hen deaths, dollars, any labor, exits; (M) monitor feedback subsystem, the information itself; (N) monitor the feedforward subsystem; (O) exit for other activities. This is a simplified system because actual management requires its practical implementation, skills, experience, a sound working system structure, and a "predictable" environment.

This system of management is modeled in Figure 6.1. When operating, this model is (or should be) "full" of materials, money, energy, information, and interactions where appropriate. It is not merely a series of steps from (A) to (O). The key to this system of management is the information and coordination of materials, money, and energy. The system's indicators, quantified and qualified flows, stocks, inputs, and outputs, provide much of the vital information and serve as an early warning subsystem.

Modifications

The term modification is used broadly to include deviations from the norm which require repair (i.e., change from present levels, returning to the norm), improvements, major structural changes, and development of totally new means and/or ends. But as Spedding (1979) has pointed out, "the bigger the change contemplated, the greater the requirement for detailed knowledge of internal workings and relationships." In addition to possession of such knowledge, it is also necessary to assume that purposes and values remain constant into the future. For example, a modification designed as an improvement in a profit-maximizing labor intensive system could turn out to be a disaster if the new objective became minimizing labor input. During heat wave conditions, the number of hen deaths is inversely correlated to labor and management input and/or to the effectiveness of an automatic cooling subsystem. Furthermore, because modifications often involve substitutions, e.g., of capital and equipment for labor, it is also necessary to assume that the benefits and costs of trade-offs and foregone alternatives are known in terms of materials, money, energy, and information.

In terms of the preceding model, repairs involve returning to (C) and/or (D) or correction of the malfunction at (G). Improvements can be ongoing modifications at (H) and/or made by returning to (A) to improve the whole, not just the parts. New constructions involve new means and/or ends in terms of this

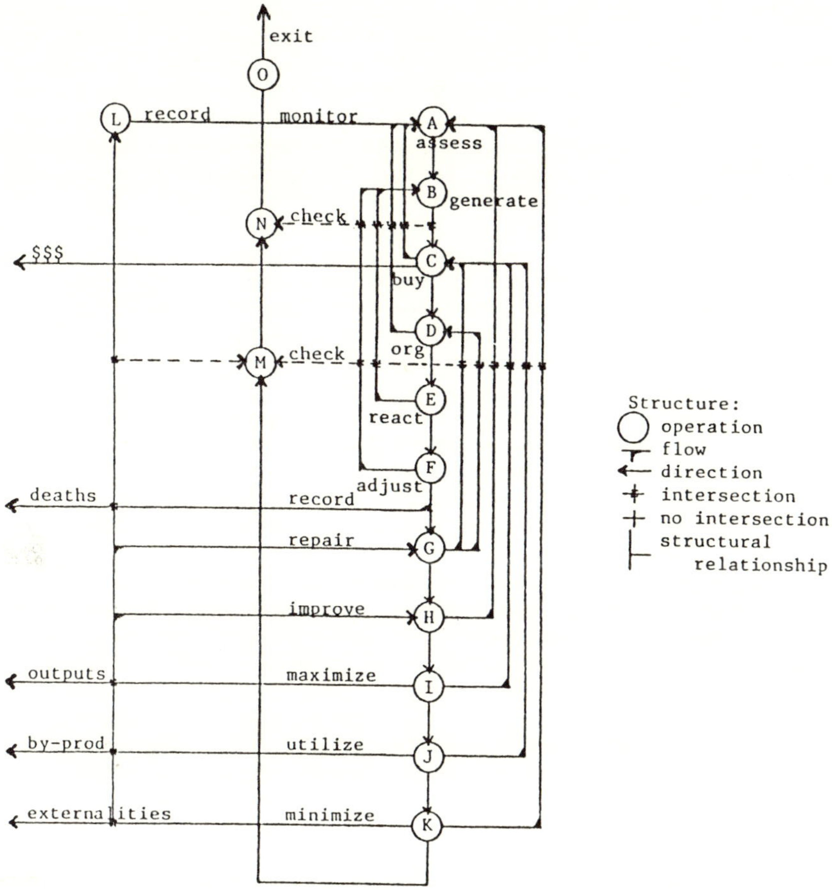

FIG. 6.1. An operational system of management.

constrained operational model. Relaxing the constraint, i.e., increasing the hen quota, would produce no increase in fixed costs and only a small increase in labor and management costs, but a large decrease in the prices received for eggs and increased egg production. Any surplus not consumed in Australia would enter the world market where prices are affected by import restrictions, subsidies, shipping, storage, and disease problems, such as avian influenza in the United States, Marex and Newcastle disease. Thus, although the system of management would be largely unaffected, a large capital outlay and/or a change in the laws governing egg marketing would be needed to significantly relax the quota constraint. Overtime, repairs, improvements, new constructions, and changes in the constraint(s) become built into the operation and structure of this system.

Repairs

This system is deemed in need of repair when a linkage, component, or part of the system fails or malfunctions. A malfunction is recognized as an abnormal change in the system's operations, performance, or indicators. Repairs are often effected in terms of their importance to the satisfactory functioning of the main subsystem or the whole system. It represents a return to the operational norm.

A key consideration is, are the repairs to mechanical or to biological subsystems? Some repairs can be effected simply. For example, a failure in the light or feed subsystems is fixed or replaced, and no real problems remain unless the situation has existed for some hours or days. Other problems such as heat stress or disease require the proper husbandry and the right equipment or drugs, as well as a few days, to correct if detected early and corrected properly. Complex repairs cannot be effected quickly. For example, to repair egg shell quality involves many considerations, interrelations, and changes if net benefits are to be made or foregone. Such changes might involve the ration, lights, water, number of eggs produced, income, extra labor, or effective "loss" of the automated egg collecting subsystem which depends upon a minimum shell hardness for "trouble-free" operation. Where possible, repairs are effected early. Social misfits, pickers, poor performers, or suspects are also removed for closer observation or isolation away from the main subsystem.

It is important to realize that some subsystem failures cannot be repaired internally. If there is a power failure or strike which affects vital supplies of electricity or feed, this system is dependent upon other people and the socioeconomic-ecologic environment. Such external problems may be "repaired" by improvements, e.g., generators, biogas production, expansion into feed production and ration mixing. Where an improvement does not generate a new norm or level of performance, the system has been repaired rather than improved.

Improvements

Improvements in all operational efficiencies (technical, biological, economic, farm, and social) of this system are made in terms of the system's purposes, values, trade-offs, and their likelihood of predictably improving the whole system. There is no point in short-term maximization of egg production or the minimization of feed inputs at the expense of the system. Thus, a component is not improved unless it will contribute to the net improvement of the whole system in the long term. This generates a new norm. Thus (H) is linked back to (A).

Improvements may begin as repairs, experiments, comparisons, copies, or innovations. They may involve planning, budgeting, prediction of results, examination of constraints to change including available resources, and consideration of consequences of changes in operations, structure, performance, and the system of management. They may end as improved efficiencies, increased stability, increased net benefits, and optimized outputs. They may also contribute to net social benefits and fewer negative externalities in the systems context.

Improvements to the main subsystem can be made in a variety or combination of ways:

- shorten linkages
- reduce entropy
- reduce deaths
- reduce wastage
- eliminate undesirable constraints on production
- relax imposed constraints
- improve technical efficiency
- improve economic efficiency
- improve biological efficiency
- improve social efficiency
- decrease dependency upon context
- improve socioeconomic-ecologic context
- improve environmental conditions for the hens (controlled environment)
- improve genetic potentials (or buy better hens)
- improve flows of nutrients, money, energy, and/or information
- improve stocks, indicators, etc.
- improve rates of transformation
- subsidize the performance of biological subsystems
- replace biological processes with mechanical ones (e.g., hatching)
- restructure the system
- reorganize components
- substitute fuel energy for labor and management
- substitute machinery for labor and management
- substitute dollars for labor and management
- substitute management for resources, inputs, etc.

However, the greater the number and variety of improvements attempted simultaneously, the slower the rate of improvement. Also, it takes longer to achieve a set of multiple objectives than to achieve a narrow, single objective by channeling all available materials, money, energy, and information into one narrow end. This system opts for slower, broader, long-term improvements.

New Constructions and Relaxed Constraints

The last major changes were made 15 years ago, before the introduction of the quota system, and are now inbuilt into the system. There is considered to be no net advantage in revolutionizing this predictable and satisfactory system at present. This system could handle 4,000 more hens with no increase in fixed costs and only a small increase in labor and management--if the quotas were increased to optimal shed capacity.

However, this can only occur with a radical change in Australia-wide egg marketing/production laws and a large significant drop in the prices producers receive for all outputs. It is not clear that these changes would make the owner or the manager better off, although consumers would benefit during periods of overproduction and very low prices. Offsetting this gain to consumers would be their loss of the marketwide internalization of externalities and the "elimination" of seasonal shortages that has benefited consumers largely at the producer's expense.

It is possible that net gains can be made with the construction of a new system of indicators, e.g., a computerized feedback-feedforward subsystem. However, such a feedback-feedforward subsystem would best be inbuilt rather than imposed onto the existing structure at a later date. Furthermore, it would increase the vulnerability of the whole system to power failures and strikes affecting electricity supplies. For these reasons such new constructions have not been implemented. Since the key to successful operation, early repair, and improvement of the whole system is the continual monitoring of the system's indicators, the skills of the manager and owner continue to be of vital importance. It is unlikely that any technology could completely replace all of the skills and knowledge needed at various times to successfully operate, repair, improve, and optimize this system.

Even this relatively isolated system is clearly affected by the region's socioeconomic-ecologic environment; for example, via Australian policies, laws, quarantine restrictions, the climate, seasonal changes, and the day's temperature. Furthermore, since feed costs are the major operating expense, world wheat, coarse-grain, and protein meal prices, plus the state's production and exports of these commodities, can also impact the system's profits. World wheat prices, as an example, reflect weather conditions in the Soviet Union, the United States, and Canada as well as these farmers', traders', and consumers' estimations of demand and supply around the world. Similarly, the replacement of biological processes with technological ones (the result of the development of hatching and rearing technologies), better management and disease prevention measures, and genetic selection and breeding, in addition to foreign investment into competing units or outlets by multinational corporations, fast food chains, and individuals, all reveal how decisions and developments in distant places can have a significant impact on such a relatively isolated business.

CONCLUDING REMARKS

Once a system's boundary and primary behavior setting has been defined, systems economics can be brought down to an applied level. Nevertheless, several important lessons can be seen as generalizations which apply to a wide variety of examples. First, the whole is not always improved by improving the performance or structure of a subsystem or component. Optimization must be holistic. Second, improvements are intended to establish new norms, but in many cases the greater the number of improvements undertaken, the slower the rate of improvement. Third, systems economists should be concerned with repairs to biological, mechanical, and socioeconomic-ecologic systems by helping to effect a gradual or rapid return to an established norm of performance or structure. Thus, it is necessary to take account of the trade-offs involved, the costs and benefits of the rate of adjustment, the predictability of the change effected, and many other considerations such as the nature of the systems being modified. However, for net benefits to be realized the cost of acquiring such information must be less than the benefits it produces.

NOTES

1. See "The Foundations of Applied Systems Economics," available upon request from Don G. Miles, Lecturer, Muresk Institute of Agriculture, Western Australian Institute of Technology, Northam, 6401, Western Australia. Revised edition forthcoming.

2. See "Wholistic Analysis, Problem Shifting Analysis, and Systems Economics" by Don G. Miles (1983). Copies available upon request.

REFERENCES

Spedding, C. R. W. 1979. *An Introduction to Agricultural Systems*. Barking, England: Applied Science.

7

The Eco-behavioral View of Human Societies: Behavior Settings, Time-allocation Matrices, and Social System Accounts

KARL A. FOX[1]

INTRODUCTION

Economic science advanced rapidly from economic indicators and index numbers in the 1920s to national income accounts and econometric models in the 1930s. These developments were facilitated by economic theory, but they were propelled by public concern about economic instability and unemployment; hence, public funds were made available for a major expansion in economic data systems for the objective measurement of these phenomena and, hopefully, for their explanation, prediction, and control. Without these data systems, the recent advances in large-scale models of national economies would have been impossible.

The range of public concerns in many countries broadened during the 1960s. The development of social indicators addressed to the new concerns was pursued with vigor and a long-term goal of comprehensive social system accounts was stated by Gross (1966). However, no one social science provided a conceptual framework for such accounts which would have satisfied the practitioners of any other, and many social scientists took comfort from the thought that the issues could be deferred until work within the social indicators tradition was far advanced.

Publication of *The OECD List of Social Indicators* (Organization for Economic Cooperation and Development 1982) represents a new level of maturity and consensus in specifying objective social indicators and relating them to well-established official data systems. The OECD List is intended to be both comprehensive and systematic and is recommended for implementation by OECD-member countries as their circumstances permit. It establishes at least a temporary plateau for objective social indicators.

It is time now to commence the active development of social system accounts. For this we need a criterion of comprehensiveness (What range of human activities should be included?), an objective method of classification that applies equally to market and nonmarket activities, and an objective unit for sampling and recording the contributions (inputs) people make to the social system and the rewards (outputs) they receive from it.

We can meet these requirements by viewing human societies from the perspective of eco-behavioral science, a term introduced by Roger G. Barker (1969; Barker and Associates 1978) in 1969 after 22 years of pathbreaking research within a somewhat narrower framework which he called "ecological psychology." His basic unit of observation is a behavior setting. Behavior settings are the natural units or "standing patterns of behavior" into which people sort themselves to get on with the business of daily life--school classes, grocery stores, meetings, government offices, social events, religious worship services, athletic events, and so on. A system of social accounts based on behavior settings can incorporate most of the existing official data systems without impairing their separate usefulness.

In adapting behavior setting concepts to the requirements of objective social accounts, we believe we are helping to extend the foundations of eco-behavioral science and to provide it with a data base which takes advantage of the many billions of dollars already invested in official data systems. If the social system of (say) the United States is viewed as a comprehensive array of behavior settings, each with its own internal dynamics and its external relations with other settings, collectively incorporating all of the living-time, behavior, and experience of the U.S. population in a given year, we believe the contexts and consequences of most private and public decisions will look somewhat different than they now do from the perspective of any existing social science. To the extent that systems scientists concern themselves with real people in real social systems, they should be interested in the modeling implications of this new view.

In most of this paper we will refer to the U.S. data systems and society with which we are familiar. However, closely comparable data systems and arrays of behavior settings exist in many other countries and proposals framed in terms of the United States should be generally adaptable in them.

THE OECD LIST OF SOCIAL INDICATORS AND ITS RELATIONS TO ESTABLISHED DATA SYSTEMS

Official data systems oriented to social concerns have been extended as new concerns have emerged and as citizens have come to believe that their governments could and should deal with them. In the United States, the catastrophic depression of 1929-1933 caused government to accept some responsibility for the aggregative performance of the economy and for providing a minimum level of social security for the aged, the disabled, and other disadvantaged groups. Economic data systems were rapidly extended and improved; Keynes's (1936) macroeconomic theory, Kuznets's (1937) national income and product accounts, Tinbergen's (1939) national econometric models, and Leontief's (1936) national input-output matrices all reinforced the view that the economy was indeed a system. Since World War II economic data systems and models have been further expanded and integrated.

As a discipline, economics was fortified by theories of the behaviors of profit-maximizing firms and utility-maximizing consumers and of the general equilibrium to which such behaviors could lead in a hypothetical economy. The variables called for by these theories--prices and quantities of commodities, money incomes of consumers, revenues and costs of firms--were observable in principle and increasingly so in fact as data systems developed.

Sociology had its share of great theorists, and it could claim comprehensiveness for its view of human societies--something economics could not. However, its very comprehensiveness was for long an insuperable obstacle to the specification of its data needs and the establishment of official data systems to meet them. This situation changed dramatically in the 1960s as government assumed broader responsibilities for health maintenance, medical care, education, the rights of women and minorities, urban renewal, community development, and the attempted elimination of poverty--in brief, for a "Great Society." The founders of the social indicators movement were quick to see the implications of these commitments for official data systems. They were interested in social measurement partly for pure science and partly as a basis for social policy. Bauer (1966) expressed these two interests succinctly: "For many of the important topics on which social critics blithely pass judgment, and on which policies are made, there are no yardsticks by which to know if things are getting better or worse." In the same volume, Gross's (1966) article "The State of the Nation: Social Systems Accounting" expressed the long-term interest of the movement in comprehensive social system <u>accounts</u> as distinct from a collection of indicators each separately designed to track a particular problem. The bill drafted by leaders of the movement and introduced by Senator Mondale in 1967 was entitled "The Full Opportunity and Social Accounting Act of 1967."

A great deal of the published work done in the name of "social indicators" during the late 1960s and early 1970s was undisciplined and eclectic--sometimes wildly so. Sophisticated social scientists and government statisticians avoided publicity during these years and concentrated on the development of data systems which would address the new social concerns while maintaining high standards of statistical quality. In particular, the OECD sponsored a Social Indicators Program which began in 1970 and published a _List of Social Concerns Common to Most OECD Countries_ in 1973. Several years of complex developmental work ensued on designing indicators to measure these concerns. _The OECD List of Social Indicators_ (1982) is the result.

The OECD List of Social Indicators is reproduced in Table 7.1. It includes 33 specific indicators grouped under eight major headings: health, education and learning, employment and quality of working life, time and leisure, command over goods and services, physical environment, social environment, and personal

Table 7.1. The OECD List of Social Indicators

Social concern	Indicator
HEALTH	
Length of Life	- Life Expectancy
	- Perinatal Mortality Rate
Healthfulness of Life	- Short-term Disability
	- Long-term Disability
EDUCATION AND LEARNING	
Use of Educational Facilities	- Regular Education Experience
	- Adult Education
Learning	- Literacy Rate
EMPLOYMENT AND QUALITY OF WORKING LIFE	
Availability of Employment	- Unemployment Rate
	- Involuntary Part-time Work
	- Discouraged Workers
Quality of Working Life	- Average Working Hours
	- Travel Time to Work
	- Paid Annual Leave
	- Atypical Work Schedule
	- Distribution of Earnings
	- Fatal Occupational Injuries
	- Work Environment Nuisances
TIME AND LEISURE	
Use of Time	- Free Time
	- Free Time Activities
COMMAND OVER GOODS AND SERVICES	
Income	- Distribution of Income
	- Low Income
	- Material Deprivation
Wealth	- Distribution of Wealth
PHYSICAL ENVIRONMENT	
Housing Conditions	- Indoor Dwelling Space
	- Access to Outdoor Space
	- Basic Amenities
Accessibility to Services	- Proximity of Selected Services
Environmental Nuisances	- Exposure to Air Pollutants
	- Exposure to Noise
SOCIAL ENVIRONMENT	
Social Attachment	- Suicide Rate
PERSONAL SAFETY	
Exposure to Risk	- Fatal Injuries
	- Serious Injuries
Perceived Threat	- Fear for Personal Safety

Source: Organization for Economic Cooperation and Development, _The OECD List of Social Indicators_ (Paris: OECD, 1982), p. 13.

safety. We believe all the objective indicators in the OECD List can be picked up and/or incorporated in social accounts based on behavior settings.

The 1982 OECD report recommends that five standard disaggregations be used in presenting nearly all indicators: age, sex, household type, socioeconomic status, and community size. It suggests optional "standard" disaggregations by ethnic group and citizenship in countries where these distinctions are relevant and also by region (i.e., by geographical location within a country) according to the classifications customary in each country.

The OECD report lists other disaggregations applicable to several indicators: branch of economic activity, occupation, type of activity, working hours, level of education, tenure status (homeowner versus tenant), and age of dwelling. It states that the breakdown of branch of economic activity should be based on the International Standard Industrial Classification (ISIC) codes at the two-digit level; that of occupation should follow the International Standard Classification of Occupations (ISCO), at the two-digit level, with three digits used where possible in coding occupational groups with a wide range of occupations such as managers; and that of levels of education should follow the International Standard Classification of Education (ISCED), which defines seven levels of education plus a residual category. The corresponding classifications used in the United States are closely comparable to the international ones cited.

The OECD List of Social Indicators is still, quite properly and explicitly, in the tradition of social indicators rather than social accounts. Each of its 33 indicators is treated as a distinct entity. Even within groups (e.g., health), the various indicators involve different units of measure, and there is no obvious way to assign "relative importance" weights to these units. Similarly, there is no obvious way to weight the relative importances of the eight major groups or social concerns.

THE NEXT STEP: SOCIAL SYSTEM ACCOUNTS BASED ON BEHAVIOR SETTINGS

Social system accounting faces two major problems: how to measure and account for nonmarket activities and how to combine social and economic indicators. Our proposed solution is accounts based on behavior settings.

Behavior settings provide the most comprehensive framework we have yet encountered for describing nonmarket as well as market activities. To make clear what behavior settings are and how they might be used as a basis for social accounts, we will begin our exposition (in the next section) at the level of a community and a complete census of its behavior settings. Similar accounts for a nation or a metropolitan region would be based on aggregates of behavior settings, linked with and interpreted in conjunction with existing data systems.

Behavior settings were discovered by Roger G. Barker, who adapted methods derived from the traditions of experimental psychology to the observation and measurement of naturally occurring behavior in a complete community (Midwest, Kansas), which he studied intensively from 1947 to 1972. Examples of behavior settings would include a bank, a Boy Scout troop meeting, the county recorder's office, a Sunday worship service, or a high school mathematics class. Each of these settings has a distinctive program of activities and (hence) a distinctive pattern of behavior by its occupants. It has a definite location in space and each of its occurrences has a definite beginning, duration, and end in time (e.g., the high school mathematics class occurs in Room 15 between 9:00 and 9:55 A.M. on weekdays). An empty classroom or a closed bank is _not_ a behavior setting.

The five settings listed belong to five different "authority systems"--private enterprise, voluntary association, government, church, and school--based on the legal status of the person or board with ultimate responsibility for their control. Only the first of these systems is market oriented; the other four are engaged in nonmarket activities. Barker applied uniform methods of observation and measurement to behavior settings in all five systems, market and nonmarket alike. Thus, his work provides a unique starting point for efforts to combine social and economic indicators and to measure and account for nonmarket activities.

Behavior settings with identical or closely similar programs (several or many banks, several or many high school math classes) are classified by Barker into categories which he calls "genotypes" (Banks, High School Mathematics Classes). Barker and Schoggen (1973) measured social change in Midwest between 1954-1955 and 1963-1964 partly in terms of the introduction of new genotypes and the disappearance of old ones; in each year they measured differences between Midwest and an English town partly in terms of the arrays of genotypes present in one town but not in the other. Barker and Gump (1964) compared large and small high schools partly in terms of the arrays of genotypes they provided.

Behavior settings can be linked with time budgets and economic accounts to form the basis for more comprehensive social system accounts. Barker's private enterprise genotypes can be identified with industries in the Standard Industrial Classification (SIC) system. The paid roles in Barker's genotype programs can be identified with occupations in the _Dictionary of Occupational Titles_ (DOT) and the Standard Occupational Classification. Barker's ratings of behavior settings on "action patterns" and "behavior mechanisms" suggest linkages (1) with categories of buildings in the new U.S. Bureau of Economic Analysis (BEA) time series on stocks of physical capital and (2) with DOT ratings of the complexity of worker functions in relation to data, people, and things and the level of physical strength required.

Much exploratory and developmental work would be needed to implement a system of social accounts based on behavior settings.

Most of the building blocks already exist in the form of published data systems, and historical time series incorporating behavior setting concepts could be constructed from these and supplementary sources. The explanatory power of accounts incorporating all nonmarket as well as market activities should greatly increase our ability to measure the effects of current social and economic policies and to predict the consequences of proposed alternatives.

Just as Tinbergen's work on econometric models followed almost immediately after publication of Kuznets's national economic accounts (with annual data from 1919 to 1935), so work on models of social systems could begin almost immediately after publication of preliminary versions of the corresponding social accounts. We will comment on modeling implications in several of the following sections.

THE USEFULNESS OF BEHAVIOR SETTINGS FOR CLASSIFYING AND DESCRIBING HUMAN ACTIVITIES IN A COMMUNITY

Existing social and economic data systems are most highly developed at the national level. However, these national aggregates are based directly or indirectly on data collected from individuals, households, firms, and other organizations. The aggregates are useful because sociologists and economists have built up extensive bodies of theory, empirical research, and personal experience concerning the attributes and behaviors of the primary decision-making units.

Experimental psychologists have concentrated on intensive studies of individuals and small groups in laboratory environments. Barker was the first psychologist trained in this tradition to study the naturally occurring behavior of people in their normal environments. Initially his research in Midwest focused on the question, "What aspects of the daily lives of children contribute positively to their personality development and mental health?" To cover all aspects would require intensive observation of the waking activities of selected children throughout the day in home, neighborhood, school, streets, playgrounds, church, stores, and other settings. This would be physically and financially feasible only in a small community which nevertheless provided a fairly wide range of situations and experiences for children. The community should be separated from its nearest neighbors by several miles of open country so that the children would spend nearly 100 percent of their time in their own community and have nearly all their interactions with other members of it. Barker chose such a community and obtained funding for his research in 1947. As a matter of empirical fact he found (Barker and Wright 1955) that children under 12 spent 98 percent of their time within the town limits; the average for all age groups of town residents combined was 95 percent. The principal "leakage" took the form of out-commuting by about 10 percent of the adult males.

Barker soon found that a child's behavior changed abruptly when he left one segment of his environment (e.g., a classroom) and entered another (e.g., a playground); a large proportion of the variance in his behavior was associated with these transitions. Within each segment the child's behavior was fairly stable, and so was the pattern of interactions among all "inhabitants" of that segment. The child's ecological environment consisted of a sequence of such patterned segments. Many of them contained significant adults (teachers, parents), whose ecological environments also consisted of patterned segments. Barker called these segments "behavior settings" and concluded that all or nearly all of the behavior and experiences of the community's residents occurred in them. As an environment for human behavior, the community *was* its behavior settings. His colleague Gump (1971, p. 134) summarized this insight as follows: "People live out their lives in a sequence of environmental units; experience in these settings *is* life. If the quality of experience is good, life expands; if it is bad, life diminishes."

Behavior settings are the basic units of organizations and communities. From the perspective of an experimental psychologist, a behavior setting is a marvelously complex entity. It imposes expectations and demands on each of its occupants according to his role in its program; minor deviations from the role-norm are countered almost instantly by pressures from other occupants and major ones lead to his ejection from the setting. Circumstances may confine a child to a few settings; if his behavior is appropriate to them, it is not likely to change unless he "migrates" on a full-time or part-time basis to other settings which impose different demands. An adult confined to an institution or restricted by poverty or physical disability to a few settings will adapt his behavior to them; he may not be deprived of food, clothing, and shelter, but he *is* deprived of a normal range of opportunities for social participation--he subsists but he does not belong to the mainstream of his society. An adult in the mainstream will choose to participate in a wider array of behavior settings which collectively define one of the normal, desirable, or acceptable life-styles of his time and place.

A few tables based on Barker's (1968) survey of the nonhousehold behavior settings of Midwest over a twelve-month period in 1963-1964 will give some indication of the relevance of his approach for social system accounts. Midwest and its trade area had a total population of about 1600, of which 830 resided in the town itself.

The figures on Total OT and Town OT (occupancy time by town residents only) for Midwest's five authority systems and the town as a whole in 1963-1964 are summarized in Table 7.2. Midwest's being a county seat accounts for the relatively large extent of the government authority system.

The total number of nonhousehold behavior settings was 884.

Table 7.2. Person-hours of Occupancy Time in Behavior Settings, by Authority System, Midwest, Kansas, 1963-1964

Authority system	Number of settings	Occupancy time: person-hours Total	By town residents	By non-residents	Percent by town residents
Private enterprise	132	734,183	531,555	202,628	72.4
Government	114	308,075	186,896	121,179	60.7
School	233	650,124	310,516	339,608	47.8
Church	193	69,753	33,173	36,580	47.6
Voluntary association	212	118,595	62,994	55,601	53.1
Total	884	1,880,730	1,125,134	755,596	59.8
			Percentages		
Private enterprise	14.9	39.0	47.2	26.8	----
Government	12.9	16.4	16.6	16.0	----
School	26.4	34.6	27.6	44.9	----
Church	21.8	3.7	2.9	4.8	----
Voluntary association	24.0	6.3	5.6	7.4	----
Total	100.0	100.0	100.0	100.0	----

Source: Compiled and reconstructed from various tables in Roger G. Barker and Phil Schoggen, Qualities of Community Life (San Francisco: Jossey-Bass, 1973).

Barker suggests that each behavior setting may be viewed as a "standing wave" or standing behavior pattern. Each person who enters the setting is analogous to a particle which becomes part of the standing pattern without losing its particle characteristics. This pattern is governed by a program which prescribes appropriate behavior for the occupants of each concentric zone of the setting. Deviations are curbed by its single leader (zone 6) or joint leaders (zone 5); parts of the program may be implemented by operatives or functionaries (zone 4). Some settings contain customers, pupils, patients, or clients (zone 3), who interact directly with persons in the more central zones; spectators or audience members (zone 2), who can do little more than express approval or disapproval of the performers in zones 4, 5, and 6; and onlookers (zone 1), who have no function in the setting and no power over it.[2]

Settings with the same program belong to the same genotype; for example, an array of three grocery stores, five eating places, and four gasoline service stations involves only three genotypes. Thus, the number of genotypes may be used to measure the variety of the town's environment.

The zone 6 leader of a behavior setting often carries the title of the genotype: banker (Genotype 15, Banks), barber (Genotype 16, Barber Shops), and attorney (Genotype 9, Attorneys Offices). In many cases these leaders have received formal training to learn the genotype's program and passed examinations to prove they knew it. Hence, many of Barker's genotypes have the built-in stability of the American occupational structure and translate readily into categories used in published data systems; this compatibility is the more impressive for being unpremeditated on Barker's part. Barker classified Midwest's 884 behavior settings into 198 genotypes.

Barker and Schoggen (1973) also provide some measures of the extent of participation in the operating and leadership functions (zones 4, 5, and 6) of Midwest's behavior settings. If all of the 884 behavior settings were operating at the same moment, a total of 10,220 persons would be needed to staff all of their zones 4, 5, and 6 positions, each of which constitutes a habitat-claim for an operative (see Table 7.3). If the same habitat-claim were operated by two or more different persons during the year, it would give rise to two or more claim-operations, one by each of the persons involved.

For the town as a whole, Barker and Schoggen also provide two other measures: leader acts, which are claim-operations performed in zones 6 (sole leader) and 5 (joint leaders) of behavior settings, and inhabitant-setting intersections (ISI). An ISI involves an individual's occupying any zone of a specified behavior setting at least once during the year. Claim-operations are a subset of the ISI, and leader acts are a subset of claim-operations; these three measures may be summarized as shown in Table 7.4.

On a per capita basis, the town's 830 residents accounted for 61.22 ISIs (50,809/830) consisting of 1.79 leader acts, 6.22

Table 7.3. Habitat-claims and Claim-operations in Behavior Settings, by Authority System, Midwest, Kansas, 1963-1964

Authority system	Habitat-claims for operatives	Claim-operations: Total	By town residents	By non-residents	Percent by town residents
Private enterprise	450	694	439	255	63.3
Government	740	1,306	453	853	34.7
School	3,999	5,316	2,149	3,167	40.4
Church	1,682	2,581	1,289	1,292	49.9
Voluntary association	3,349	4,352	2,312	2,040	53.1
Total	10,220	14,249	6,642	7,607	46.6

Source: Compiled and reconstructed from various tables in Roger G. Barker and Phil Schoggen, *Qualities of Community Life* (San Francisco: Jossey-Bass, 1973).

Table 7.4. Inhabitant-Setting Intersections, by Zones Within Behavior Settings, Midwest, Kansas, 1963-1964

Measure	Inhabitant-setting intersections: Total	By town residents	By non-residents	Percent by town residents
Leader acts (zones 5 and 6)	2,104	1,482	622	70.4
Other claim-operations (zone 4)	12,145	5,160	6,985	42.5
Total claim-operations (zones 4, 5, and 6)	14,249	6,642	7,607	46.6
Other inhabitant-setting intersections (zones 3, 2, and 1)	115,831	44,167	71,664	38.1
Total inhabitant-setting intersections, all zones	130,080	50,809	79,271	39.1

Source: Compiled and reconstructed from various tables in Roger G. Barker and Phil Schoggen, *Qualities of Community Life* (San Francisco: Jossey-Bass, 1973).

other claim-operations, and 53.21 other ISIs in zone 3 (customers, pupils), zone 2 (audiences, spectators), and zone 1 (onlookers). In terms of life-paths linking successive behavior settings, the average life-path intersected 61 different non-household settings during the survey year. This implies a high degree of selectivity of people for behavior settings and vice versa, because on the average a resident entered only 100(61/884) or 6.9 percent of the available settings. Some reasons are obvious, e.g., a certain school class is restricted to a certain age group. Other reasons are less so and include customer loyalty, church affiliation, or role expectations.[3]

Assigning weights to the various measures of community participation and integration is not attempted here. The schools, churches, and voluntary associations of Midwest provide a great many opportunities for children, adolescents, and retired people to participate in the leadership and implementation of behavior settings approved by the community; these three authority systems accounted for 88.4 percent of all habitat claims for operatives and 86.0 percent of all claim-operations. A minute percentage of these claim-operations was performed by paid professionals (teachers, coaches, ministers) and the rest by amateurs.

Nonresidents contributed slightly more than half of the Total OT of schools and churches in Midwest and only slightly less than half of the Total OT of voluntary associations. Apparently the attendance and membership areas of these three authority systems were virtually coextensive and contained about the same number of residents in the open country as in the town. These same open-country residents served as customers for about half of the retail sales and personal services of Midwest's private enterprises; a large part of the occupancy time of private enterprises attributed to town residents reflected their roles as proprietors and employees.

As a full convenience trade center with an elementary school, a high school, three or four churches, and a number of voluntary associations (not to mention the county courthouse), Midwest and about 50 square miles of the countryside surrounding it formed a relatively complete and self-contained community. If each ISI is viewed as a line on a large map connecting a particular individual to one of the town's behavior settings, the array of settings connected to an open-country resident probably would be nearly identical with the array connected to a town resident of the same age and sex. Beyond a certain radius, very few country residents would be connected with Midwest's behavior settings; rather, they would be connected with similar arrays of settings in other towns 10 miles or so from Midwest.

A community with this degree of completeness and closure is the smallest territorial unit for which a complete set of social accounts might be justified. If Midwest lost its high school, over 20 percent of the total occupancy time contributed by nonresidents would be diverted to another location; if it also lost its elementary school, another 20 or 25 percent of nonresident OT would be diverted. The resulting travel patterns of open-country residents to new consolidated schools might also encourage shopping and recreation at a center or centers other than Midwest.

Although Barker did not survey the households of Midwest in detail, he was clear on the points that household activities could also be partitioned into behavior settings and that his approach lent itself to an exhaustive accounting for the living-time of Midwest's residents. Thus, in Barker and Wright 1955, p. 84, he noted that 2030 behavior settings were identified in Midwest during July 1, 1951-June 30, 1952 and that 1445 of them were located in the homes of the town; the other 585 were found in its more public behavior areas. Further, in Barker and Wright 1955, pp. 97-98, he observed that Midwesterners during the survey year spent 5,130,000 hours in family settings; 1,030,658 hours in community settings; and 330,620 hours in settings outside the corporate limits of the town.

MICROANALYTICAL SIMULATION MODELS AND SOCIAL ACCOUNTING MATRICES AT THE COMMUNITY LEVEL

Fox and Ghosh (1980, 1981) described a conceptual model of a small community in which the second-by-second activities of each resident could be represented (1) by his locational coordinates in three-dimensional space, (2) by his location in some well-defined architectural entity (e.g., Room 15 of the high school), (3) by his presence in a specific behavior setting (the 9:00 A.M. algebra class is in session in Room 15), and (4) by his behavior within that setting (his behavior indicates that he is the teacher). His life-path during the year would literally intersect a series of behavior settings, each in a particular role; the number of different nonhousehold settings intersected would be his ISI and the number of hours he spent in each setting would be his contribution to its occupancy time (OT).

Fox and van Moeseke (1973) represented a rational individual as trying to choose an optimal life-style (the time-allocation vector x^*) during the coming year subject to the limitations of his endowment (the vector b) and his environment (the matrix A). Each column of A represents a specified role in a specified behavior setting. The elements a_{ij} of column j (j = 1, 2, ..., n) are input coefficients; a unit of time spent in the jth role-and-setting absorbs a_{ij} units of b_i, the ith element of the endowment vector (i = 1, 2, ..., m). Thus, the individual seeks to maximize his utility function u(x) subject to $Ax \leq b$, $x \geq 0$. If x is measured in hours, the elements of the optimal life-style vector x^* will sum to 8760 hours in a 365-day year. The elements of b would include time (8760 hours), income from property and transfer payments, occupational skills, health status, and some others. This model is stated briefly but rigorously in van Moeseke's chapter in the present volume.

The actual allocation of an individual's time among behavior settings, as observed in a Barker-type survey, should reveal his preference structure for behavior settings just as his actual purchases of consumer goods should reveal his preference structure for them. Thus, observed changes in the occupancy times of behavior settings by well-defined population aggregates should be subject to study by the methods of statistical demand analysis, as presented in Fox 1958, but with appropriate adjustments in the price and income concepts as described in Fox and van Moeseke 1973 and Fox 1974.

Within a given community, residents having a number of attributes (age, sex, years of schooling completed) and statuses (in school or not, employed or not, living in private homes rather than nursing homes) in common could be grouped for purposes of accounting and modeling. We believe the 830 residents of Midwest could be classified into about 150 attribute-and-status groups which would also be applicable to other U.S. communities. Barker's 884 behavior settings could be grouped into authority systems: within each authority system multiple settings in any genotype could be aggregated to the genotype total and in some cases two or more genotypes could be combined; genotypes accounting for very small amounts of occupancy time could be consolidated into "miscellaneous" categories. The resulting time-allocation matrix (TAM) for the community might have about 150 columns (groups of behavior settings) and a similar number of attribute-and-status rows.

As many genotypes are designed specifically for children or adolescents and many workplaces are entered only by adults, the TAM would contain many zero elements; each row would represent the time-allocation vector (TAV) of a particular attribute-and-status group in Midwest in 1963-1964. Given the distribution of persons among attribute-and-status groups in another community in the same region, we could compute an expected TAM for it on the explicit assumption that its TAVs per person were the same as those of Midwest for each group (row) i, i = 1, 2, ..., 150. Communities at successively higher levels in the central place hierarchy of the region would have successively wider arrays of genotypes; this has been amply documented for retail trade and consumer-oriented services--see, for example, Fox and Kumar 1965 and Fox 1974--and is probably true for the nonmarket authority systems as well. The "expected TAM" for a previously unsurveyed community could then be modified and interpreted on the basis of a limited amount of information specific to that community.

An authority system includes one or more organizations (individual firms, individual schools, individual government agencies, individual churches, individual voluntary associations). Hence, simulation models of organizations should have a prominent place in eco-behavioral studies at the community level. Some organizations consist of a single setting (e.g., a small retail store); others may consist of a number of settings that can be grouped into one or two major genotypes plus a few minor ones (e.g., most of the total occupancy time of Midwest's elementary school is accounted for by 13 settings of the genotype Elementary School Basic Classes).

James R. Prescott (1980, 1985) proposed a dynamic microanalytical simulation model consistent with Barker's data for Midwest in most respects but condensing the 884 settings into about 60 "prototype settings." Each prototype setting would be modeled in some detail. Its flow chart would specify exogenous variables which impinge on the setting's performance, variables endogenous to the setting which measure its performance in the current year, and forward linkages which will influence the setting's performance in the succeeding year. The model as a whole would specify causal (hence dynamic) relationships within Barker's behavior setting structure and also provide a comprehensive set of social accounting tables for the community. If and when implemented, Prescott's model would incorporate approaches pioneered by Orcutt (Orcutt et al. 1961) and by Forrester (1969). The main features of Prescott's proposed model are presented in Chapter 9 of this volume.

IMPLEMENTATION OF SOCIAL SYSTEM ACCOUNTS AND MODELS AT NATIONAL AND REGIONAL LEVELS

In a book just published (Fox 1985), we have made detailed suggestions toward the implementation of social system accounts based on behavior settings. At the national level, we show how data embodying behavior setting concepts can be linked, merged, or fused with official data systems such as those in the OECD List. For example, data for behavior setting genotypes can be merged with data for SIC (Standard Industrial Classification) industries (U.S. Office of Management and Budget 1978). We propose a matrix with a row for each genotype and a column for each SIC industry such that the living-time of the U.S. population in a given year is allocated exhaustively among genotypes and also among industries, with the latter augmented to include the occupancy times of unpaid persons (e.g., pupils, customers, spectators, and household members) in addition to gainful workers.

Paid roles in the programs of behavior setting genotypes can be identified with occupations in the *Standard Occupational Classification Manual* (SOC) published by the U.S. Office of Federal Statistical Policy and Standards (1977) and the *Dictionary of Occupational Titles* (DOT) published by the U.S. Employment and Training Administration (1977). Three digits in the SOC and DOT codes are identical; they refer to the complexity of a worker's function in relation to data, people, and things respectively--the demands that a typical job in a certain occupation imposes on anyone who tries to fill it. Levels of job complexity are highly correlated with the levels of specified worker traits (e.g., general educational development, specific vocational preparation, and general, verbal, and numerical aptitude) required for average performance in the relevant occupation. These relationships are spelled out in the U.S. Manpower Administration's (1972) Handbook for Analyzing Jobs.

Occupations are also characterized by strength required or heaviness of work. We note that the three categories of job complexity plus strength required seem to correspond roughly to Barker's categories of behavior mechanisms--thinking, talking and affective behavior, manipulation (use of the hands), and gross motor activity--which people use in carrying out their roles in behavior settings. Barker rates behavior mechanisms for entire settings rather than for individual roles. Some developmental research would be required to adapt Barker's rating scales so that they represented true aggregations or transformations of the SOC-DOT ratings of worker functions (required behavior inputs) for all persons in the setting.

The U.S. Bureau of Labor Statistics (1981) has published a national industry-occupation employment matrix with a row for each of 425 occupations and a column for each of 260 industries; all gainful employment in the U.S. economy is allocated both among the occupation-rows and the industry-columns. We suggest that quasi-occupations (student, customer, unpaid housekeeper, and the like) can be created to describe the activities of unpaid participants in behavior settings; many such activities are performed for pay by some persons and are included in the SOC and DOT systems. The quasi-occupations plus gainful employment would produce an exhaustive allocation of living-time among roles (occupations and quasi-occupations) and also among industries. Note that private households is one of the 260 SIC-type industries.

Data on stocks of physical capital in the United States (annually from 1929 to 1979) recently published by the U.S. Bureau of Economic Analysis (1981) can be interpreted as the circumjacent milieus of behavior settings and the durable behavior objects used in implementing their programs. Several categories of structures (e.g., religious buildings, educational buildings, hospital and institutional buildings, state and local government buildings, commercial buildings) are the primary locations of certain of Barker's action patterns which embody the purposes for which the various behavior setting genotypes were created: religion, education, physical health, government, and business for the types of structures cited. Commercial buildings can be subdivided, with the help of additional data sources, into food stores and restaurants (action patterns: nutrition as well as business), barber and beauty shops (action pattern: personal appearance), bowling alleys and motion picture theaters (action pattern: recreation), and others. The three remaining action patterns listed by Barker are aesthetic, professionalism, and social contact; the last two are very widely distributed and the aesthetic action pattern also appears in a variety of contexts.

Changes in stocks (in constant 1972 dollars) of the various types of structures during 1929-1979 are consistent with changes in gainful employment in the clusters of industries which use those structures. With additional effort, it should be possible to allocate these stocks to specific industries and thence to behavior setting genotypes. The same should apply to stocks of equipment. Changes in stocks of the 10 categories of consumer durable goods mirror dramatic changes in the technology of household production and in patterns of indoor and outdoor recreation and leisure. In many cases, the durable good used completely dominates a particular activity (temporary role) and the time allocated to it; the stock data should be very helpful in reconstructing uses of time in household settings.

If data on the consumption of services and nondurable goods were also rearranged to conform to behavior setting genotypes, along with the corresponding financial flows, the result of all the procedures outlined would be a rough, preliminary but comprehensive system of social accounts at the national level based on behavior settings.

The matrices and submatrices of this system could be linked experimentally with existing national models of various types: large-scale econometric models as conceptualized in Fox 1956 and implemented in the Brookings quarterly econometric model of the United States (Duesenberry et al. 1965) and its many descendants and counterparts, the input-output matrices of the U.S. Bureau of Economic Analysis (1979), demographic models of the type pioneered by Stone (1971, 1981), simulation models of the type developed by Stone and Brown (1962) and their associates, and the social accounting matrices (SAMs) developed by Stone, Pyatt, Roe, Thorbecke, and others.

We also discuss alternative approaches to comprehensive social accounts for urban-centered regions. The county data base developed by the U.S. Bureau of Economic Analysis during the past decade provides an excellent starting point, as do its more detailed estimates of employment and earnings by industry for Standard Metropolitan Statistical Areas (SMSAs) and for BEA Economic Areas; the latter areas partition the United States exhaustively into about 183 urban-centered regions, each delineated as a cluster of contiguous whole counties and each containing an integral number of home-to-work commuting fields or Functional Economic Areas (FEAs), as proposed by Fox and Kumar (1965).

The "expected TAM" approach described earlier could probably be extended upward successfully from small towns like Midwest through small cities (often county seats of 5,000 to 25,000 population) with trade areas approximating counties to FEA central cities (usually with 30,000 to 300,000 people) and complete FEAs (typically with 150,000 to 500,000 residents). BEA Economic Areas of up to 2,000,000 people could be accounted for as clusters of FEAs plus some additional industries and genotypes in the largest city if its population exceeded 300,000. Fullerton and Prescott (1975) developed a simulation model for Iowa with 120 geographical units (counties or parts of counties) which could be clustered to form FEAs, BEA Economic Areas, or other types of regions. Expected TAMs for Iowa counties and FEAs could be compared and possibly linked with components of the Fullerton-Prescott model for the same areas.

Alternatively, published data from the U.S. censuses of population and housing could be used to extend some elements of a social accounting system from the national level through BEA Economic Areas, FEAs, and counties down to townships, villages, and towns in rural areas and to census tracts, enumeration districts, and blocks within SMSAs and urbanized areas. These same data are currently used by local governments in conjunction with primary data needed for their various functions (street, water, and sewer system maintenance; planning and zoning; traffic control; public health; police and fire protection; public school administration; parks and playgrounds; abatement of excessive noise levels and air pollution; and perhaps others). Local governments could, if they chose, adapt behavior setting accounts to the analysis of alternative policies in their own departments. Within a comprehensive behavior setting and time-allocation framework, they should be better able to distinguish between policies which merely shift a problem between neighborhoods or departmental jurisdictions and policies which are likely to solve a problem _in situ_ and/or with minimal adverse effects on other neighborhoods and programs.

ACCOUNTS IN TERMS OF NATURAL OR CUSTOMARY UNITS OF ALL SOCIAL SYSTEM OUTPUTS

Each specific behavior setting within a genotype is a complex entity existing in four dimensions--occupying, on each occurrence, a three-dimensional physical space and extending over a certain interval of time. All inputs to the social system are made in or to behavior settings, and all outputs from the social system are produced in behavior settings. The inputs are contributions made by members of the society, and the outputs are rewards received by them.[4] The total value of the inputs _is_ the total value of the rewards; the gross social income _is_ the gross social product.

Up to this point, our proposed system of accounts is completely objective--an allocation of person-hours of occupancy time among population subgroups (attribute-and-status categories), among occupations and quasi-occupations (unpaid roles), and among behavior setting genotypes cross-classified with SIC-type industries augmented to include the occupancy times of customers, students, household members, and other persons in unpaid roles. The problems of classification and measurement are inherently no more difficult than those dealt with in the economic censuses, the census of population and housing, the Standard Industrial Classification, and the Standard Occupational Classification. Monetary values are referred to only (1) within those genotype-and-industry "cells" included in the national income and product accounts and (2) in connection with estimates of the values of physical capital (including consumer durable goods) allocable to each cell and hence to each genotype.

The next step is more difficult but still inherently objective: to list and classify the outputs of a social system which constitute its gross social product and to define a unit of measure for each output. The list would include changes in the health, education, and skills of individuals; changes in stocks of physical capital, including consumer durable goods; current consumption of purchased services and nondurable goods; current consumption of services and nondurable goods produced in households and nonmarket organizations for their own use; numbers of crimes and accidents of various types; person-hours of exposure to specified levels of noise and air pollutants; and other outputs initially more difficult to define.

At this stage, the gross social product would be a vector of outputs, each measured in its own natural or customary unit. Most of the 33 OECD indicators could be included in or derived from this output vector, interpreted to include also the distributions of the various outputs among households. Each output could be disaggregated to the level of genotype-and-industry cells. Within each cell, a very basic problem could be studied: Can the vector of outputs from each cell (and hence from a typical behavior setting in the relevant genotype) be shown to result from the vector of inputs in or to that cell? Are there structural relationships between inputs and outputs such that changes in the amounts of specified inputs would lead to predictable changes in the amounts of specified outputs?

If such input-output relationships could be demonstrated and if proposed public policies could be interpreted as increasing the amounts of inputs in some cells and reducing them in others, then alternative policies could be compared in terms of the changes in output vectors expected from each contemplated set of changes in input vectors. As in Jan Tinbergen's (1952) theory of economic policy, a policymaker could then apply his own relative weights (values or pseudoprices) per unit to each of the relevant inputs and outputs and take the action that seemed most desirable in those terms. If the choice among policies required prior debate in a parliament or similar body, members with different value systems might arrive at different rankings of the alternatives. However, the demonstration of stable relationships between inputs and outputs would help to separate questions of fact from questions of values.

Because of space limitations, we will not discuss the possibilities of social accounts involving a unique system of prices or pseudoprices for all social system outputs.

POSSIBILITIES FOR EXPERIMENTATION WITH SOCIAL SYSTEM ACCOUNTS AND MODELS BASED ON BEHAVIOR SETTINGS BY INTERNATIONAL AGENCIES, BY LOCAL GOVERNMENTS, AND BY MARKET AND NONMARKET ORGANIZATIONS

Experimentation with social accounts and models based on behavior settings could proceed at several levels and on many independent initiatives.

Official data systems are most fully developed at the national level. Comparability among the official data systems of many countries has been promoted by international organizations (United Nations, OECD) since the late 1940s, so that experimental accounts for one country should demonstrate potentials and problems that would be relevant to many others.

At some stage, international organizations might undertake the task of promoting a consensus on those aspects of the accounts ready for widespread implementation at a given time. The United Nations' (1975) publication *Towards a System of Social and Demographic Statistics*, prepared by Stone and reflecting the suggestions of statisticians from many countries, makes concrete proposals for accounts and data systems covering 19 areas of economic and social concern; pilot efforts should be made to reformulate these as (or in) a comprehensive eco-behavioral system.

Local governments could experiment with accounts based on behavior settings to see if they clarify some of their planning and administrative decision problems. Hopefully, unintended consequences of proposed changes in the physical, economic, or social environments of the community could be recognized and demonstrated within a behavior setting and time-allocation framework for the community as a whole or for any subdivision of it that was nearly self-contained with respect to a proposed change and its more obvious impacts.

An independent line of experimentation and research, which might be called microsocial accounting, could be carried on within organizations. It would involve attempts to identify and measure the inputs and outputs of each type of setting in an organization using Barker's rating scales, SOC-DOT measures of job complexity and worker traits, and the organization's financial and other accounts and output measures. Some components of existing simulation models of organizations could be reformulated in terms of categories of behavior settings. Simulation and optimization models for university departments reported in Fox 1972 and 1975 might be reviewed from this perspective.

Barker and his former students and colleagues have made extensive applications of behavior setting concepts to schools, hospitals, churches, and some other kinds of organizations. However, they have not yet tried to link these concepts with the economic accounts of organizations or with the organizational counterparts of comprehensive social accounts. Organizations would be justified in implementing and maintaining such accounts and related models if they were sufficiently helpful in planning and decision making and in explaining themselves to employees, members, and other constituencies.

SOME BROADER IMPLICATIONS OF BEHAVIOR SETTINGS FOR THE SOCIAL SCIENCES

In our judgment, the implications of behavior settings for the social sciences are far reaching. We have stated them more fully in Fox 1984.

We believe that the behavior setting concept may come to play as important a role in the social sciences as the cell concept does in biology. It seems to us that the interests of several disciplines converge in behavior settings. All roles are played in them; all organizations are composed of them. Felson (1979) asserts that all sociologically interesting phenomena involving direct physical contact between persons occur in behavior settings, and that they appear to be ideal units for describing and modeling social processes. Behavior settings in nonmarket organizations are empirically valid analogs of the economist's markets. Small group phenomena occur in behavior settings; they can be viewed from the standpoints of group dynamics, transactional analysis, game theory, and the theory of teams. Kurt Lewin's (1951) concept of an individual's life space remains intact as the means by which a behavior setting secures the behavior appropriate to it.

Each individual in a setting can also be viewed as an organism in an environment-organism-environment continuum or E-O-E arc, a conception Barker (1968, pp. 137-139) attributes to Egon Brunswik. Brunswik used the E-O-E arc as a basis for classifying representative schools and problems of psychology; since Barker's ecological psychology, with behavior settings as a focal concept, encompasses the whole E-O-E arc plus environmental phenomena which shape and transmit influences from the termination of one arc to the origins of others, links between other social sciences and psychology can be established, tested, and evaluated in a behavior setting context.

Wicker (1979) has provided ecological psychology with its first textbook, and Wicker (1986) is suggesting major refinements in behavior setting concepts. Hopefully, the discipline will now expand more rapidly as a teaching field and ecological psychologists will find it easier to convince colleagues and students from other departments and professional schools of the relevance of their offerings. Perhaps an alternative name for the discipline should be emphasized: as Barker (1978) states, it is an *eco-behavioral science*. In our own view, it can contain all economic behavior and its claims to comprehensiveness in describing human activities in social systems are as legitimate as those of sociology and anthropology.

In Barker's view (1978, pp. 286-287),

> the fundamental significance of behavior settings for the behavior sciences comes from their position within the topological hierarchy of entities ranging from cell, to organ, to person, to behavior setting, to institution (in some cases), and to community. Within this included-inclu-

sive series, behavior settings are proximal and circumjacent to people (people are components of behavior settings), and behavior settings are proximal and interjacent to institutions and communities (they are components of institutions and communities). Although we have only the beginning of an understanding of behavior settings, we can see that enlightenment must move in two directions: inward to relationships between behavior settings and their human components and outward to relationships with institutions and communities. In both directions, there are important potential applications. People control their lives to an important extent (1) by creating and influencing the programs of the behavior settings of their communities and (2) by selecting, so far as possible, the settings into which they allow themselves to be incorporated. A person's greatest strength is at the boundary of a setting; once he "joins," he has to cope with much greater forces than those operating at the boundary. Knowledge of a community's behavior settings should be a strong weapon in the armory of those professionals who counsel individual persons.

CONCLUDING REMARKS

Official data systems are not discipline oriented. Barker's description of human activities and communities in terms of behavior settings is singularly free of borrowings from sociology, anthropology, economics, or any traditional field of psychology. He started from a base in experimental psychology under Calvin Stone and Kurt Lewin and psychological measurement under Lewis Terman, but he turned his skills in a direction entirely his own--to the systematic observation of naturally occurring human behavior in complete communities. He continued in this direction from 1947 to 1972 with substantial research support and is still professionally active at age 82. Until 1968 he described his research as ecological psychology--i.e., as a distinctive field within psychology. Since 1969 he has recognized the need for "an eco-behavioral science independent of psychology" but certainly not coextensive with any other established science.

Barker's research program has been one of the most original in the recent history of the social and behavioral sciences. Its legacy is an eco-behavioral view of human societies that is comprehensive in scope yet concrete and operational in detail.

NOTES

1. Most of the research underlying this chapter was supported by the National Science Foundation under research grants SOC 74-13996 and SOC 76-20084; this support is gratefully acknowledged.

2. "Zones" in the present context are not spatial entities but define specified degrees of power and types of roles in any given setting. Some examples are teacher (zone 6), pupils (zone 3); dentist (zone 6), assistant (zone 4), patients (zone 3); music director (zone 6), musicians (zone 4), audience members (zone 2); and construction foreman (zone 6), workmen (zone 4), onlookers (zone 1).

3. Barker and Schoggen (1973, pp. 385-397) present measures of various aspects of selectivity in a chapter on "biases between differential habitats and inhabitant subgroups."

4. Of course, some inputs are deleterious (acts of arson or violence) and some outputs are negative (destruction of physical capital and injuries to persons).

REFERENCES

Barker, R. G. 1968. Ecological Psychology: Concepts and Methods for Studying the Environment of Human Behavior. Stanford, CA: Stanford University Press.

_____. 1969. "Wanted: An Eco-Behavioral Science." In E. P. Willems and H. L. Raush, eds., Naturalistic Viewpoints in Psychological Research. New York: Holt, Rinehart and Winston. Reprinted with revisions in Barker and Associates, Habitats, Environments, and Human Behavior. San Francisco: Jossey-Bass. 1978.

Barker, R. G., and Associates. 1978. Habitats, Environments, and Human Behavior. San Francisco: Jossey-Bass.

Barker, R. G., and P. V. Gump, eds. 1964. Big School, Small School: High School Size and Student Behavior. Stanford, CA: Stanford University Press.

Barker, R. G., and P. Schoggen. 1973. Qualities of Community Life: Methods of Measuring Environment and Behavior Applied to an American and an English Town. San Francisco: Jossey-Bass.

Barker, R. G., and H. F. Wright. 1955. Midwest and Its Children: The Psychological Ecology of an American Town. New York: Harper and Row. Reprinted 1971 by Archon Books, Hamden, CT.

Bauer, R. A., ed. 1966. Social Indicators. Cambridge: MIT Press.

Duesenberry, J. S., G. Fromm, L. R. Klein, and E. Kuh, eds. 1965. The Brookings Quarterly Econometric Model of the United States. Amsterdam: North-Holland.

Felson, M. 1979. "How Should Social Indicators be Collected, Organized, and Modeled?" Contemporary Sociology 8 (January): 40-41.

Forrester, J. W. 1969. Urban Dynamics. Cambridge: MIT Press.

Fox, K. A. 1956. "Econometric Models of the United States." Journal of Political Economy 64: 128-142.

_____. 1958. Econometric Analysis for Public Policy. Ames: Iowa State University Press. Reissued 1977.

_____, ed. 1972. Economic Analysis for Educational Planning: Resource Allocation in Nonmarket Systems. Baltimore, MD: Johns Hopkins University Press.

_____. 1974. Social Indicators and Social Theory: Elements of an Operational System. New York: John Wiley.

_____. 1975. "Practical Optimization Models for University Departments." In H. Correa, ed., Analytical Models in Educational Planning and Administration. New York: David McKay.

_____. 1984. "Behavior Settings and Eco-Behavioral Science: A New Arena for Mathematical Social Science Permitting a Richer and More Coherent View of Human Activities in Social Systems. Part I, Concepts, Measurements and Linkages to Economic Data Systems, Time-Allocation Matrices, and Social System Accounts." Mathematical Social Sciences 7: 117-138. "Part II, Relationships to Established Disciplines, and Needs for Mathematical Development." Mathematical Social Sciences 7: 139-165.

_____. 1985. Social System Accounts: Linking Social and Economic Indicators through Tangible Behavior Settings. Dordrecht and Boston: D. Reidel.

Fox, K. A., and S. K. Ghosh. 1980. "Social Accounts for Urban-Centered Regions." International Regional Science Review 5: 33-50.

_____. 1981. "A Behavior Setting Approach to Social Accounts Combining Concepts and Data from Ecological Psychology, Economics, and Studies of Time Use." In F. T. Juster and K. C. Land, eds., Social Accounting Systems: Essays on the State of the Art. New York: Academic Press.

Fox, K. A., and T. K. Kumar. 1965. "The Functional Economic Area: Delineation and Implications for Economic Analysis and Policy." Regional Science Association Papers 15: 57-85.

Fox, K. A., and P. van Moeseke. 1973. "Derivation and Implications of a Scalar Measure of Social Income." In H. C. Bos, H. L. Linnemann, and P. de Wolff, eds., Economic Structure and Development: Essays in Honor of Jan Tinbergen, pp. 21-40. Amsterdam: North-Holland Publishing Company and New York: American Elsevier.

Fullerton, H. H., and J. R. Prescott. 1975. An Economic Simulation Model for Regional Development Planning. Ann Arbor, MI: Ann Arbor Science Publishers.

Gross, B. M. 1966. "The State of the Nation: Social Systems Accounting." In R. A. Bauer, ed., Social Indicators. Cambridge: MIT Press.

Gump, P. V. 1971. "The Behavior Setting: A Promising Unit for Environmental Designers." Landscape Architecture 61: 130-134.

Keynes, J. M. 1936. The General Theory of Employment, Interest

and Money. New York: Harcourt, Brace, and Company.
Kuznets, S. 1937. National Income and Capital Formation, 1919-1935. New York: National Bureau of Economic Research.
Leontief, W. W. 1936. "Quantitative Input and Output Relations in the Economic System of the United States." Review of Economic Statistics 18: 105-125.
Lewin, K. 1951. Field Theory in Social Science: Selected Theoretical Papers. Edited by D. Cartwright. New York: Harper. Reprinted 1975 by Greenwood Press, Westport, CT.
Orcutt, G., M. Greenberger, J. Korbel, and A. Rivlin. 1961. Microanalysis of Socioeconomic Systems: A Simulation Study. New York: Harper.
Organization for Economic Cooperation and Development. 1973. List of Social Concerns Common to Most OECD Countries. Paris: OECD.
_____. 1982. The OECD List of Social Indicators. Paris: OECD.
Prescott, J. R. 1980. "A Behavior Setting Approach to Microanalytical Simulation Models at the Community Level." Unpublished manuscript, Department of Economics, Iowa State University, Ames.
_____. 1985. "A Behavior Setting Approach to Microanalytical Simulation Models at the Community Level." Chapter 8 in K. A. Fox, Social System Accounts. Dordrecht and Boston: D. Reidel.
Stone, R. 1971. Demographic Accounting and Model-Building. Paris: Organization for Economic Cooperation and Development.
_____. 1981. "The Relationship of Demographic Accounts to National Income and Product Accounts." In F. T. Juster and K. C. Land, eds., Social Accounting Systems. New York: Academic Press.
Stone, R., and A. Brown. 1962. A Computable Model of Economic Growth. London: Chapman and Hall. Paper No. 1 in Programme for Growth Series, published for the Department of Applied Economics, Cambridge University.
Tinbergen, J. 1939. Statistical Testing of Business Cycle Theories: Volume I. A Method and Its Application to Investment Activity; Volume II. Business Cycles in the United States of America, 1919-1932. Geneva: League of Nations Intelligence Service.
_____. 1952. On the Theory of Economic Policy. Amsterdam: North-Holland.
United Nations Department of Economic and Social Affairs. 1975. Towards a System of Social and Demographic Statistics. New York: United Nations. Prepared by R. Stone.
U.S. Bureau of Economic Analysis (Department of Commerce). 1979. The Detailed Input-Output Structure of the U.S. Economy: 1972. Two volumes. Washington, DC: Government Printing Office.
_____. 1981. Revised Estimates of Capital Stocks and Related

Measures for Fixed Non-Residential Private and Residential Capital, Government-Owned Fixed Capital, and Durable Goods Owned by Consumers, 1925-79. Washington, DC: National Income and Wealth Division, Bureau of Economic Analysis.

U.S. Bureau of Labor Statistics (Department of Labor). 1981. The National Industry-Occupation Employment Matrix, 1970, 1978, and Projected 1990. Two volumes. Washington, DC: Government Printing Office.

U.S. Employment and Training Administration (Department of Labor). 1977. Dictionary of Occupational Titles: Fourth Edition. Washington, DC: Government Printing Office.

U.S. Manpower Administration (Department of Labor). 1972. Handbook for Analyzing Jobs. Washington, DC: Government Printing Office.

U.S. Office of Federal Statistical Policy and Standards (Department of Commerce). 1977. Standard Occupational Classification Manual. Washington, DC: Government Printing Office.

U.S. Office of Management and Budget (Executive Office of the President). 1978. Standard Industrial Classification Manual, 1972. Washington, DC: Government Printing Office.

Wicker, A. W. 1979. An Introduction to Ecological Psychology. Monterey, CA: Brooks/Cole. Republished by Cambridge University Press in 1984.

_____. 1986. "Behavior Settings Reconsidered: Temporal Stages, Resources, Internal Dynamics, Context." In D. Stokols and I. Altman, eds., Handbook of Environmental Psychology. New York: John Wiley. In press.

8

The Dollar Values of Social Variables: Two Models of Social Income

PAUL VAN MOESEKE[1]

INTRODUCTION

In Chapter 7 of this volume, Fox proposes a new approach to the design of social accounts for communities, urban-centered regions, and nations. For Barker's (1968) community of Midwest in any given year, Fox's accounts would imply a primary data matrix with a row for each resident and a column for each behavior setting. Each non-zero element (say) t_{ij} would be the number of hours spent by the ith resident in the jth setting in the course of the year.[2] This time-allocation matrix would be purely descriptive; it would require no information about the attributes of either residents or settings apart from arbitrary identification numbers i (i = 1, 2, ..., m) for the m residents and j (j = 1, 2, ..., n) for the n settings. Obviously, these numbers would be of no help in "explaining" the observed t_{ij}.

Information about the attributes of each resident (age, sex, years of education, and others) would suggest plausible ways of grouping the rows; for example, the rows for most 6-year-olds would show a large time allocation to one particular behavior setting which they evidently occupy in common and smaller non-zero allocations to several other settings in a pattern distinctive of 6-year-olds.[3] Combinations of two or more attributes should further increase the similarities of time-allocation patterns within each resulting subgroup of residents.

Information about the attributes of each behavior setting (its program, its prominent action patterns, the authority system to which it belongs, and so on) would suggest plausible ways of grouping the columns: first, perhaps, into genotypes (settings with identical programs) and then into clusters of genotypes with the same prominent action patterns (religion, education, recreation, social contact, and others) or combinations of such patterns (religion and social contact, education and physical health, and so on). If the t_{ij} were first aggregated over rows within each subgroup of residents and then over columns within each cluster of genotypes, the result would be a time-allocation matrix (TAM) for the community. The row-aggregate for any subgroup of residents divided by the number of residents in the subgroup would describe its average or typical life-style. The unit of account would, of course, be person-hours per year.

The time-allocation matrix does not require any theory of resident choice. It makes no use of specifically economic data such as prices of goods and services sold in market-oriented behavior settings and the wages and property incomes of individual residents and their households. Fox proposes to integrate these variables (as embodied in standard economic data systems) with the time-allocation matrix in some fashion. He mentions the task of listing and classifying "the outputs of a social system which constitute its gross social product" and defining a unit of measure for each output. Some of these outputs are strictly economic, are measured in dollars, and are included in the national income and product accounts; others are not (e.g., changes in the health, education, and skills of individuals; numbers of crimes and accidents of various types; person-hours of exposure to specified levels of noise and air pollutants). Fox stops short of assigning dollar values to these other outputs, saying that "because of space limitations, we will not discuss the possibilities of social accounts involving a unique system of prices or pseudoprices for all social system outputs."

In this chapter, we present two approaches to assigning dollar values to social variables in a behavior setting and time-allocation framework. The first ascribes an ordinal utility function to each (adult) resident, as in currently received economic theory. The second is completely objective; it makes no use of utility functions and is more in keeping with Fox's emphasis on directly observable variables in Chapter 7.

A PARTLY OBJECTIVE MODEL: DERIVATION AND IMPLICATIONS OF A SCALAR MEASURE OF SOCIAL INCOME

In this model, we introduce a scalar measure of an individual's social income (SI) which includes returns in terms of social media of exchange other than money, such as professional standing and political power, in addition to money income from property and transfer payments.[4]

We show that such a scalar measure exists if the individual is assumed to optimize the allocation of his time among alternative behavior settings under a number of social constraints. SI is computed with the help of a mathematical programming model: since one of the constraints is financial, the dual variables pertaining to the remaining constraints, and hence SI, can be equally expressed in dollars.

A number of desirable, and empirically meaningful, properties are derived by mathematical programming techniques.

Outline of Mathematical Derivation and Implications

From a sociological viewpoint, the individual is active in a number of behavior settings belonging to the economy, the polity, the church, the family, the club, and so on. Within each behavior setting, his activity is guided--and restricted--by inputs and outputs (or contributions and rewards) in terms of a number of media of exchange such as money, influence, votes, and professional standing.

We assume that the individual optimizes the allocation of his time among alternative behavior settings under a number of constraints pertaining to several media--money included. The resulting programming model theoretically allows the derivation of a scalar measure, called social income (SI) and expressed in dollars, of the individual's rewards in terms of all social media of exchange resulting from his activities in all relevant behavior settings. Summation over individuals would then yield a figure, expressed in dollars, for the social income of any specified population aggregate (nation, region, state, age, sex, occupation, or other grouping).

Several empirically meaningful implications of the programming model can be derived: the individual's utility need only be defined up to a monotonic transformation; SI changes proportionately with the general price level in the economy; the individual's choice is invariant under proportional changes (in particular, changes in the unit of measurement) of inputs and outputs of any medium of exchange; his choice further satisfies the elasticity rule and the Le Chatelier principle. A quadratic approximation to the individual's utility function can be specified. We omit these derivations for reasons of space and also to keep the chapter on a fairly simple expository level.

The Model

The individual divides one period of time (the current accounting period) over n behavior settings, hereafter interchangeably referred to as _settings_ or _activities_, spending the fraction x_j of the unit period on the jth activity. The n-tuple x_j, $j = 1, 2, \ldots, n$, is denoted by x. Formally, an _individual_ is a triple $(u:R^n+ \rightarrow R; A; b)$, where u is his utility function; A and b are real matrices, respectively, $m \times n$ and $m \times 1$; b denotes the endowment (or resources) in terms of the different media of exchange; and the elements a_{ij} of A are input coefficients: a unit of the jth activity absorbs a_{ij} units of b_i. The matrices x, A, b express the individual's _life-style_, _environment_, and _endowment_, respectively.[5]

He faces the programming model:

$$\text{(P)} \quad \text{maximize } u(x) \tag{8.1}$$

$$\text{subject to} \quad Ax \leqq b \tag{8.2}$$

$$x \geqq 0 \tag{8.3}$$

The set $X \equiv \{x \geqq 0 | Ax \leqq b\}$ is called the feasible set of possible activity levels (time allocations to alternative settings).

By way of illustration, we write out the first three rows of (8.2):

$$-p_1x_1 + p_2x_2 + \dots + p_nx_n \leqq y \tag{8.4}$$

$$x_1 + x_2 + \dots + x_n \leqq 1 \tag{8.5}$$

$$-w_1x_1 - w_2x_2 - \dots - w_nx_n \leqq -w \tag{8.6}$$

and we assume that x_1 denotes time spent at work; x_2, time spent shopping at the grocery store; and so on. Income constraint (8.4) is the reduced form of $p_2x_2 + \dots + p_nx_n \leqq y + p_1x_1$, stating that expenses incurred in activities 2 through n cannot exceed money income (from property and transfer payments y and current personal services p_1x_1, where p_1 denotes the wage rate). The meaning of time constraint (8.5) is obvious. Constraint (8.6) is the reduced form of $w_1x_1 + w_2x_2 + \dots + w_nx_n \geqq w$: in the case of a local politician, for example, election requires at least w votes; activity 1 is estimated to yield w_1 votes per unit of time spent at work (such as a law practice or union activity), w_2 votes per unit of time spent at the grocery store, and so on. Put another way, the left side of (8.6) is a linear approximation to the assumed functional relationship $w = w(x_1, \dots, x_n)$ between votes obtained and time invested in alternative behavior settings. Such linearization is neither more nor less rebarbative in a social than in an economic context, where linear activity analysis (Koopmans 1951) in general and input-output tables (Leontief 1951) in particular are standard tools in approximating production functions.

Analogously, in the case of a research worker, w may express an output requirement (e.g., pages or papers published), and the w_j may denote estimated average yields from time spent in such behavior settings as work, professional contacts, and relaxation.

As illustrated by (8.4) to (8.6), the a_{ij} may denote inputs or outputs according to whether $a_{ij} > 0$ or < 0. Furthermore, the b_i denote endowments or requirements according to whether $b_i > 0$ or < 0.

Estimation of Social Income

We make the standard assumption that u is concave (i.e., has the usual properties of risk aversion and nonincreasing returns). By the saddlepoint theorem (Uzawa 1958), x^* solves (P)--assuming the Slater regularity condition: $Ax° < b$ for some $x° \geqq 0$--if and only if there is a real n-tuple $v^* \geqq 0$ such that (x^*, v^*) is a saddlepoint of the Lagrangian $L(x, v) = u(x) + v(b - Ax)$; that is, if and only if

$$u(x) + v^*(b - Ax) \geqq u(x^*) + v^*(b - Ax^*)$$
$$\leqq u(x^*) + v(b - Ax^*) \qquad (8.7)$$

for all $x \geqq 0$, $v \geqq 0$. Clearly, the second inequality holds if and only if

$$v^*(b - Ax^*) = 0 \qquad (8.8)$$

The coordinates x_j, v_i of x, v are called primal and dual variables, respectively.

The standard interpretation of v^* as a price system for endowments b_i (in terms of maximand u) is well known. Consequently, the solution of the model implies the valuation of total endowment at

$$v^*b \equiv \Sigma v_i^* b_i = v_1^* y + \dots + v_m^* b_m \qquad (8.9)$$

We define social income as

$$SI \equiv v^*b/v_1^* \quad (v_1^* > 0) \qquad (8.10)$$
$$= (v_1^*/v_1^*)y + (v_2^*/v_1^*)b_2 + \dots + (v_m^*/v_1^*)b_m$$

which evidently has the same dimension as y, namely, dollars.[6] Total income (TI), including income from current personal services, is then $p_1x_1^* + SI$. If u is known, the value of SI is given by (8.10): we showed in Fox and van Moeseke 1973 that the value of SI is given by (8.10) if u can be specified up to a monotonic transformation.

Income from current personal services, $p_1x_1^*$, and income from property and transfer payments, y, are standard items in the national income and product accounts. These items are, in principle, observable for each single adult and household in a community or other population of interest. If each single adult and household optimized as in the present model and reported its total income, these total incomes could be added up to yield a community total income, measured in dollars.

We readily concede the difficulty of making this approach

operational; however, it does link the unfamiliar data systems and social accounts of Barker and Fox with the standard assumptions and demonstrations of utility theory which are familiar to economists and may therefore contribute to their understanding of the Barker-and-Fox innovations.

A STRICTLY OBJECTIVE MODEL: MEASURING THE SOCIOECONOMIC INTERFACE

In this model, we dispense with utility functions entirely. We pose the question, Is it possible to assign objective (dollar) values to an individual's social position? This can be done by quantifying his life-style in terms of the time and money spent in different activities (behavior settings), each of which contributes to the several requirements of his social status, such as professional, family, and community commitments.

The tool used is an elementary cost-minimizing linear program. Its dual yields dollar values for both the agent's time and his social requirements; it also implies a socioeconomic theory of saving and impatience. Finally, one can predict an agent's behavior pattern, hence his consumption pattern, from his social position and economic environment. The model is therefore a contribution to objective consumption theory. Simple numerical examples illustrate the approach. An alternative time-minimizing program is considered.

The model below describes a social agent, on the one hand, in terms of the activities on which he spends his time and money, and on the other hand, the parameters of the social position he occupies, such as professional, political, religious, and family requirements. It is therefore, quite literally, an attempt at quantifying the so-called socioeconomic interface.

A social agent spends, on average, certain fractions of his waking hours in various activities such as work, professional contact, leisure, and interaction with family, club, polity, and church. These activities fulfill a number of social commitments inherent in his position as, say, an author, husband, club officer, town councillor, church elder, and so on. Every activity, of course, carries an economic price tag. It is therefore possible, in principle, to determine the activity mix, or behavior pattern, that will minimize costs given the agent's social requirements. The latter in turn acquire dollar values or rents implied by the cost of the activities they generate; so does the individual's time. The values so derived add up to his total income (TI).

In the present model, measurement of social parameters is now not only objective but also practicable. Actual measurement would be difficult in the previous, partly subjective model where, even in the simplest case, viz. the approximation of utility by a quadratic function, identification of a large number of parameters would be required. The agent would have to be able to specify $n(n+3)/2$ behavior patterns among which he was indifferent, where n is the number of possible activities or behavior settings. Even in the case of only four activities he would have to imagine 14 such patterns.

The Minimum-cost Model

For convenience we take a 16-hour waking day as the unit of time. The agent spends <u>on average</u> a fraction $x_j \geqq 0$ (j = 0, 1, ..., n) of his waking day at activity j. So the (n+1)-tuple $(x) = (x_0, x_1, \ldots, x_n)$ is his <u>life-style</u> or <u>behavior pattern</u>. The 0-th coordinate x_0 denotes the time fraction spent at work. The remaining n-tuple $(x_1, \ldots, x_n)$ is denoted x.

Each activity has an economic cost: activity j costs $\$c_j$ per day (or $\$c_j/16$ per waking hour, assuming a 16-hour waking day). Work normally yields a net income after tax and work-related expenses; this is a <u>negative</u> cost: we write $-c_0$, taking $c_0 > 0$. The (n+1)-tuple (c) summarizes the agent's <u>economic position</u>. A given activity, such as leisure, will cost more or less per day according to one's economic status. Again the n-tuple $(c_1, \ldots, c_n)$ is denoted c.

The agent's <u>social position</u> is given by an m-tuple b of parameters $b_1, \ldots, b_m$ which indicate the requirements of his social standing relative to his profession, family, polity, club, church, and so on. These may be expressed in such units as publications, outings, votes, and attendances.

Finally, activity j satisfies requirement i to the extent of a_{ij} units per unit of activity. The m x (n+1) matrix A of coefficients a_{ij} quantifies the agent's <u>environment</u>. Since it relates activities, hence cost, to social position, it represents the <u>socioeconomic interface</u>.

Some b_i may be endowments rather than requirements so that $b_i < 0$: one can think of free tickets that come with certain positions or election funds and media appearances to which a politician is entitled. Similarly, $a_{ij} < 0$ means that activity j draws on an endowment rather than contributing to a requirement. The time constraint

$$X_0 + x_1 + \ldots + x_n \leqq 1$$

is actually of this nature, so that, for the sake of uniformity, we shall write it in the reduced form (8.11) with signs and inequality reversed. For convenience and emphasis it has been stated apart from the A and b matrices.

We assume the agent minimizes net cost subject to a time constraint and his social constraints so that he faces the linear program

(P) minimize $-c_0x_0 + cx$

subject to	$-x_0 - ux \geqq -1$	$v_0 \geqq 0$	(8.11)
	$A(x) \geqq b$	$v \geqq 0$	(8.12)
	$(x) \geqq 0$		(8.13)

where u is the n-tuple of units (1, ..., 1) and the dual variables v_0 and $v = (v_1, \ldots, v_m)$ appear to the right of the corresponding constraints.

Denote by (x*) a solution to (P); then

$$y = -c_0x_0^* + cx^* \tag{8.14}$$

is the agent's <u>net</u> expenditure. An alternative program, minimizing time spent without increasing expenditure, suggests itself:

(P_t) minimize $x_0 + ux$

subject to $c_0x_0 - cx \geqq -y$ (8.15)

and (8.12), (8.13).

It is easy to see that any solution (x^t) of (P_t) solves (P):

<u>Proposition</u>: (x^t) solves (P).

<u>Proof</u>: By (8.14), (8.15) (x^*) is clearly feasible in (P_t); hence,

$$x_0^t + ux^t \leqq x_0^* + ux^* \leqq 1.$$

Consequently, (x^t) is feasible in (P). Substituting (x^t) for (x) in (8.15) yields, by (8.14),

$$-c_0x_0^t + cx^t \leqq -c_0x^* + cx^*$$

so that (x^t) is also optimal in (P). QED.

We will <u>not</u> refer to this alternative program below. However, following the numerical examples, there are some comments on the case where the agent is subject to a budget constraint.

Note that we can predict the agent's behavior (x) from his economic position (c) and his social position (b), both of which can be observed. Conversely, his life-style or behavior pattern (x), while not so readily amenable to direct observation, can be tested for consistency against the parameters c_j and b_i of his economic and social position. The approach is in strong contrast with classical utility theory where only the general characteristics of a class of hypothetical utility functions can be derived indirectly from a number of postulates regarding the consumer's revealed preference (vide Samuelson 1947, Ville 1951-1952, Uzawa 1960, van Moeseke 1969), whose empirical validity is hardly subject to experiment.[7]

The matrix A is, of course, a linear approximation to the socioeconomic production functions

$$b_i = b_i(x_0, \ldots, x_n) \qquad i = 1, \ldots, m$$

as in the previous, partly subjective model. Hence, for example, an author may see b_i as an output requirement and the a_{ij} as average yields (in pages or papers published) from time spent in different activities such as paid work, professional contacts, creative leisure, and so on. Of course, realism restricts the application of fixed coefficients to small variations.

Total Income, Saving, and Impatience

The objective function of the dual program is

$$\text{maximize } -v_0 + vb$$

and the solutions, indicated by asterisks, by the duality theorem relate the marginal values (or rents) of the social requirements to costs:

$$-c_0x_0^* + cx^* = -v_0^* + v^*b \tag{8.16}$$

Since the left is in dollars so, evidently, is the right: v_0^* is the dollar value of the agent's time, and $v^*b = v_1^*b_1 + \ldots + v_m^*b_m$ is the value of his social position. As in the partly subjective model, the amount corresponding to the latter plus money income,

$$v^*b + c_0x_0^* \tag{8.17}$$

is termed total income (TI).

Observe that these values are objectively measurable and derived directly, this time, from an observed cost function.[8]

By (8.16)

$$TI = c_0x_0^* + v^*b = cx^* + v_0^*$$

so that total income adds the value of time to the value of consumption.

Again, duality provides an interesting social theory of saving: (8.16) can be rewritten

$$c_0x_0^* - cx^* = v_0^* - v^*b \tag{8.18}$$

The left of (8.18) is net income - expenses = saving; the right is value of time - value of social requirements.[9] Consequently, the agent saves or dissaves according to whether (8.18) is positive or negative or, equivalently, whether his time is more valuable than his social requirements or vice versa. In particular, if the agent dissaves, or is a net borrower, the value of his social requirements exceeds the value of his time and the difference measures his impatience. Presumably, this attitude would be typical of aspiring executives and young couples generally. Impatience too becomes measurable in dollars.

Note finally that, for most wage earners at least, worktime is a 9-to-5 job, hence a fixed time fraction α. This alters the program slightly but does not affect it in essentials. One imposes the additional constraint

$$x_0 = \alpha$$

equivalent to the twin constraints

$$x_0 \leqq \alpha \qquad (\text{or } -x_0 \geqq -\alpha)$$

$$x_0 \geqq \alpha$$

only one of which can be tight. If the former is, which means that the agent would take on more paid employment if he could, the effect is to subtract an amount $\nu\alpha$ from the previous formula for TI, where ν is the corresponding dual variable. If the latter inequality holds, one adds $\nu\alpha$.

Parable of the Struggling Author: A Numerical Illustration

To fix the ideas, we conclude with a numerical example of two social requirements and four activities: while it makes no pretense at realism, it does illustrate the concepts involved on the basis of reasonable figures. We hope, of course, that the matter will be pursued in detail at some later stage on a statistical level commensurate with institutional resources.

Consider a struggling author who spreads his waking time over paid work (as reader or subeditor for a publishing house), professional contacts such as writers' conventions and entertainment, creative leisure (when he does most of his writing), and family entertainment. The amount of paid work is assumed to be variable to some extent. (Refer to our earlier remark on linearization as an approximation to small variations.) Our author's economic and social position, as well as his environment, are summed up in Table 8.1.

The two requirements of his social position (last column) as author and family man are, respectively, an average output of a minimum two pages per day and at least three outings (movie, picnic, and so on) a month. These requirements may to some extent be self-imposed, as long as they can be observed.

The first row of figures indicates an average net return from gainful employment of \$80 per 16 hours, i.e., gross income

Table 8.1. Socioeconomic Matrix*

Activity	0. Paid work	1. Professional contact	2. Creative leisure	3. Family entertainment	Daily requirement or supply
Net cost ($)	-80	50	20	20	---
Time spent	1	1	1	1	1
Pages written	1	1	3	0	2
Family outings	0	0	0	2.5	0.1

*All data averaged per waking day of 16 hours.

minus income tax minus work-related expenses such as commuting, eating out, extra clothes, and so on.

If, as in the solution to the minimum-cost program for Table 8.1, the agent works on average during 44% of his waking hours, his net income is $12,848 per annum or about $25,000 gross. Per diem costs for professional contacts (motel), creative leisure (including rent of a holiday home or caravan, for example), and family entertainment are $50, $20, and $20, respectively. The third row of figures indicates that his literary productivity is three times higher in activity 2 (creative leisure) than in activities 0 and 1, which leave little time for private writing. The bottom row tells us that the average outing claims about 16/2.5 = 6.4 hours; at $20 per day of 16 waking hours, the average outing therefore costs $8. For simplicity all other "basic" costs, such as rent of home and food consumed at home, are assumed covered from the earnings of a working spouse.

We solve the linear program

(P1) minimize $-80x_0 + 50x_1 + 20x_2 + 20x_3$

$$\text{subject to} \quad -x_0 - x_1 - x_2 - x_3 \geq -1 \quad \Big| \quad v_0 \qquad (8.19)$$

$$x_0 + x_1 + 3x_2 \geq 2 \quad \Big| \quad v_1 \qquad (8.20)$$

$$2.5x_3 \geq 0.1 \quad \Big| \quad v_2 \qquad (8.21)$$

$$x_0,\ x_1,\ x_2,\ x_3 \geq 0 \qquad (8.22)$$

where the dual variables on the right of the vertical bar have been juxtaposed to the corresponding constraints for ready reference.

The primal and dual solutions to (P1) are

$$x_0^* = 0.44 \qquad x_1^* = 0 \qquad x_2^* = 0.52 \qquad x_3^* = 0.04$$

$$v_0^* = 130 \qquad v_1^* = 50 \qquad v_2^* = 60$$

The first line quantifies the behavior pattern or life-style: the agent spends 44% of his time at work, none in professional contacts, 52% in creative leisure, and 4% at family outings. He values his time at \$130 per diem and his writing and family commitments at \$50 per page and \$60 per outing, respectively.

The dollar value of the objective function is

$$-(80 \times 0.44) + (50 \times 0) + (20 \times 0.52) + (20 \times 0.04) = -24$$

for the primal and

$$-(130 \times 1) + (50 \times 2) + (60 \times 0.1) = -24$$

for the dual: the agent <u>saves</u> \$24 per diem. By (8.17) his total income (TI) amounts to

$$(50 \times 2) + (60 \times 0.1) + (80 \times 0.44) = 141.20$$

or \$141.20 per diem.[10]

<u>Dissaving</u> occurs if, for instance, net income is reduced from \$80 to \$50 and a higher-style leisure is chosen at \$50 rather than \$20: the objective becomes

$$\text{(P2)} \quad \text{minimize } -50x_0 + 50x_1 + 50x_2 + 20x_3$$

and the new solutions are

$$x_0^* = 0.44 \qquad x_1^* = 0 \qquad x_2^* = 0.52 \qquad x_3^* = 0.04$$

$$v_0^* = 100 \qquad v_1^* = 50 \qquad v_2^* = 48$$

The value of the objective function becomes 4.8 so that the agent <u>dissaves</u> \$4.80 per diem: the amount measures his <u>impatience</u> in that the value (\$50 × 2) + (\$48 × 0.1) of his social requirements now <u>exceeds</u> the value (\$100) of his time by this much.

Imposing the Budget Constraint

What happens if, instead of allowing for (dis)saving, we enforce the budget constraint as in the standard static consumption model of economic theory? The latter leaves no room for savings by postulating nonsaturation of a hypothetical increasing utility function in commodity space.

Since costs are now <u>given</u> by the budget constraint, we shall assume that the agent minimizes the time, rather than the money, spent on his social requirements, subject to the condition that he keep within his income. Program (P2) is replaced by

$$\text{(P2}^+\text{)} \quad \text{minimize } x_0 + x_1 + x_2 + x_3$$

$$\text{subject to } \quad 50x_0 - 50x_1 - 50x_2 - 20x_3 \geq 0$$

and (8.20), (8.21), (8.22). The solutions are

$$x_0^+ = 0.512 \qquad x_1^+ = 0 \qquad x_2^+ = 0.496 \qquad x_3^+ = 0.040$$

$$v_0^+ = 1/100 \qquad v_1^+ = 50/100 \qquad v_2^+ = 48/100$$

The agent spends more time at paid work (51.2% instead of 44%) and enjoys correspondingly less creative leisure (49.6% instead of 52%) since he has to earn the extra $4.80 previously borrowed. However, note that, since budget and time constraints cannot be enforced simultaneously in this model, the total time requirement is 1.048, i.e., 4.8% more than the 16-hour waking day previously assumed. Enforcing the budget constraint, rather than the time constraint, may therefore be less realistic.

In (P2) the unit marginal value of time was $100; that of the two social requirements, $50 and $48. In ($P2^+$) the objective function is expressed in time units and so, therefore, are the marginal values of the constraints. Since a unit of time was worth $100 in (P2), one dollar is worth 1/100 of a time unit in ($P2^+$); similarly, the (P2) values of the two social requirements are scaled down by a factor of 100 in ($P2^+$).

While the primal solutions to programs (P) and (P^+) are, of course, different, the duals are seen to be closely related. This intuitive result is general and can be formalized. Indeed, interchanging the roles of time and money (from constraint to objective and vice versa) in (P), one gets

$$(P^+) \quad \text{minimize } x_0 + ux$$

$$\text{subject to } \; c_0x_0 - cx \geqq 0$$

and the original constraints (8.12), (8.13). Assuming $v_0^* > 0$, one can show that $1/v_0^*$, v^*/v_0^* is a dual solution to (P^+) if v_0^*, v^* is a dual solution to (P). The proof, however, is somewhat beyond the scope of this chapter.[11]

In principle, the results of similar models for all single adults and households in a community could be added up to yield community totals, measured in dollars. We do not, of course, underestimate the problems involved in making this objective approach operational. However, we might learn a great deal through pilot efforts to implement it on a small scale. The cost of such efforts would be negligibly small in relation to the many billions of dollars already invested in existing economic and social data systems in many countries and the hundreds of billions no doubt currently misallocated due in part to our lack of convincing evidence as to the equivalent economic values of social variables.

NOTES

1. Most of the research underlying this chapter was performed at the Australian National University during my tenure of the Professorial Fellowship in Economic Policy of the Reserve

Bank of Australia, whose generous support is gratefully acknowledged. I am indebted to Jean Goldsmith of Massey University for numerical assistance.

2. Each non-zero element would also denote an "inhabitant-setting intersection" (ISI) in Barker's primary data set.

3. The common setting in which most 6-year-olds spend a large block of time is First Grade Academic Subjects in Midwest's elementary school.

4. This model was originally published in Fox and van Moeseke 1973; we excerpt and revise here a few paragraphs from that paper.

5. Note that x records the proportions of the individual's time spent in each of the n behavior settings (a complete time budget), hence summarizes his life-style. Each column of the matrix A lists the amounts of each of m (economic and social) exchange media absorbed per unit of time spent in a particular setting as an environment for the individual's behavior. The characterization of b as the individual's endowment is straightforward.

6. Assuming $v_1^* > 0$ by (8.2), (8.8) implies that money constraint (8.4) is binding. Since v_i^* can be interpreted as the marginal utility u/b_i of the ith endowment (proof in van Moeseke 1965), the assumption means that money is a scarce commodity for the individual; v_i^* is, of course, the marginal utility of money to the individual.

7. On the (in)determinacy of utility functions, see Basu 1982.

8. The <u>values</u> of the v_i^* in the present approach need not, in general, coincide with those of the subjective model partly because the constraints are not the same.

9. Here we use the term "social requirements" (per unit of time) rather than "social position," which expresses the same notion but is not intuitively associated with flows over time.

10. As suggested by Becker (1965) "full income" is substantially above money income.

11. The reader may refer to a more technical article on a related approach, to be circulated as a research report in the *Massey Economic Papers*: P. van Moeseke, "Time and Money: Min-cost/Min-time Equivalence," forthcoming. A shorter version will appear as P. van Moeseke (1986), "Time and Cost Budgets," *Mathematical Social Science*, forthcoming.

REFERENCES

Barker, R. G. 1968. *Ecological Psychology: Concepts and Methods for Studying the Environment of Human Behavior*. Stanford, CA: Stanford University Press.

Basu, K. 1982. "Determinateness of the Utility Function:

Revisiting a Controversy of the Thirties." Review of Economic Studies 49: 307-311.

Becker, G. 1965. "A Theory of the Allocation of Time." Economic Journal 75: 493-517.

Fox, K. A., and P. van Moeseke. 1973. "Derivation and Implications of a Scalar Measure of Social Income." In H. C. Bos, H. Linnemann, and P. de Wolff, eds., Economic Structure and Development: Essays in Honor of Jan Tinbergen, pp. 21-40. Amsterdam and New York: North-Holland Publishing Company.

Koopmans, T. C., ed. 1951. Activity Analysis of Production and Allocation. New York: Wiley.

Leontief, W. 1951. The Structure of American Economy, 1919-1939. 2nd ed. New York: Oxford University Press.

Samuelson, P. 1947. Foundations of Economic Analysis. Cambridge: Harvard University Press.

Uzawa, H. 1958. "The Kuhn-Tucker Theorem in Concave Programming." In K. J. Arrow, L. Hurwicz, and H. Uzawa, eds., Studies in Linear and Nonlinear Programming. Stanford, CA: Stanford University Press.

______. 1960. "Preference and Rational Choice in the Theory of Consumption." In K. J. Arrow, S. Karlin, and P. Suppes, eds., Mathematical Methods in the Social Sciences. Stanford, CA: Stanford University Press.

van Moeseke, P. 1965. "A General Duality Theorem of Convex Programming." Metroeconomica 17: 161-170.

______. 1969. "Revealed Preference: Equivalence Theorem and Induced Pre-Order." In K. A. Fox et al., eds., Economic Models, Estimation and Risk Programming: Essays in Honor of Gerhard Tintner. Berlin and New York: Springer.

Ville, J. 1951-1952. "The Existence Conditions of a Total Utility Function." Translation by P. Newman. Review of Economic Studies 19: 123-128.

9

Community Dynamics: Microanalytical Simulation Models with Behavior Settings as Basic Units

JAMES R. PRESCOTT

INTRODUCTION

It is 16 years since Roger Barker (1969) expressed the need for an eco-behavioral science. His paper was addressed to his fellow psychologists and stressed those requirements of the new science which could not be met with the facilities, data, and methods then available and/or familiar to psychologists. Psychology was predominantly an experimental science which generated its own data under laboratory conditions. The new science would observe naturally occurring behavior "in the field." Its practitioners would learn to collect, record, preserve, and analyze ecological data and would gain useful insights in so doing from the biological sciences, sociology, anthropology, economics, and other disciplines.

The basic units of eco-behavioral science are behavior settings. Barker's (1968) Ecological Psychology, despite its title, is the classic work on eco-behavioral science. Earlier statements are to be found in Barker and Wright 1955 and Barker and Gump 1964. Barker and Schoggen 1973 is heavily data oriented but also makes further advances in theory and methods. Barker and Associates 1978 devotes about 140 pages to ecological psychology (therein defined as the study of individual behavior in natural settings) and another 100 pages to eco-behavioral science--the study of behavior settings as such. Bechtel (1977) and Bechtel and Ledbetter (1976) have applied the method of behavior setting surveys to problems of architecture and community and neighborhood planning. Wicker (1979) has written the first textbook on eco-behavioral science, though it still uses the older (and better known) title of "ecological psychology."

Interest in behavior settings seems to be growing rapidly. Wicker's 1979 textbook has been republished by the Cambridge University Press in 1984. Wicker (1986) has written a major article on the dynamic aspects of behavior settings. Schoggen (1986) is preparing a book entitled Behavior Settings, which will constitute a major revision and extension of Barker's 1968 classic. Fox has published an article (1983) and a book (1985) proposing a system of social accounts based on behavior settings. Fox (1984) has also proposed behavior settings and eco-behavioral science as "a new arena for mathematical social science" and urged readers from several disciplines to participate in "this new scientific enterprise." Articles by Prescott (1985) and Sengupta (1986) present alternative approaches to modeling eco-behavioral systems.

Barker sees eco-behavioral science as independent of psychology and not coextensive with any other established discipline. Fox views eco-behavioral science as "metadisciplinary": it has interfaces with all or most of the social and behavioral sciences and with many applied fields but does not threaten to displace or compete with any of them. At the micro level, it offers a new unit--the behavior setting--for exploratory use by research workers in any discipline in addition to the units currently favored in addressing particular problems. The behavior setting concept might thus be added to the methodology of each discipline without disturbing its internal structure or significantly increasing its communications with other fields.

At the macro level, eco-behavioral science provides a framework for implementing social system accounts and models which are beyond the capacity of any one discipline. Gump (1971, p. 134) stresses the comprehensiveness of eco-behavioral science: "People live out their lives in a sequence of environmental units; experience in these settings is life." No established science can lay claim to this entire domain--nor can eco-behavioral science. But eco-behavioral science can provide a comprehensive framework for classifying and describing the immediate environments, social and physical, of all human behavior and measuring the allocation of time by all members of a society or community among these environments.

Behavior settings occur in time and space. People are social, political, economic, cultural, and religious; they are interested in health, education, personal appearance, and recreation; they pursue their activities in enclosed spaces and open ones. Within the comprehensive descriptive framework of eco-behavioral science, most members of most disciplines might continue to address their present problems in their present ways. But some would be encouraged to study the combined effects of different segments of the environment upon the well-being of population subgroups--for example, the combined effects of homes, neighborhoods, recreational facilities, youth organizations, and schools on the well-being of school-age children in different parts of a community. The time allocations among types of behavior settings could be estimated and the salient attributes of the settings quantified by Barker's methods.

Moreover, the employment statuses, work schedules, and commuting patterns of parents would not only affect their own well-being but also impinge on the well-being of their children. So, parents and school children, homes, neighborhoods, youth organizations, recreational facilities, schools, workplaces, sidewalks, and transportation facilities would be seen as components of an interacting eco-behavioral system. This system in turn would interact with other population subgroups and types of settings in homes, neighborhoods, and workplaces and also in churches, shopping centers, clinics, and other places. At this stage, the community as a whole would be seen as an eco-behavioral system. (We have in mind here a town-and-trade area or other urban-centered region of 1,000 to 500,000 population which constitutes a relatively self-contained ecological unit.)

This conception of a community in terms of behavior settings and population subgroups is plausible enough. Ruggles (1981, p. 465) had commented as follows on a paper by Fox and Ghosh (1981):

> The concept of the space-time behavior setting can provide a comprehensive basis for classifying and analyzing human behavior. There is considerable validity in the proposition that accounts drawn up on this basis do delineate the human activity of a society, and that differences observed over time and space can reveal how a given society changes with the passage of time or how the pattern of life in different countries varies. Certainly, this vision of social accounting is on a grand scale worthy of Darwin, Marx, and Veblen.

Ruggles went on to say, correctly, that such accounts "would be quite difficult to implement on a large scale" and that "it is not at all clear at this stage just what such accounts would look like and what they would contain" (p. 465). But this was also true of the national income and product accounts until Simon Kuznets and his predecessors at the National Bureau of Economic Research had worked on them for more than a decade and of Leontief's input-output accounting matrices until he (and later the Bureau of Labor Statistics) had worked on them for a similar period.

In Chapter 7 of this volume and in his 1985 book, Fox has made substantial progress in defining the scope and content of his proposed accounts. Kuznets and Leontief made extensive use of data from economic censuses which had, of course, been collected for other purposes. Indications of usefulness based on highly aggregated and imperfect data pointed the way to successive improvements in the relevant data systems. Tinbergen's econometric model of the United States, and later models by Klein and his associates, led to subsequent improvements in data systems relevant to business cycle analysis and policy. By the early 1960s, input-output matrices were being used as benchmarks for the national income accounts, and both were being incorporated in large-scale econometric models.

In the present context, Barker's 1963-1964 survey data for the town of Midwest provide the best available starting point for social system accounts and models based on behavior settings. The special features of eco-behavioral systems should stand out very clearly.

For example, only 132 of Midwest's 884 nonhousehold behavior settings are in the private enterprise "authority system" or sector. Even in these settings, conventional economic accounts would exclude customers, clients, and patients, retaining only the proprietors and employees. The conventional accounts would pick up about 30 full-time equivalent employees in the 233 settings sponsored by the school system but omit the 380 full-time students as well as the parents and friends who turn out for extracurricular events. Perhaps 50 employees would be found in the 114 settings controlled by various levels of government, but the churches with 193 settings and the voluntary associations with 212 would hardly account for 10 paid employees between them. Only those settings (a window-and-door assembly shop, the county machine shop, and certain others) which contained no persons except paid employees, managers, and proprietors would enter the conventional economic accounts intact.

Hence, conventional economic accounts and models would ignore most of Barker's eco-behavioral information. If they simply included or excluded whole settings, we might hope to model Midwest as a combination of two subsystems, one economic and the other noneconomic. But the reality is much more complex: the economic accounts would contain mere fragments of a great many settings (teachers without students, dentists without patients, and the like), whereas only complete settings are observed in practice.

Barker's 1963-1964 data constitute an "eco-behavioral census" of Midwest's nonhousehold settings. Fox (1980) incorporated these data into a preliminary set of time-use accounts. If Barker's census were repeated every year, these accounts would become time series of annual observations, analogous to Kuznets' time series on the U.S. national income and its components. Tinbergen incorporated the latter time series in an econometric model designed to give causal explanations for changes in national income, employment, and other variables from year to year. By analogy, we may visualize a dynamic eco-behavioral model of Midwest which would incorporate annual data on time allocations among its various categories of settings and would be designed to give causal explanations for changes in these allocations from year to year.

Attempts to implement such a model would teach us a great deal about the potential usefulness of social system accounts and time series based on behavior settings. Prescott (1980) submitted a research proposal for this purpose; it was not funded in

1980 and drastic cuts in the 1981-1982 budgets of the relevant agencies made it pointless to pursue the matter further at that time. A revised version of the proposal has been published in Prescott 1985.

In this chapter, we use the concept of such a model as a framework for discussing systematically what we know, and what we need to know, about the characteristics of individual behavior settings in order to give causal explanations of changes in their performance levels over time. The performance levels of individual settings are constrained by their direct relationships to some other settings and also by indirect relationships to more remote ones.

The concept of a dynamic eco-behavioral model of Midwest may also be viewed as adding a new dimension to community studies. It seems likely that eco-behavioral models of complete communities will be most useful in urban-centered regions of moderate population size in which many residents do in fact enter the same behavior settings. As the ratio of acquaintances to strangers declines, the holistic sense of community may decline with it. Eco-behavioral models of communities at successively higher levels in the urban hierarchy should provide new insights into the effect of population size upon human relationships and ways of mitigating those effects to the extent that they are perceived as undesirable.

MODELING THE BARKER COMMUNITY OF MIDWEST

Barker's social accounting system for the town of Midwest is unique in both coverage and conception. Though official data systems exist for private enterprises and government, his includes churches, voluntary associations, and a good deal more on schools than is found in the U.S. Census of Governments. The individual reporting unit distinguished in most official systems (manufacturing establishments, stores, etc.) may also contain many behavior settings. Similarly, the variables collected and structural detail on the internal characteristics of behavior settings extend well beyond traditional financial accounting variables that are given most emphasis in government data systems.

Though comprehensive, structural comparisons seem to be the strength of Barker's system; less power is found in specifying causal interrelations among behavior settings and norms for assessing both individual setting and system performance. Thus Barker and Schoggen (1973) are able to provide penetrating contrasts of Midwest and Yoredale (a small English town), and similarly well-documented structural comparisons of small and large schools are found in Barker and Gump 1964. It is, however, less easy to analyze the degree of success in individual setting operation and the major variables influencing performance. (The theory of manning is an exception here so will be reviewed briefly below; see Wicker 1979.) Also, there are dimensions of internal setting structure and inter-setting relationships which could usefully be added to Barker's system. The ultimate objective would be causally specified hypotheses which could be empirically modeled.

With the National Science Foundation's support during 1974-1980, Fox and his associates have made extensive use of data systems at the community, regional, national, and world levels. At the community level, Fox (1980) has synthesized a data set from secondary data sources published by Barker (termed the Fox-Barker [FB] data set) to illuminate the socioeconomic structure of this community. Despite these extensive empirical applications, the primary data from the 1963-1964 survey of Barker's community have not yet been used to comprehensively model the town of Midwest. Indeed, we know of no comprehensive sociometric model of a community of any size.

In our view such a model should (1) specify causal relationships within Barker's behavior setting structure and (2) provide a comprehensive set of social accounting tables for a small community. The value of a social accounting system is substantially enhanced if such causal hypotheses are testable, for, in their absence, we shall never know if or why attendance at the Boy Scout meeting is abnormally low or high, why a community has an unusually high dropout rate in the school authority system, or the relative importance of parental attitudes and the quality of teaching in determining high school grade distributions. The power of a data system depends (at least in part) on showing how specific variables in specified tables can be used to test accepted theories; this is often lacking even in well-established government data systems.

Modeling Strategies

The alternative types of model structures depend on research objectives. Land use-transportation models of the type discussed by Brown et al. (1972) have been applied to larger urban regions with very specialized land uses and transit networks. Regional simulations that combine input-output and demographic cohort-survival techniques also have been applied to labor markets, states, and larger regions (see, for example, Fullerton and Prescott 1975). Though time-use accounts incorporated into these types of models would render them capable of testing numerous hypotheses of interest, they are very economics oriented and designed for larger regions than the small town studied by Barker. For the town of Midwest our objectives would be the following:

1. Expand the FB data set to include assignments of time to all of Barker's behavior settings and allow for reaggregation of these activities into approximations of the 87 time-use categories employed by the SRC (Survey Research Center) in its study of Americans' use of time in 1975-1976 (see SRC 1977, 1978). Utilize the Barker data set in conjunction with the FB data.

2. Provide a typology for the operation of behavior settings along with measurable performance norms. This would include both the internal and external influences on a given setting in achieving specified objectives.

3. Provide a modeling typology and flow charts for sets of behavior settings within each of Barker's five authority systems (church, school, private enterprise, government, and voluntary associations). The typology may include 10 to 12 major types of settings within each authority system. The flow charts would specify the predetermined and/or exogenous variables that causally influence the dependent variables (social indicators or performance norms) and, in turn, become predetermined variables in future simulated periods.

4. Combine the modeling elements in (3) above with the assignments in the FB data set to simulate behavior settings and the resulting use of time by individuals in Barker's community.

These objectives suggest the use of two computer-modeling packages. (1) MICROSIM provides a capability for using all individuals in the FB data set and simulating life histories of members in the community; this is a modern version of the original work initiated by Guy Orcutt (Orcutt et al. 1961) at Harvard University. (2) The Forrester-type of model structure provides for dynamic simulation by specifying tabled functions between causally related variables. It is quite flexible, allowing the models to set constraints (variable limits) and identify poorly specified equations which might be causing counter-intuitive results. This type of model would be more applicable to objectives (2) and (3).

Caldwell (1980) provides a case for the use of microanalytical simulation as an appropriate methodology for modeling social accounts. First, it allows for direct representation of individuals and families. Thus, stock attributes can be accumulated over time (e.g., experience in leadership roles, skills, experiences, educational attainment, etc.); these cannot be carried in currently implemented regional and land use-transportation models. Second, life histories can be represented so individual comparisons can be made over time. We might want to know how behavioral capacities change (and how diffuse they are throughout the community) when certain behavioral settings are added, deleted, or replaced by other settings. Third, the complexity of society should be representable so that assumptions as to behavior setting causal relationships can be varied. As indicated below, the modeling would have to include new behavioral hypotheses with varied impacts on the individuals in Barker's community as represented in his 1963-1964 data.

The Forrester-type model seems appropriate for modeling the operation of behavior settings. In _Urban Dynamics_, Forrester (1969) was able to attain a believable representation of a very complex social organism; as in his effort, various data gaps may be present in specifying causal hypotheses. Analogous to his major systems for population, housing, and enterprises, we could envisage the five Barker authority systems plus a household sector with prototypes (as discussed below) within each of these systems. The FB and Barker data sets are extremely rich and disaggregated, but many of the causal relationships might have to be judgmentally specified as was the case in Forrester's work. The Forrester framework allows for such specifications as well as the individual testing of smaller model components.

Alternative spatial and temporal bases might be considered for the community simulation. Fox has chosen to close the FB data set by bringing certain out-commuting activities within the region's boundaries, but it would seem desirable to preserve some spatially competitive jobs and residential locations; these adjustments should not be difficult to make. A daily simulation could be considered with highly disaggregated locations for households and behavior settings; this would allow one to analyze individual person-and-setting intersections as well as placing individuals in specific settings at particular times. Several seasonal and within-week prototype simulations could be developed. However, it seems that the most needed work is on the determinants of behavior setting attendance (and related performance measures), and this suggests a long time-unit without the locational detail.

Data Sources

Barker and his associates have produced a community data set which is unparalleled in detail (see, e.g., Barker and Schoggen 1973). By implication from published sources, this data set includes detailed ratings on action patterns and behavior mechanisms for all behavior settings, the number of participants by zone in these settings, and the distribution of time spent in the settings for each individual. Any model which utilized either individuals or behavior setting data would substantially benefit from his unpublished information.

Even if some data for individual time use were not available, a complete time-use file could be generated from the FB data set. Fox (1980) describes his synthesis as follows:

> In Table 9.1, while observing these distributional constraints, I have allocated the 830 town residents among 285 households and a nursing home. The entries in the table indicate the age, sex, marital status and relationship (to the household's head) of each member of the household. The entries 1, 2 and 3 above the household identification numbers represent Barker's Socioeconomic Classes 1, 2 and 3, with the number of persons in Class 3 increased by 26 to include the black residents. The entries below each household column indicate years of education completed by each household member (head, wife, parent or other relative) aged 20 years or over.

In this reference, Fox goes on to describe similar assignments to the rural farm sector and the specific allocation of jobs to households. He conjectures that there might be something like 2,000 constraints in Barker's published data for 1963-1964 alone. These would be more than sufficient to replicate a complete time-use distribution for each of the 1,500 individuals in town-and-trade area. The data set need not exactly replicate the time-use distributions of Midwest's residents in a given year but only be believable; 2,000 constraints in the form of time-use control totals for 884 behavior settings in 198 genotypes should suffice. Data gaps in the Barker set should be estimable in a consistent framework.

STRUCTURAL AND CAUSAL HYPOTHESES

Prior to specifying causal relationships, it is useful to review some normative concepts due to Barker and analyze several ways by which behavior settings could be classified. The _theory of manning_ does examine some of the consequences of under- and overmanned behavior settings as they relate primarily to the participants within the setting itself. Also, there are structural characteristics used primarily in economics and regional geography which offer a way to categorize settings (and genotypes) for modeling purposes; another possibility is to use Barker's authority systems and group distinctive clusters of genotypes. In a final section, we illustrate possible causal structures for several prototypes of settings.

Theory of Manning

Wicker (1979) provides a discussion of manning theory with the effects of under-, optimally, and overmanned behavior settings. When a setting is undermanned, people take various actions to protect the setting program from disruption. There are also secondary impacts which are a consequence of the primary actions designed to preserve the adequate completion of the setting's program; additional psychological impacts may occur because of interpretations given to the primary and secondary reactions to undermanning. Wicker suggests that small schools tend to have undermanned behavior settings with the result that students feel more challenged, experienced, and valued in these activities.

Manning theory distinguishes between the _maintenance minimum_ (the smallest number of people needed to carry out the program) and _capacity_ (the largest number of persons that can be included and still sustain the program). (This is somewhat analogous to the minimum and maximum range of a good in central place theory.) When the number of participants is less than the maintenance minimum, presumably the setting's program must be modified, and this would also be true for overmanned settings, where participant numbers exceed capacity. Between these limits are adequately manned settings. (See Wicker 1979, p. 140, for a more detailed discussion of the theory.) Empirical measures include, for example, students per behavior setting and responsible roles per student; the applied research discussed in this reference primarily relates to schools and churches.

Several comments are pertinent here. (1) Attendance is a performance norm consistent with the manning studies cited in Wicker 1979 and is used (with others) in the flow charts discussed below. (2) The consequences of under- and overmanned settings relate primarily to the individual setting's operation and interrelationships among participants. Thus, individuals in undermanned settings perform more diversified tasks, feel more significant, apparently have little time to be concerned over differences among other participants, and tend to think of themselves in terms of their jobs. While this emphasis may be appropriate to the psychologist, there are many intersetting relationships which will also influence setting attendance. For example, setting complementarities may exist where an overmanned school play tryout is due in part to the private drama lessons given by a highly regarded teacher. Additional characteristics are suggested in the next section.

Behavior Setting Operation

Barker provides static measures of action pattern and behavior mechanism ratings in each behavior setting; less attention is paid to structural characteristics within and among settings which might be useful in distinguishing prototypes for modeling purposes. Fourteen setting characteristics are distinguished below and are split into (1) individual setting attributes, (2) determinants of the number and sizes of settings, and (3) among-setting relationships. Rating scales could be developed for these characteristics with cluster analyses grouping behavior settings into prototypes for modeling.

Individual setting attributes. These include (1) task organization (horizontal and vertical), (2) task specialization (common or committee activities), (3) sequential dependence, (4) input complexity, (5) output complexity, and (6) zonal satisfaction.

The first three attributes relate to internal organization and the interdependence of successive occurrences for given settings. The den meetings during the Cub Scout pack meeting are horizontally integrated; if subcommittee chairpersons are on the executive committee, then we have a vertically integrated setting. Some settings may combine both organizational attributes, increasing the setting's complexity and the preparation times of leaders. The proliferation of subcommittees may be efficient if both the specialized tasks and skills of members exist; a common meeting will usually suffice for simpler setting objectives. Sequential dependence may also influence setting attendance. Missing a single class period may be much more crucial to good student performance in a mathematics course than in one on art history. The ability of setting leaders to find appropriate organizational structures may have a substantial influence on the participation by all zonal members in the setting's occurrences.

The last three characteristics include the production technology of the setting and various measures of zonal satisfaction (i.e., the degrees of satisfaction of setting leaders [zone 6] or coleaders [zone 5], performers or functionaries [zone 4], and customers [zone 3] or spectators [zone 2] with the setting's performance; see Fox's Chapter 7). For input complexity, we distinguish fixed and variable inputs in addition to inputs required outside the formal occurrence and hence unmeasured by Barker's methods. The church bake sale and playing tag in the vacant lot provide sharp contrasts in input complexity, with the former requiring substantive efforts before and outside of the setting itself. Fixed inputs are essential to the production of setting outputs, whereas variable inputs may be adjusted to relative scarcities. Carnivals are multiproduct settings with a wide array of outputs, whereas the ice cream stand in the park has a more limited product line. Also, note that outputs of some settings will be inputs to future occurrences in the same (or another) setting. Finally, zonal satisfaction will influence setting attendance but should be related to numerous facets of the setting's operation; this may include the leader's enthusiasm, organizing ability, attention to members' complaints, and the like.

Number and sizes of settings. The determinants of these include (7) scale economies, (8) setting divisibility, (9) market thresholds, and (10) setting competition.

The first two attributes relate to technological constraints on the size of individual settings. Scale economies may be exhausted when Wicker's "capacity" is reached, so added competitive settings are likely to develop when settings are overmanned. At scales where adequate manning occurs, there is a lower probability that new competitive settings will be successful. Membership divisibility may also set limits on the size (or growth) of individual settings. The bridge club should ideally be divisible by four and the chess club by two, with similar constraints placed on the various athletic settings distinguished by Barker. Eleven players are required to have the A football team, but an additional 11 must be found for the B team. The required inputs for these activities may show similar discontinuities. If the bridge club grows by four members, an additional four chairs and a card table are needed.

The last two characteristics influence the existence and number of settings that will be found in communities of alternative sizes. The market threshold is analogous to the maintenance minimum number of participants in manning theory; there must be some minimum community size which will produce enough participants to enact the settings' program. This concept suggests that there are probably hierarchies of settings among communities of different sizes in the four authority systems excluding private enterprises; hierarchies in the latter are well documented in central place studies. Setting competition will also influence attendance. There appears to be only one option for young boys in Cub Scouts, whereas girls may be Bluebirds or Brownies. Competition may stimulate leaders in organizing setting activities, or it may produce too many poorly manned settings in which programs are inadequately executed.

Among-setting relationships. These include (11) substitutes and complements, (12) linkages (forward and backward), (13) benefit incidence, and (14) policy channels.

Relationships among settings appear to be the least well studied by the ecological psychologists thus far. School dances are complementary with the private teacher giving dance lessons; the quality and quantity of both mutually reinforce the attendance at both settings. Settings within genotypes, alternatively, may be highly competitive so are close substitutes. The barbershop, beauty salon, and grocery store employees of a community probably would place themselves in this category. High tavern attendance may reduce movie house ticket sales and could even decrease the production of outputs in work-related settings. Settings may also have significant forward (demand) and backward (supply) linkages. The talented ninth-grade pianist is a product of the combined efforts of pupil and teacher and supplies a valuable input to the school operetta. The quality of the latter is dependent on numerous linkages in the community such as dance lessons, drama coaching, and music lessons on numerous instruments. The quality of the inputs to the operetta depend on the variety of settings and the abilities of their teachers over a number of years prior to the production.

The last two characteristics are concerned with policy. Some settings produce outputs that are more generally linked to other settings or individuals in the community. In 1950-1951 the town of Midwest had a chest X-ray unit and cancer control clinic providing free examinations to citizens. These settings are usually publicly supported, and their number and output levels are a partial measure of the community's interest in redistributing behavioral income (in this case the enjoyment of good health) among residents. We also may want to distinguish key settings (or individuals active in these settings) through which important policy actions are implemented. These may be settings with key community leaders, citizens' committees, elected organizations such as the municipal council, and the executive committees of public-spirited organizations.

Prototype Settings

The 14 characteristics discussed above are only one way to group behavior settings for modeling purposes. A priori, we should be able to reduce the number of setting prototypes far below the 884 settings in 198 genotypes that Barker distinguished in his 1963-1964 survey. The ninth- and tenth-grade English classes will probably not differ substantially in the educational processes internal to these settings; other settings differing only by age group include athletic contests, school classes, Cubs through Boy Scouts, and so on. It might be possible to group different athletic contests (e.g., football and basketball) together for modeling purposes. The following are suggestions for major prototypes within each of the five authority systems:

Schools. School classes are the major educational settings, and it may be necessary to distinguish classes on the basis of input complexity (e.g., science and shop classes versus lecture sections). Athletic practices and performances and club meetings will be important extracurricular activities in the school system. Special events (class plays, band concerts, assemblies, dances, etc.) will comprise several prototypes with perhaps two others for educational and noneducational excursions. The occupancy time in a rather broad class of settings may be primarily determined by the activity groups discussed above; this would include the various administrative offices distinguished by Barker, time in hallways, and so forth.

Churches. Worship services and Sunday School classes are the two most important prototypes. Special events will include weddings, funerals, social events, and fund raisers (e.g., the church bake sale). Additional settings include study groups, fellowship meetings, and prayer and meditation services; it seems likely that these can be modeled in a common "meetings" format.

Private enterprises. As discussed below, separate models could be specified for the demographic and economic systems, the latter to include profits, sales, costs, and the equilibrium number of enterprises in each genotype. Many of Midwest's enterprises are residentiary with sales levels influenced by export income in farming and, to a much lesser extent, manufacturing; business implement and services sales are probably even more closely related to export earnings. Since the latter is exogenous, it might be simpler to handle the economic characteristics in a single prototype model. Some enterprises may have significant social influences. Cafes and restaurants provide social gathering places for the town's inhabitants; a drugstore near the high school provides a similar function for students after school is over. Bars, pool halls, and movie theaters are often settings where interpersonal conflicts are resolved. Perhaps three or four prototypes would be developed in addition to the economic model.

Government. Several groups of activities can be distinguished here. Some offices provide regular services to virtually every household. Auto license bureaus and tax assessment offices are examples, and visitations will be primarily determined by economic and demographic variables. Police, fire prevention, and the courts are "social control" activities. The age-quality of the housing stock, school dropout rates, unemployment rates, and income are some variables that we expect to influence police and fire prevention activity levels. Other governmental activities will influence other settings and draw on the community for leadership. The agricultural extension agent will give presentations at various agricultural clubs and business meetings, and the mayor (and the other elected officials) will be expected to appear at numerous community functions. Modeling the election process is suggestive here; polling places are a separate genotype in the 1963-1964 survey.

Voluntary associations. A wide variety of motivations probably typifies this system. Sewing clubs and bridge parties accommodate the social and specialized interests of members. Voluntary work in charitable organizations probably provides some prestige in leadership roles and "public-spirited" rewards to lower zone participants in collecting door to door, for example. Professional and business-related interests probably typify participants in the Junior Chamber of Commerce, Rotary Club, Lion's Club, and others. Thus, attendance (or membership) may depend on annual dues, the level of budgetary allocations to publicly oriented projects, and the extrinsic premium in the private sector to membership (or leadership) in such organizations.

This discussion suggests the presence of about 30 basic prototypes; perhaps double this number would emerge ultimately. Cluster analysis applied to Barker's ratings on action patterns and the 14 rating categories discussed above would be another method in identifying prototypes. Though some prototypes may include common variables, the modeler would want to specify plausible differences in parameter values that might occur among settings; a given percentage decline in farm income may have a larger impact on twelfth-grade compared to ninth-grade dropout rates, for example.

Causal Relationships

After specifying model prototypes, the next task would be to compile flow charts which specify causal relationships. Figure 9.1 provides an example of how one prototype (basketball game at the high school) might be modeled. As above, we assume the existence of separate economic and demographic models to provide explanatory variables. Some of these are listed as possible predetermined variables on the left-hand side of the flow chart, with the dependent variables including various performance measures; the latter include attendance, membership, won-lost record, and others and can be modeled as deviations from "normal" magnitudes.

Figure 9.1 is illustrative of possible variables that might influence this setting's performance norms. In the basketball game, we distinguish nonstudent attendance, student attendance,

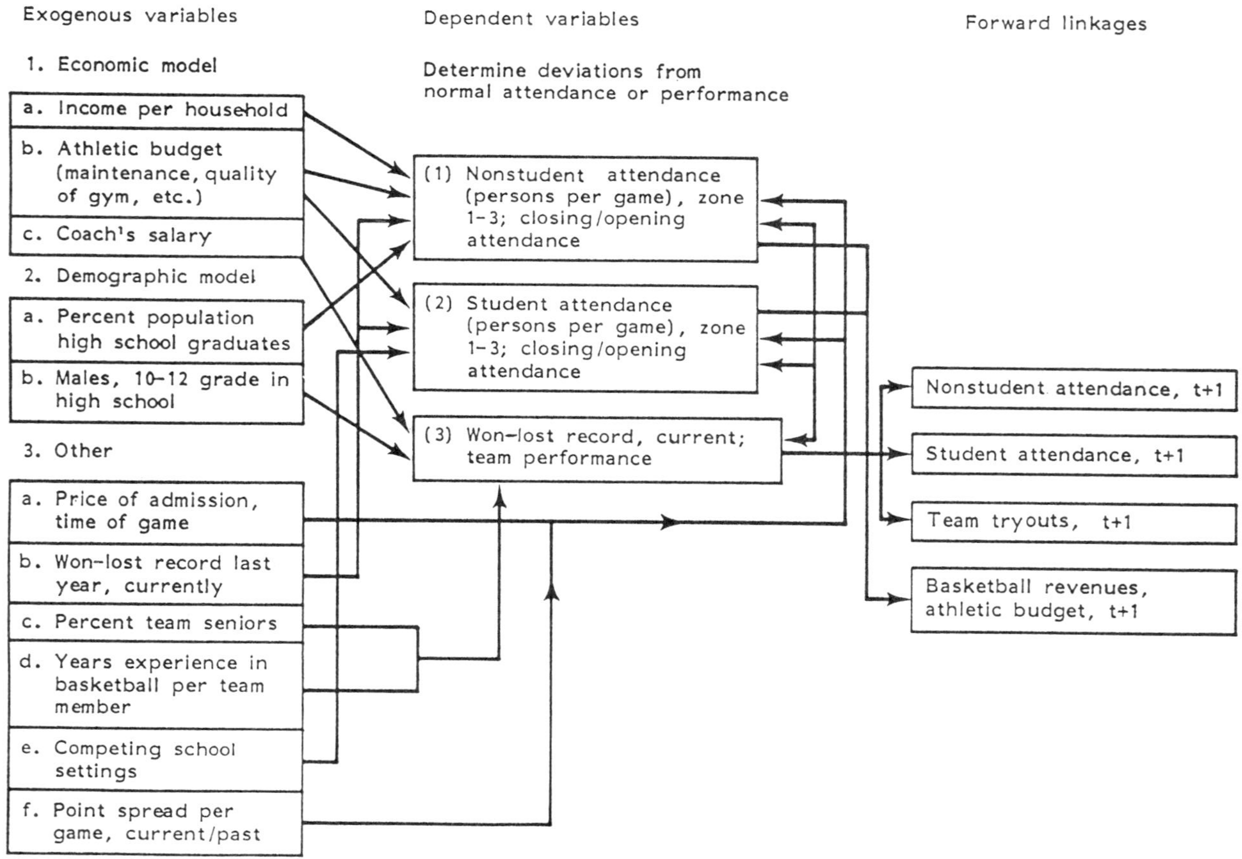

FIG. 9.1. Athletic contests flow chart: basketball game at the high school.

and the team won-lost record. Persons per game is the attendance norm, though the ratio of closing to opening attendance is another measure of interest. Nonstudent attendance may be influenced by income, price of admission, and other variables measuring "interest" (percent of town population who graduated from the high school, last year's won-lost record, and/or average point spread per game). Student attendance may be influenced by these variables in addition to the scheduling of competing extra-curricular activities. Other attendance determinants may include the quality of the gymnasium (age and seating capacity) and coaching ability. The team's won-lost record will be determined by coaching ability, experience of the team (percent seniors and basketball experience per team member), and perhaps by the size of potential player pool (males in grades 10-12). The three dependent variable categories are simultaneously determined with the current won-lost record influencing attendance and vice versa through the enthusiasm and size of audience. The current dependent variables then influence attendance, team tryouts, and basketball revenues in future time periods.

Figure 9.2 provides another example of possible variables that might influence the "school classes" prototype. Here we distinguish average daily attendance, the dropout rate, and grade distributional measures (e.g., percent of high grades) as performance norms. (Other measures are possible; standard test scores and percent of seniors with college scholarships are examples.) Educational attitudes (occupational or socioeconomic distribution or percent of population with 12 or more years of education) may influence both average daily attendance and grade performance. Measures of how the local economy is performing (farm income and/or unemployment) may at least partially determine the dropout rate. Illnesses or major flu epidemics will lower average daily attendance, with native intelligence of the students a partial determinant of grade performance. Births, deaths, and net migrants determine the size of enrollments, and the three dependent variables have forward linkages to variables listed on the right-hand side of Figure 9.2.

A final flow chart (Figure 9.3) suggests relationships which might be present in attendance at church worship services. Age groups are distinguished, as well as revenue attained from collections at the service. Age distributions from the demographic model determine potential participants, while parental influence (percent with surviving parents in the community) and personal tragedies (percent widowed and/or percent with deaths in the immediate family) condition religious attitudes. The latter may also be influenced by both occupational hazards and the extent to which natural phenomena determine family income (percent in blue collar occupations and/or farming). Income per household and percent aged 65 and over have influences of opposite sign on worship service collections, while zones 4, 5, and 6 preparation times influence attendance (pastor's variables [zone 6] and zones 4 and 5 [performers'] preparation times). The

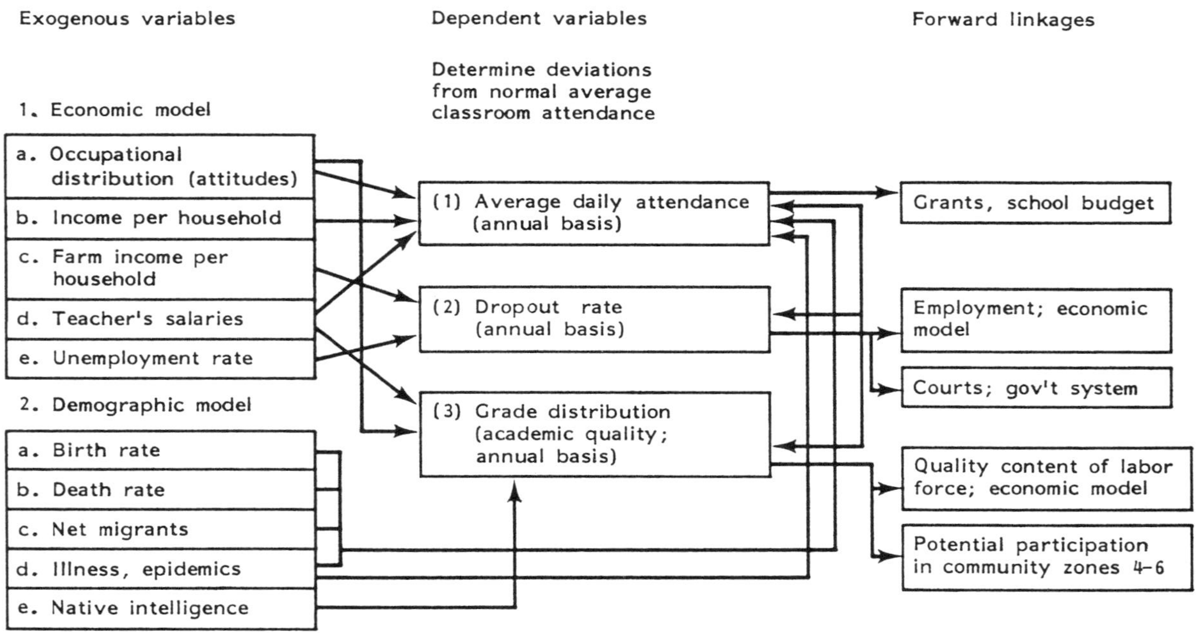

FIG. 9.2. School classes flow chart.

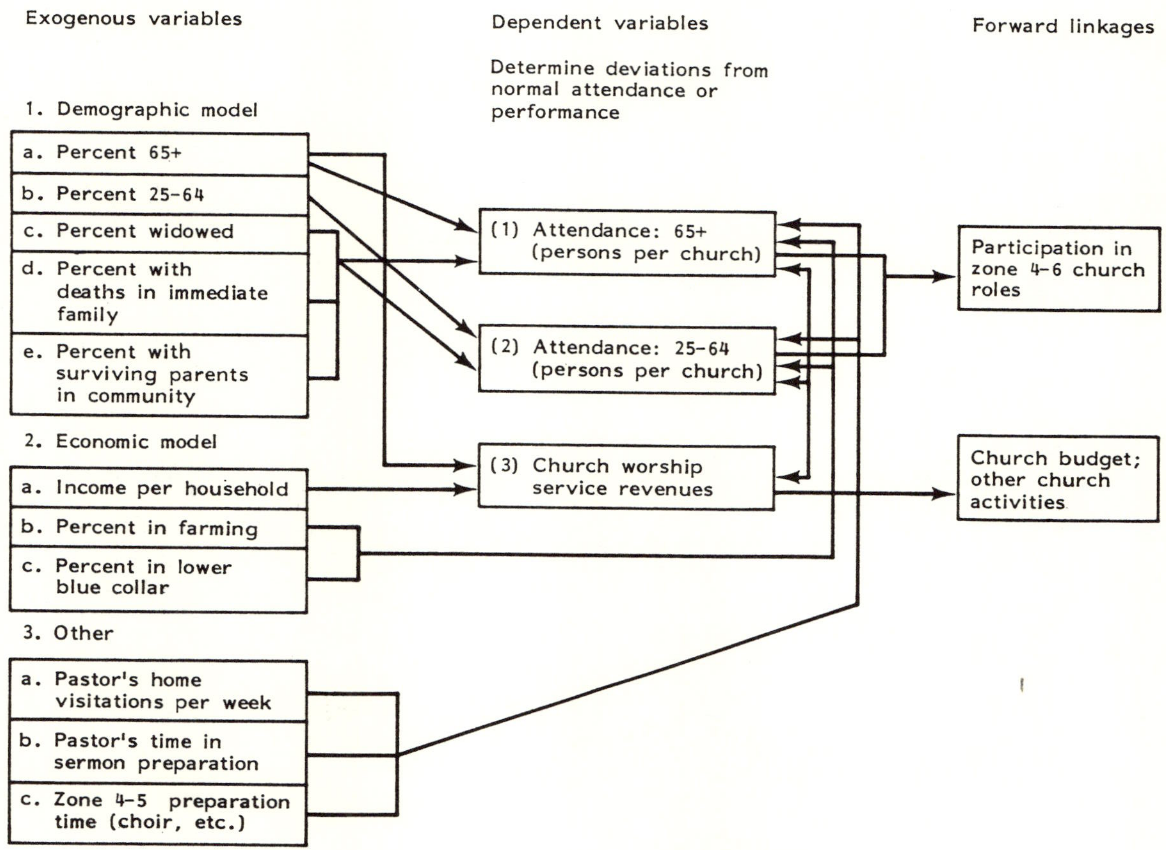

FIG. 9.3. Church worship services flow chart.

dependent variables are again jointly determined, though church income may be less important in determining attendance than the opposite causal relation.

The above are initial examples of plausible causal linkages involved in behavior setting prototypes. If related to individuals' time use, such a system would include both individual household and behavior setting time uses as the basis for a community's social accounts. Consideration should also be given to administrative control prototypes that allocate resources among behavior settings; the elementary school's academic offerings and activities are something more than just the operation of its individual behavior settings. In addition, we note that by establishing causal linkages we have gone a long way toward specifying believable reallocations of time use in the household data set. If a farm income decline of 20 percent increases dropouts by a fixed number of males in the tenth through twelfth grades, then farm families with the qualifying progeny are debited time in school and credited with time in primary job; other effects are also possible, of course.

CONCLUDING COMMENTS

In this chapter we have sketched a modeling strategy for empirically estimating a system of time-use social (or eco-behavioral) accounts for a community. Though Barker's system includes a substantial number of behavior settings, specifying prototypes would be one way to make the task more manageable. Several other problems might concern the modeler of such a system:

1. Generality may be limited with the data based on the activities and social structure of a small midwestern town. A counter argument is that the meticulous distinction of 884 behavior settings most surely covers the overwhelming percentage of settings common to communities of a similar size across the United States. Also, if we believe in a hierarchical theory of central places as applied to noneconomic settings, then the Barker settings are found in nearly all U.S. urban communities of Midwest's population or larger. The modeler using Barker's data will miss the New England town meeting, but little more.
2. Data availibility could be a problem in specifying flow charts similar to those discussed above. Detailed data were collected by Barker, but logical specifications of causal relationships may reveal new data needs. The pastor's sermon preparation time is clearly not available in census publications and also may be excluded from Barker's data. However, even just the specification of these causal linkages would be of substantial value in future empirical work on community social accounts.

A final point should be noted. Had we a widely accepted system of causal equations describing every important aspect of human behavior, we would be much closer to a consensus on what should constitute a system of social accounts. As all human behavior occurs in behavior settings, the latter must be a logical contender as the basic unit of such accounts. As yet, the causal linkages and their impact on setting performance in Barker's system must be specified.

REFERENCES

Barker, R. G. 1968. Ecological Psychology: Concepts and Methods for Studying the Environment of Human Behavior. Stanford, CA: Stanford University Press.

______. 1969. "Wanted: An Eco-Behavioral Science." In E. P. Willems and H. L. Raush, eds., Naturalistic Viewpoints in Psychological Research. New York: Holt, Rinehart, and Winston.

Barker, R. G., and Associates. 1978. Habitats, Environments, and Human Behavior: Studies in Ecological Psychology and Eco-Behavioral Science from the Midwest Psychological Field Station, 1947-1972. San Francisco: Jossey-Bass.

Barker, R. G., and P. V. Gump, eds. 1964. Big School, Small School: High School Size and Student Behavior. Stanford, CA: Stanford University Press.

Barker, R. G., and P. Schoggen. 1973. Qualities of Community Life: Methods of Measuring Environment and Behavior Applied to an American and an English Town. San Francisco: Jossey-Bass.

Barker, R. G., and H. F. Wright. 1955. Midwest and Its Children: The Psychological Ecology of an American Town. New York: Harper and Row. Reprinted 1971 by Archon Books, Hamden, CT.

Bechtel, R. B. 1977. Enclosing Behavior. Stroudsburg, PA: Dowden, Hutchinson and Ross.

Bechtel, R. B., and C. B. Ledbetter. 1976. The Temporary Environment: Cold Regions Habitability. Hanover, NH: U.S. Army Cold Regions Research and Engineering Laboratory. Special Report 76-10, October 1976.

Brown, J. H., J. R. Ginn, F. J. James, J. F. Kain, and M. R. Strazheim. 1972. Empirical Models of Urban Land Use: Suggestions on Research Objectives and Organization. New York: National Bureau of Economic Research.

Caldwell, S. B. 1980. "Choosing Among Modeling Strategies for Social Accounts." Paper presented at the Social Science Research Council Workshop on Social Accounting Systems, Washington, DC, March 24-26, 1980.

Forrester, J. W. 1969. Urban Dynamics. Cambridge: MIT Press.

Fox, K. A. 1980. "The Fox-Barker (FB) Data Set: An Interim Report." Unpublished paper, Department of Economics, Iowa State University, Ames.

______. 1983. "The Eco-Behavioral View of Human Societies and Its Implications for Systems Science." International Journal of Systems Science 14: 895-914.

______. 1984. "Behavior Settings and Eco-Behavioral Science: A New Arena for Mathematical Social Science Permitting a Richer and More Coherent View of Human Activities in Social Systems:

Part I, Concepts, Measurements, and Linkages to Economic Data Systems, Time-Allocation Matrices, and Social System Accounts." Mathematical Social Sciences 7: 117-138.

Part II, Relationships to Established Disciplines, and Needs for Mathematical Development." Mathematical Social Sciences 7: 139-165.

______. 1985. Social System Accounts: Linking Social and Economic Indicators Through Tangible Behavior Settings. Dordrecht and Boston: D. Reidel.

Fox, K. A., and S. K. Ghosh. 1981. "A Behavior Setting Approach to Social Accounts Combining Concepts and Data from Ecological Psychology, Economics, and Studies of Time Use." In F. T. Juster and K. C. Land, eds., Social Accounting Systems: Essays on the State of the Art. New York: Academic Press.

Fullerton, H. H., and J. R. Prescott. 1975. An Economic Simulation Model for Regional Development Planning. Ann Arbor, MI: Ann Arbor Science Publishers.

Gump, P. V. 1971. "The Behavior Setting: A Promising Unit for Environmental Designers." Landscape Architecture 61: 130-134.

Orcutt, G., M. Greenberger, J. Korbel, and A. Rivlin. 1961. Microanalysis of Socioeconomic Systems: A Simulation Study. New York: Harper.

Prescott, J. R. 1980. "A Behavior Setting Approach to Microanalytical Simulation Models at the Community Level." Unpublished manuscript, Department of Economics, Iowa State University, Ames.

______. 1985. "A Behavior Setting Approach to Microanalytical Simulation Models at the Community Level." Chapter 8 in K. A. Fox, Social System Accounts. Dordrecht, Holland: D. Reidel.

Ruggles, R. 1981. "The Conceptual and Empirical Strengths and Limitations of Demographic and Time-Based Accounts." In F. T. Juster and K. C. Land, eds., Social Accounting Systems: Essays on the State of the Art. New York: Academic Press.

Schoggen, P. 1986. Behavior Settings: A Revision and Extension of Barker's Ecological Psychology. In preparation.

Sengupta, J. K. 1986. "Modeling Eco-Behavioral Systems." Mathematical Social Sciences 11: 1-31.

Survey Research Center. 1977 and 1978. Data Tapes from the Survey of Americans' Use of Time in 1975-76. Ann Arbor, MI: University of Michigan.

Wicker, A. W. 1979. _An Introduction to Ecological Psychology_. Monterey, CA: Brooks/Cole. Republished by Cambridge University Press, 1984.

______. 1986. "Behavior Settings Reconsidered: Temporal Stages, Resources, Internal Dynamics, Context." In D. Stokols and J. Altman, eds., _Handbook of Environmental Psychology_. New York: Wiley. In press.

10
Summary and Overview

KARL A. FOX and DON G. MILES

In the introduction we said that the objectives of this book are to describe, develop, and advocate a systems approach to economics and to illustrate the prospective scope and power of this approach. We urged experimentation with courses or seminars in systems economics or systems approaches to multidisciplinary research. And we defined systems economics provisionally as "what systems economists do."

We have presented nine examples of their work. We will summarize their major themes, draw some implications for the study and development of systems economics, and conclude.

A SUMMARY OF THE CONTRIBUTIONS

Boulding describes the world as "a very self-contained general system in three dimensions of space and one of time." (It is significantly open only to inputs of energy from the sun and outputs of transformed energy and heat to space.) Using vivid imagery, he discusses problems of describing or "mapping" successively more complex systems. If we wish to predict future states of a system we must go beyond "maps" to models--dynamic models which relate at least two successive state descriptions. He distinguishes between strict equilibrium and quasi-equilibrium systems; ecosystems, he says, are very nice examples of the latter.

Ecosystems consist of many different populations in interaction with each other. Any change in the parameters of such a system will change the position of the equilibrium. This change may create an empty niche for a species which would have an equilibrium population if it existed. The empty niche might be filled by genetic mutation of some species within the system or by immigration of members of a suitable species from another location. A further change in parameters might close the empty niche before either of these events occurs; but if it is filled, all the other niches change. If a niche shrinks to zero, the corresponding species disappears from a local ecosystem or becomes extinct if the ecosystem in question is coextensive with its range. This is evolution, and evolution consists in "the filling of empty niches through parametric change."

The more complex a system is, the more difficult it is to apply simple concepts of cause and effect and to predict the outcome of any particular event. "This is especially true . . . in systems that have fundamental indeterminacy, as evolutionary systems have and, indeed, any system has which involves information or its derivatives as an essential feature." However, such a system will have limits and constraints (physical laws, conservation principles, and identities or near-identities) which may make it reasonably predictable in the large, though not in detail. And it may be possible through human ingenuity to change systems in directions which make them more predictable. "A good deal of experience and empirical knowledge consists of finding where in the real world the essential identities and limitations apply."

Boulding then proceeds to apply all of these concepts to the economy regarded as an ecosystem and part of the general system of the world. He translates all the familiar entities of economics into the terms of general systems theory. At one stage of his exposition, the economy looks "a little bit like an ecosystem of commodities, but it also looks like a quasi-ergodic (quasi-equilibrium) system." At the next stage, he describes the economic system as an evolutionary system, as well as an ecological one, because the parameters change through technical innovation and other factors. He finds the concept of the empty niche "very useful in explaining the particular forms which economic development takes."

There are some features of the economy which are not found in the biosphere: know-how embodied in large numbers of different workers producing a complex artifact; money and financial institutions; and debt (negative assets) which permits an enormously complex structure of property. Hence, the economy is capable of pathologies (inflation, deflation, and unemployment) that have no biological parallel. But in spite of these important differences, the basic processes of biological and societal evolution are remarkably similar.

Boulding's statements about "the economy as an ecosystem" are based on great professional depth and sophistication in economics. He published his first article on economic theory in 1932 (when he was 22). He published the first modern textbook on economic theory in 1941 and received the John Bates Clark Medal of the American Economic Association in 1949 for outstanding contributions to economics prior to age 40. The first six recipients of this biennial award were, in chronological order, Samuelson, Boulding, Friedman, Tobin, Arrow, and Klein. Boulding is the only one of these six who has not yet received the Nobel Prize in economic science. He served as president of the American Economic Association in 1968. The ideas presented in his contribution are elaborated in three recent books (Boulding 1978, 1981, 1985a).

Lawlor's essay complements Boulding's. Lawlor first surveys the development of general systems theory as a new scientific outlook in the life sciences, spearheaded by von Bertalanffy beginning about 1949. von Bertalanffy made the simple but crucial distinction between open and closed systems. A closed system is isolated from its environment. Given its initial conditions and the laws governing the interactions of its elements, such a system will reach a completely determinate final equilibrium. The laws of thermodynamics apply rigorously to closed systems--for example, to physical or chemical experiments conducted in vacuums or closed containers.

In contrast, a living organism is an open system, maintaining itself in a continuous inflow and outflow (interchange) with its environment. So long as it lives, the organism is never in a state of chemical and thermodynamic equilibrium but rather in a steady state which differs from such an equilibrium. And an organism (an open system) can reach its particular steady state from different initial conditions and in different ways.

Lawlor then briefly reviews the development of general equilibrium theory in economics. On the one hand, the economy is treated as a closed system: its final equilibrium (a vector of relative prices) is completely determined by its initial conditions (endowments, technology, and preferences). On the other, the economy is conceived of as an open system that takes inputs from the physical and social environment and transforms them into outputs to the larger social system. From the standpoint of general systems theory, this is a fundamental anomaly.

Lawlor holds that this anomaly results from a defect in the framing of the general equilibrium problem from Walras on--"the lack of any theory of the process by which Walras's equilibrium might actually come about and be maintained." Drawing on the work of Hayek, Lawlor concludes that the problem boils down to one of social-level facts concerning the processes by which knowledge and information are acquired in a social setting. How do economic actors acquire knowledge of both the objective and subjective data that cause them to change their plans? Why do general equilibrium theorists so consistently ignore institutions such as the press (the purpose of which is to communicate knowledge) and advertising (intended to change preferences)?

Lawlor suggests that "a complete system specification of a general economic equilibrium, one that included a social-specific role for knowledge acquisition (or control), could possibly clear the theoretical ground for that union of economists and other social theorists that has been called for so many times since Comte first proposed a science of society." It might also provide a framework within which the proposals of a variety of heterodox thinkers within economics could be developed and accommodated without abandoning all of the structuring and centering insights which have emerged from the work on general equilibrium theory.

Gardner's essay also complements Boulding's. Boulding uses verbal artistry to evoke mental images of systems concepts. But mathematics is also a language--an essential one if we are to advance from descriptive maps or images of systems to explanatory and predictive models.

Gardner defines a system as "any process that transforms inputs into outputs." For example, a production function is a paradigm case of a system. A system may have some or all of nine major properties: (1) It has memory if any of its inputs are dated earlier than any of its outputs; (2) it is either discrete or continuous; (3) it is invertible if the roles of inputs and outputs can be reversed (i.e., if they can be treated as either dependent or independent variables in a mathematical model of the system); (4) it is causal if current values of outputs depend only on past values of inputs; (5) it may be deterministic or stochastic; (6) it is time invariant if the relationship between inputs and outputs does not depend explicitly on time; (7) it may be stable if it approaches an equilibrium value (say P^*) from an initial value in the neighborhood of P^* or globally stable (equifinal) if it approaches P^* from any initial value whatsoever; (8) it may be linear or nonlinear; and (9) it may be controllable or not.

Obviously, a great many combinations of these properties are possible. Gardner uses the von Neumann production system to illustrate some of these properties: "From a systems point of view, it represents production as a discrete, deterministic, time invariant system with memory." Gardner then discusses the stability (equifinality) of systems based on the ideas of Liapunov, the controllability of systems, and the treatment of causality in econometric models. He briefly outlines the logic of comparing (economic) systems and concludes with an empirical model demonstrating the existence of repressed inflation in the Soviet economy.

Gardner concludes that "today's graduate student in economics must know a nontrivial amount of systems theory, whether he has the benefit of a course in the subject or not. . . . Systems theory is vital to research at the forefront of economics and promises to grow in importance in the years to come."

Gardner's illustrations fall within the accepted boundaries of the economy. His models are adapted to the regularly spaced time series observations familiar to economists and to engineers concerned with controlling physical systems and, apart from stochastic elements, seem to imply a high degree of permanence in the structural relationships among variables. This type of systems theory should be readily teachable within an economics department to students who are also taking econometrics and/or mathematical economics.

In contrast, Sengupta views the economy as part of a complete social system. Like Boulding, he views society as a social ecosystem. He goes beyond Boulding in adopting an objectively observable and measurable unit of social activity--the behavior setting--which applies equally to market-oriented and nonmarket systems.

The behavior setting concept, originated by the psychologist Roger Barker in 1950, is fully described in Fox's essay (Chapter 7). Put simply, behavior settings are the natural units or standing patterns of behavior into which people sort themselves to get on with the business of daily life--retail stores, offices, school classes, religious services, meetings, athletic events, and so on. Behavior settings are the immediate social and physical environments of human behavior and collectively absorb an exhaustive allocation of the living-time of members of a specified social system or community in each unit of calendar time. Barker defined the study of *individual* behavior in everyday activities as ecological psychology and the study of complete behavior settings and systems of settings as eco-behavioral science. Though Barker's work was completely independent of Boulding's, his eco-behavioral view of human societies reinforces Boulding's and provides the starting point for Sengupta's contribution.

Sengupta points out that economics provides very limited tools for analyzing social behavior. Social dynamics are certainly important for predicting market demand, but "no theory of social dynamics has filtered into most economists' concept of management and managerial efficiency." Social dynamics are crucial for explaining why the same innovation succeeded in one culture while failing in another; mechanistic growth models shed no light on this. Economists should ask themselves why economic theory "has not delved deep into social behavior to turn itself into a viable social theory."

In several specific areas economic theory has extended its market-oriented boundaries. But these developments are all based on the *economic method*, which comprises three aspects: a market system, a choice mechanism, and a set of constraints. The economic method applies quite well to private enterprises and may apply in part to the resource allocation decisions of nonprofit agencies (schools, hospitals, and some others) producing goods and services. But there are many types of behavior settings, accounting for a very large proportion of social activity "in which there are no markets, no observable prices, and it is not known if there are any optimization objectives implicit in the agents' behavior. There may be constraints due to the environment, although these may not be clearly known." This is the situation in ecological systems, which are so vividly described by Boulding.

Sengupta then introduces the concepts of diversity, variety, truncation, and rigidity which have been found useful in characterizing the distributions of species in ecosystems and in explaining the viability of individual species within such systems. Populations of identical or similar behavior settings are analogous to species in their interactions within the social ecosystem.

The bulk of Sengupta's paper illustrates some basic elements of a general theory of behavior settings in which variety occupies a central place. We regard this as a major step toward the operational modeling of social systems consisting of both economic and noneconomic settings. Sengupta also applies the ecological concept of variety to product-differentiation by firms within an industry. Finally, he makes a strong case for Marshall's representative firm as an ecological concept, by redefining it as a "representative cluster of behavior settings" against which all other individual clusters may be compared and contrasted. The clusters may indeed constitute firms within an industry (in which case he illustrates three uses of the representative firm concept in microeconomic theory), or they may constitute nonmarket organizations of a given generic type.

Johnson's essay takes recent articles by two economists, McCloskey and Kirzner, as his points of departure. McCloskey deplores the modernist methods of the economic research establishment; Kirzner calls for a complete restructuring of neoclassical economic theory to incorporate structural dynamics. Thus Johnson, like Lawlor, addresses himself to methodological issues of great current concern to economists. He examines the McCloskey and Kirzner arguments in the light of 35 years of research by agricultural economists, himself included.

Johnson distinguishes three major categories of research in which agricultural economists have been involved. Problem-solving (PS) research is holistic; the problem must be grasped in its entirety or it cannot be solved. Subject matter (SM) research (e.g., modeling the agricultural sector of an economy) is less holistic than PS research. Both PS and SM research are usually multidisciplinary. Disciplinary research (DISC) is reductionist, the opposite of holistic. Its tools are drawn from a single discipline (economics), its subject is internal to the discipline, and its results are of interest only to members of the discipline.

Johnson observes that agricultural economists doing research, consulting, and advising work have repeatedly encountered the difficulties stressed by McCloskey and Kirzner. However, he reports trends toward holism in modeling problem and subject matter domains relevant for agricultural development. He finds that agricultural economists researching practical problems (which are generally multidisciplinary) and multidisciplinary subjects have made some progress in meeting the criticisms of McCloskey and Kirzner. Finally, he lays out essential characteristics of models of problem and subject matter domains, reflects on the evaluation of such models, and proposes a compromise with McCloskey.

On the one hand, Johnson finds several of McCloskey's objections to modernism unconvincing or overdrawn. On the other, he finds substantial correspondence between iterative, interactive general systems simulation analyses of PS and SM domains and what is advocated by McCloskey and Kirzner.

Johnson's discussion of the development of general systems simulation models of the agricultural sectors of Nigeria and South Korea is particularly enlightening. These models gave practical effect to many of the systems properties described by Gardner. They include physical, biological, economic, demographic, and social components, as in Boulding's evocative descriptions of general systems. And in different components or different versions, they incorporated both optimizing and nonoptimizing features--as would be required in Sengupta's proposed models of social systems containing both economic and noneconomic behavior settings.

Miles provides a succinct, closely integrated description of a small, constrained poultry farm, designed to illustrate many of the concepts of systems economics. His flow diagram reinforces the verbal description and could be used as the basis for mathematical formulations of the system incorporating relevant properties enumerated by Gardner and/or for a general systems simulation model as discussed by Johnson. The poultry farm, with 10,000 hens, is a remarkably complex system with biological, structural, mechanical, and electrical components; physically vulnerable to local heat waves and disruptions of electrical power, feed, transportation, and labor supplies; and economically sensitive to political and regulatory as well as market forces. Information flows are extremely important and the manager must often respond very quickly to deviations of system components from performance norms. The system is holistic in that "improvements" in a particular component may actually impair the efficiency of the system as a whole, and attempts at simultaneous improvements in several components may prove disastrous.

Fox's essay complements Sengupta's in its emphasis on behavior settings as basic units of social activity. The development of national economic accounts provided a rationale for improving economic time series relevant to the description of economic change. These time series made it possible for Tinbergen, Klein, Stone, and others to experiment with dynamic models of the economy for purposes of prediction, policy analysis, and (in principle) control.

Fox proposes a similar development of social system accounts, time series, and models. He asserts that social accounts with behavior settings as basic units can take advantage of the many billions of dollars already invested in existing data systems. Classifications of types of behavior settings can be closely related to standard classifications of industries; classifications of roles in behavior settings can be closely related to standard classifications of occupations. In any given year, Fox's accounts would take the form of time-allocation matrices (TAMs) with categories of behavior settings as columns and categories of persons (by age, sex, occupation, education, and other attributes singly or in combination) as rows. Different TAMs would use the same set of columns but alternative sets of rows. Each row of a TAM would be the time-allocation vector (TAV) of a population subgroup; on a per capita basis, it would summarize the average life-style of that subgroup.

Fox holds that surveys actually conducted by Roger Barker and his associates in certain American and English communities have demonstrated the feasibility of social accounts based on behavior settings. Barker's unit of account, person-hours of occupancy time, should be acceptable to social scientists generally on a descriptive level. A small retail firm or a local voluntary association may consist of a single behavior setting; if so, the behavior setting _is_ a firm in the one case or a nonmarket organization in the other. Larger firms and nonmarket organizations consist of several or many behavior settings. Hence, social accounts based on behavior settings are quite compatible with data systems based on firms and organizations.

van Moeseke presents two models for estimating the dollar values of social variables. The first expresses the attempt of an individual to determine an optimal allocation of his time during the next accounting period (year). He must allocate his time exhaustively among an array of behavior settings which constitute his social and physical environment, subject to the limitations of his endowment (occupational skills, health, rights to income from property and transfer payments, etc.) and perhaps to certain social requirements and/or personal output goals. This leads to a mathematical programming problem, the solution of which is his optimal time-allocation vector or life-style. The individual is assumed to have an ordinal utility function; since one of the constraints is financial (and binding), each of the other constraints can also be valued in dollars. The sum of the dollar values ascribed to the nonfinancial constraints is his social income (SI); his total income (TI) is the sum of his money income and SI. Under certain assumptions, TI and its components could be aggregated over individuals, yielding dollar estimates of total income and social income for residents of a community, region, nation, or for any population subgroup; the difference between aggregate total income and aggregate social income is _personal income_ as defined in the national economic accounts.

van Moeseke's second model is completely objective; it dispenses with utility functions entirely. The individual's social status imposes several requirements, such as professional, family, and community commitments. These must be met by expenditures of time and money in different activities (behavior settings). The solution to a cost-minimizing linear program yields dollar values for both the individual's time and his social requirements; it also implies a socioeconomic theory of saving and impatience.

van Moeseke does not develop the systems implications of his models other than the possibility of aggregating time and money expenditures and the dollar values of social requirements over individuals to arrive at aggregates for all members of a community or society. His models pose an interesting problem of reconciliation with the existence of nonmarket behavior settings which, as such, may have no discernible optimizing objectives. Is this consistent with an assumption that each individual participant in such settings is guided by his search for an optimal life-style or by the need to meet the requirements of his social position? Perhaps there is no conflict in the case of van Moeseke's second model, though there might be in that of his first.

Prescott's essay complements those of Fox and Sengupta in its emphasis on behavior settings as basic units of social activity. As these are essentially ecological (eco-behavioral) units, Prescott's emphasis is also consistent with Boulding's depiction of economy and society as ecosystems. While Sengupta uses ecological concepts explicitly and applies them to social systems in general, Prescott proposes a simulation model based on Barker's data for a specific American community in a particular year.

Prescott's model would be comparable in some respects to the general systems simulation models described by Johnson. Prescott has had extensive experience with large-scale economic simulation models of metropolitan areas and other regions. In modeling Barker's community, he would propose to combine some features originated by Forrester (1969) in his Urban Dynamics and others embodied in a microanalytical simulation system (MICROSIM) based on the approach initiated by Orcutt et al. (1961).

As procedures for handling the economic and demographic components of urban models are well established, Prescott would deal with these in a fairly conventional way. The model as a whole would include submodels for perhaps 60 prototype behavior settings, each of which would represent a number of similar settings reported in Barker's survey. Flow diagrams for three such prototype settings are included in the essay.

If implemented, Prescott's proposal should lead to a major breakthrough in the modeling of social systems. We know of no other approach, no other data base, and no other basic unit that promises such rapid progress in the modeling of social ecosystems.

SOME IMPLICATIONS FOR THE STUDY AND DEVELOPMENT OF SYSTEMS ECONOMICS

Boulding's essay provides a view of the world as a general system. Miles' presentation of wholistic analysis in Appendix 1 parallels Boulding's view. Both views have already been taught at the Western Australian Institute of Technology (Muresk campus) as part of the final year undergraduate subject Environmental Economics 401.

We believe it is essential that systems economists learn to think about the world in this way. Boulding (1985a), in The

recommends data systems of high statistical quality in a societal perspective.

Systems economists should also develop an acquaintance with literature on the internal structures of firms and other organizations. Coase 1937 is still a classic on the nature of the firm; we believe it provides a starting point for an eco-behavioral view of firms and other organizations as clusters of behavior settings. Prescott's essay lists 14 characteristics of behavior settings which link them (in our judgment) with organization theory and the theory of the firm; Prescott groups the 14 into (a) individual setting attributes, (b) determinants of the numbers and sizes of settings, and (c) among-setting relationships. Systems economists should also become acquainted with the general features of existing types of simulation models of firms and other organizations.

Johnson's essay emphasizes general systems simulation models of the agricultural sectors of Nigeria and South Korea. His essay, and the references cited in it, should provide starting points for studying the main features of models simulating the interactions of (a) human communities and their natural environments and (b) firms and other organizations with their natural environments.

Systems economists should also learn the main features of systems theory as developed for application (a) in the physical sciences and engineering and (b) in the life sciences. Gardner's essay and its references provide an entry into the physical science tradition, which should be accessible to students with some background in mathematical economics and econometrics. Odum 1983 is a leading textbook on systems theory in the life science tradition, with special emphasis of ecological systems.

In Appendix 2, Fox surveys classic examples of systems thinking: some in the physical sciences, some in the life sciences, and some in the social and behavioral sciences.

CONCLUDING REMARKS

How much should any one systems economist know? We think he or she should be acquainted with the whole range of ideas and types of models mentioned above on a fairly general level. After choosing a major field of application within economics or agricultural economics, a systems economist should go very deeply into the systems ideas and models most relevant to that field.

Johnson, in his essay, concludes that "a theory (economic or not) involving institutional, technological, and human change and the accumulation of conventional capital would be so massive it would encompass within itself all existing academic disciplines. To this author, such a theory seems to be beyond the grasp of mere mortals."

In their introduction, Fox and Miles quoted Shackle's (1967) description of three episodes of intense creative activity in economic theory. These bursts of intellectual energy and their consequences for theory were contained within the economics discipline. Systems economics can be expected to improve problem-solving and multidisciplinary research involving several fields of applied economics. It may, as Lawlor's essay suggests, encourage economic theorists in attempts to model the economy as an open system. It may also, as urged by Boulding and others, lead to further theoretical developments in "evolutionary economics."

The most dramatic consequence of systems economics should be to facilitate cooperation between economists and other social scientists in the cumulative development of social system accounts, models, and data. Cooperation in the description and empirical modeling of firms, other organizations, communities, urban-centered regions, and nations should also lead to some integration of theories and translatability of terms and concepts across disciplines. Systems economics, as such, would simply prepare those economists and agricultural economists who studied it for such cooperation; the multidisciplinary endeavor as a whole would need a much more appropriate title--perhaps social systems accounting and modeling.

Gross (1966) prophesied that the development of social systems accounting would take several decades. Some progress has been made, and much more could be made, with proper research support and arrangements for intensive cooperation among social scientists from several disciplines. Overarching theories of man and society can wait--perhaps forever, so far as operational models and data systems are concerned.

We must somehow grasp and hold on to Boulding's conceptualization of the world as a total system. At the necessary level of aggregation, this is not beyond the grasp of mere mortals--and it must be grasped if mere mortals are to survive.

REFERENCES

Barker, R. G. 1968. Ecological Psychology: Concepts and Methods for Studying the Environment of Human Behavior. Stanford, CA: Stanford University Press.

Barker, R. G., and P. Schoggen. 1973. Qualities of Community Life: Methods of Measuring Environment and Behavior Applied to an American and an English Town. San Francisco: Jossey-Bass.

Boulding, K. E. 1978. Ecodynamics: A New Theory of Societal Evolution. Beverly Hills, CA: Sage.

_____. 1981. Evolutionary Economics. Beverly Hills, CA: Sage.

_____. 1985a. The World as a Total System. Beverly Hills, CA: Sage.

_____. 1985b. Human Betterment. Beverly Hills, CA: Sage.

Braudel, F. 1981, 1982, 1984. Civilization and Capitalism,

15th-18th Century. Volume 1, 1981: *The Structures of Everyday Life: The Limits of the Possible*. Volume 2, 1982: *The Wheels of Commerce*. Volume 3, 1984: *The Perspective of the World*, translated by Sian Reynolds. New York: Harper and Row. Originally published in French in 1979.

Coase, R. H. 1937. "The Nature of the Firm." *Economica* (New Series) 4: 386-405.

Forrester, J. W. 1969. *Urban Dynamics*. Cambridge: MIT Press.

Gross, B. M. 1966. "The State of the Nation: Social Systems Accounting." In R. A. Bauer, ed., *Social Indicators*. Cambridge: MIT Press.

Mitchell, B. R. 1976. *European Historical Statistics, 1750-1950*. New York: Columbia University Press.

Odum, H. T. 1983. *Systems Ecology: An Introduction*. New York: Wiley.

Orcutt, G., M. Greenberger, J. Korbel, and A. Rivlin. 1961. *Microanalysis of Socioeconomic Systems: A Simulation Study*. New York: Harper.

Organization for Economic Cooperation and Development. 1982. *The OECD List of Social Indicators*. Paris: OECD.

Shackle, G. L. S. 1967. *The Years of High Theory: Invention and Tradition in Economic Thought, 1926-1939*. Cambridge: Cambridge University Press.

Stone, R. 1971. *Demographic Accounting and Model-Building*. Paris: Organization for Economic Cooperation and Development.

United Nations Department of Economic and Social Affairs. 1975. *Towards a System of Social and Demographic Statistics*. New York: United Nations. Prepared by R. Stone.

APPENDIX 1
Wholistic Analysis, Problem Shifting Analysis, and Systems Economics

DON G. MILES

The essays by Johnson and Lawlor introduced the concepts of holism and reductionism. These concepts have figured prominently in controversies over the objectives and methods of research in the life sciences and in social sciences other than economics.

Few economists have paid much attention to such controversies or to the philosophy of scientific method in general. Glenn Johnson is an exception; he has been a serious student of the philosophy of science since the 1950s, and this has given direction to an immensely productive career in agricultural economics. Michael Lawlor shares in the current resurgence of interest in the history of economic theory; in its resurgent form, this field requires a high level of expertise in the philosophy of scientific method.

This appendix reflects the author's efforts during the mid-1970s and early 1980s to think through for himself, with the help of a limited amount of self-directed reading, the conceptual issues involved in interpreting and modeling complex socio-economic-ecologic systems. Much of this thinking was done before the author had decided to specialize in economics. His world view was not limited by practical considerations of course requirements, availability of data, or conformity to standards of scientific rigor in particular disciplines. To a considerable extent his thinking paralleled Boulding's, but unfortunately was not backed up by Boulding's enormous erudition and unmatched felicity of expression.

The first section of this appendix is a review of holistic thinking based on Phillips (1976) and other published sources. The second summarizes a broad conceptual framework originated by the author in the mid-1970s and called by him "wholistic analysis." The third describes a somewhat more limited framework also originated by the author in the 1970s and called "problem shifting analysis." The term _systems economics_ was coined by the author as a direct result of his research on the frameworks already mentioned.

HOLISTIC THINKING, A REVIEW

Holism is not new. A review of the literature reveals that at least seven holistic approaches exist to analyze, explain, or predict socioeconomic-ecologic problems and issues.

Perhaps the most famous is the whole organism approach. Phillips (1976) classifies this as Holism I and links it to Hegel's principle of internal relations--although Phillips also notes the organism approach may have been used in Roman times. Holism I is identified by five characteristic propositions:

a. That reductionist, physicochemical analytical approaches are inadequate when applied to a biological organism, to an economy, or to reality as a complex whole;

b. That parts cannot be completely understood if considered in isolation from the whole;

c. That parts are dynamically interrelated or interdependent;

d. That the whole affects the nature of its parts; and

e. That as Aristotle stated, "The whole is more than the sum of its parts." Holism I (including von Bertalanffy's general systems theory) maintains that if one only has knowledge of the parts, then at least some of the properties of organic wholes or systems cannot be predicted or explained (Phillips 1976, pp. 33, 34, 36).

Synthesis, as defined by Kant, i.e., the action of combining and unifying isolated data into a cognizable whole, and mathematical systems models such as Lange's (1965) differ from Holism I. Both synthesis and Langeian systems approaches maintain that if one adequately accounts for all the parts, including interaction, feedback loops, ramified inputs and outputs, transformations, changes over time, reactions, and structure, then the properties of wholes or systems can be predicted or explained. Furthermore, both synthesis and the Langeian approach avoid the problems of metaphysical finalism. As Lange noted, some holists impute to wholes some specific substantial factor or value (e.g., a soul, spirit, or vital force) which allegedly imparts to wholes some distinct properties (new qualities) and modes of action (laws of behavior) which influence the direction of development, usually towards wholeness, and which cannot be empirically tested. Thus both synthesis and Langeian methods differ from the holistic beliefs of von Bertalanffy (1968), Jung (see Hannah 1971, p. 2), Moulyn (1957, pp. 189-190), Smuts (1926/1973) in _Holism and Evolution_, and Teilhard de Chardin (1965).

What distinguishes synthesis from Langeian systems models is that synthesis, which is usually descriptive, does not really avoid the reductionist, mechanistic error of viewing a whole as entirely due to the properties of its parts. For example, as Phillips (1976) has also explained, "it is logically impossible to deduce or predict the production of a colorless, odorless, and tasteless liquid (i.e., H_2O) from premises that only refer to the properties of the gaseous elements of hydrogen and oxygen." But Langeian systems models, which are mathematical and explicit, can avoid the mechanistic error. By using a system or set of active components, a set or matrix of transformations which define the mode of action of the system, and a matrix of modes of action of components, Lange (1965) demonstrates that a system is endowed with a specific mode of action or law of behavior which is a feature of the system as a whole. This law of behavior depends not just on the mode of action of the individual components and the transformation of input and output states of the components but also on the network of couplings of components, i.e., on the explicit structure of the whole system.

Holism I, synthesis, and Langeian systems approaches can be distinguished from Holism II. According to Phillips (1976), Holism II maintains that the properties of organic wholes or systems, <u>after</u> they have been found, cannot be explained in terms of the properties of parts. Weiss's (1967) paper "1 + 1 ≠ 2" reportedly adds that the brain shifts between telescopic and microscopic vision and that increasing perspective (decreasing precision) reveals new, relevant, unexpected information about wholes not revealed by the detailed examination of their parts.

The implication of Holism II is that the analyst should start with some model of totality, a whole, or complete system and proceed to identify some generalizations, principles, or properties about the whole before examining the significance, nature, and limitations of smaller components or the linkages between greater and lesser (sub)systems. But the problem is, as William James once noted, that everything would have to be known before anything could be known or done. Furthermore, science has proven that a great deal of relevant and reliable information can be obtained by studying things in relative isolation or, as first introduced by Greniewski (1955), in relatively isolated systems. Thus what distinguishes Holism II from Holism I, synthesis, Langeian systems models, and Holism III is Holism II's difficult but clear belief that the analyst should start with or at least study the whole before attempting to explain the properties of the parts. In some ways, Holism II is similar to the biologist's examination of the species, then the individual, then its organs, a cell, the nucleus, and lastly DNA before offering any sweeping explanations or predictions about the nature and significance of DNA.

Phillips (1976, p. 35) only briefly identifies Holism III as concepts pertaining to field theory. This classification immediately includes the works of Lewin (1951), Smuts (1926/1973), Bews (1937), and probably some books on transactional analysis, human ecology, and ecology. At the bottom of page 1, Smuts (1973 reprinted edition) points out that "the concept of fields is absolutely necessary in order to get back to the fluid plastic facts of nature." Bews (1937) tries to make a stronger plea:

> Wisdom was honored (by the Greeks) above all specialized knowledge, and wisdom is not to be distinguished in its essence from the all-round holistic or practical ecological viewpoint. How then is wisdom to be acquired, or in other words, what are the methods of human ecology? (p. 9)
>
> The construction or synthesis which we must attempt is not merely an aggregation of facts so arranged that we know where to find each again if we want it. The main point is to seek each new fact in such a relationship to all other facts already collected that it will no longer ever be considered or even thought of by itself. (p. 43)
>
> It is man together with his environment that constitutes the whole. (p. 45)

Lewin (1951) described individual and small-group behavior in terms of field theory. However, apart from some emphasis and focusing on fields, Holism III becomes difficult to distinguish clearly from some other holistic approaches. Perhaps it is for this reason that Phillips also mentions the need for such holists to use additional terms like hierarchy and noosphere to describe wholes and their properties as being another characteristic of Holism III. But many holists have encountered this problem. Languages, including English, mathematics, sociology, and Indonesian, structure and compartmentalize reality in ways that make it necessary to invent concepts and words to describe what the "language" consciously or unconsciously either omits or doesn't value. Most holists are concerned with things, methods, processes, paradigms, structures, or (world) views which have traditionally been ignored.

Using Phillips's (1976) definition of Holism III, it is difficult to separate field theory from works such as Spedding 1979, Teilhard de Chardin 1965, Dewey 1938, and Bradley 1962 and works by holists who ascribe or impute a special substantial factor or value to the whole. Teilhard de Chardin's (1965) work, for example, does not satisfy both of Phillips's distinguishing characteristics of Holism III unless one assumes that a noosphere is also a field.

In order to resolve this confusion, it seems reasonable to identify Holism IV as those holistic approaches Lange (1965) described as metaphysical finalism. Thus Holism IV maintains that the end point or goal of development, evolution, or holism is wholeness. This new classification immediately includes Jung, who advocated giving up the hopeless search for perfection and replacing it with wholeness, and Smuts, whose central theme was that people evolve toward wholeness. The problem that Smuts's work (1926/1973) could be classified in both Holism II and IV does not really need to be resolved because several holists employ or advocate a variety of techniques and can be grouped on the basis of which combination(s) they use.

The development of holism has contributed to the development of systems thinking and vice versa. von Bertalanffy's General Systems Theory is a landmark work which has been classified as being almost synonymous with Holism I (or H_1). Both approaches are identifiable by the five characteristics of Holism I defined by Phillips (1976).

Similarly, O. Lange's Wholes and Parts is another example of holistic thinking (H_5). A native of Poland (born 1904), Lange had made brilliant contributions to economic theory during the late 1930s and early 1940s while on the faculties of the University of Michigan and the University of Chicago. He was well versed in neoclassical economic theory, general equilibrium theory, and welfare economics. Lange believed that these theories could be used effectively in a socialist state to avoid most of the economic distortions which might otherwise result from centralized planning. Back in Poland from 1945 until his death in 1965, Lange taught (and advised the Polish government on) the theory of resource allocation in a socialist economy and helped introduce new, largely Western developments in cybernetics, quantitative methods, and general systems theory while maintaining his commitment (which began in the 1920s) to the principles and objectives of socialism.

Thus of the seven holistic approaches listed below, at least five are of some relevance to systems economists and are starred accordingly:

- H_0 Synthesis, "building" cognizable descriptive wholes
- H_1* Holism I, the whole organism approach
- H_2* Holism II, wholes first
- H_3* Holism III, field theories
- H_4 Holism IV, metaphysical finalism
- H_5* Langeian systems approaches, mathematical totalities
- H_6 Holistic practices, including holistic medicine
- H_7* Wholistic analysis, relatively free of academic bias (to be discussed below)

Moreover, the development of systems theory (and modern biology) has helped structure holism. Some examples of systems thinking relevant to systems economists are presented in several chapters of this volume.

Wholistic analysis (H_7) can be distinguished from Holism I, II, and III, synthesis, Langeian systems models, and other holistic approaches by its development. It is a conceptual framework that was developed by the author to analyze, predict, explain, and integrate dimensions of the world food problem, agriculture, and human ecology. Though not unlike Boulding's work, it was independently thought through. Most of its development resulted from the author's spending nearly three years visiting 38 foreign countries, interacting with people from many different walks of life, doing self-directed research, and from creative thinking. This nontraditional foundation represented both a reason for interest in wholistic analysis and a professional weakness in the model.

Problem shifting analysis and systems economics (as the author conceived it) are byproducts of this development of wholistic analysis. Each consciously attempts to help make people better off and aware of the consequences of decisions within and beyond their control. Problem shifting analysis also defines a new private and social optimum based on the complexities, market imperfections, and nature of the modern world. Systems economics also attempts to establish a useful framework for understanding how and anticipating when world and national events affect the lives of individuals. Both problem shifting analysis and systems economics are empirically stronger models than wholistic analysis. Only systems economics has generated sufficient professional interest to enlist contributors in producing the present volume and to suggest a proposed university course on the subject.

The next two sections will summarize the author's conceptualizations of wholistic analysis (H_7) and problem shifting analysis.

WHOLISTIC ANALYSIS

No description of life is as whole or as complete as life itself. Words are a mere shadow of reality, often as limited as the visible in the known spectrum of light, as limited as the audible in the known range of sound, as limited as our perception and thinking. Even scientific information is only a partial description of what exists and is happening, and scientific measurement is only a partial measure of what occurs. Acts such as differentiating, identifying, naming, measuring, or analyzing do not separate the unit or part from the whole. Everything differentiated and measured remains part of the whole with innumerable relations to other parts and to the vast macro and micro universes in which every system is affected both by the workings of its own sub(systems) and by the greater system(s) of which it is just a division, component, or process. The whole is also greater than the sum of its identifiable parts.

Thus, in a world where even the most isolated consumer or food producer can be profoundly affected by some decision made in a distant national or international capital city (e.g., changing commodity prices, trade policy, war) and by the very workings of the solar system (e.g., seasons, day length, temperature, winds, rainfall), how should we partition the macro and micro universes? There are no final answers. All people are elements (of carbon, hydrogen, oxygen, nitrogen, sulphur, phosphorus, potassium, calcium, trace elements, vitamins, etc.) reorganized and reconstructed from the soil, the waters, the sun, plants, animals, and information into carbohydrates, proteins, hormones, enzymes, consciousness, needs, wants, norms, values, culture, civilization, and other accumulations (of materials, energy, income, and solutions to problems) over time and space. This living and soon-to-be-living populace can be seen as a living extension of the entire history of humankind and of the evolving environment as well as a major stock of transformed and reconstructed materials, energy, money, and information. Thus, inorganic elements disappear into organic life, things disappear into events, and events disappear into systems. It is as though the boundaries of each entity, each whole, reach unseen into distant dimensions of time, space, and existence.

Unfortunately this whole n-dimensional continuum of time, space, and existence cannot be adequately explained by a neat logical sequence of words. To begin with one component, information, we can see how this has grown and evolved throughout the entire history of humankind as an essential element of life. The few people who originally perceived, experienced, and survived by food gathering or hunting manifested such information simply by living. This information gave birth to the toolmakers, the herders, and the farmers. Many of these people, perhaps a few thousand, fed a growing populace with food, information, technologies, and ideas of management, organization, and urbanization. Others probably migrated and settled in new areas, developed new skills, and domesticated alternative plants and animals. Increasing interaction within and between groups via social organization, wars, plundering neighbors (for land, wealth, or power), industrialization, and/or trade probably increased information flow and conceptual horizons. Some ideas and achievements were no doubt lost, while others were valued and accumulated in cities, administrative, religious, and educational centers. Accumulated information did not get used up with use; it grew and could thus be described as an infinite resource. Old and new information influenced people, political decisions, management, development, innovation, philosophy, and science. It is most unlikely that such information was accumulated, analyzed, and embodied in a neat logical sequence. It grew as a living extension of change, the past, and the socioeconomic-ecologic environment since it was and is a prerequisite for successful living, learning, technology, management, business, and government.

Furthermore, there is an enormous fund or stock of information in the minds of peasants, employees, employers, and the elderly, which is largely untapped and neglected. Who knows what solutions to different present and future personal, national, or world problems live and die in the minds of even the less isolated individuals? These people can potentially affect the accumulation of solutions to trivial or important problems. The addition (or loss because of deaths) of important insights or solutions to problems can even influence the lives of future generations on distant continents. History is full of examples of individual and collective contributions to knowledge.

Other components of this whole n-dimensional continuum of time, space, and existence include matter, energy, and income.

These components, like information, can be seen as essential components of life. Although each embodies and exhibits characteristically different natural processes and structures, these four essential components of life are clearly interactive and interdependent. The extent of this interaction is described in the following paragraphs.

As the earth turns, sunlight, nutrients, water, and air are processed and transformed by plants, animals, and microorganisms. They are harvested (usually in accordance with the earth's seasons and the day's weather) by primary producers, often after the cultivation and husbandry needed to improve the transformation processes and to increase the diversion of nutrients, energy, information, and income to human purposes. This produce thus embodies effort, employment, experience, managerial expertise, innovativeness, capital, technology, raw materials, pesticides, herbicides, fertilizers, information, market awareness and farmer response, research, trials, demonstrations, education, institutional organization, laws and policies as well as utilized soil organic matter, soil moisture and elements, photosynthetic productivity, and seasonal and environmental conditions (including the weather, growing periods, and insect or weed competition which diverts these embodied components away from human purposes).

The amino acids, calories, vitamins, minerals, and the water content of foods also form information and take on qualities such as digestibility, flavor, nutritional adequacy, storage life, and price. As produce or food this is passed by trade, middlemen, distribution systems, and consumers for use or further transformations. Vast transactions are often determined by marginal changes in current or prospective prices, currency exchange rates, financial or political decisions, and by new information. Production, marketing, trade, distribution, consumption, utilization, and residuals mean that materials, money, energy, and information can flow across personal, farm, city, county, state, national, international, and historical borders. These flows link even the most isolated consumer or food producer with external environments, economies, cultures, other systems, and with one another. Furthermore, the embodied elements of food are, eventually and during the whole process outlined above, reprocessed in the biological and social environments. Thus today, humankind is a major living stock of transported and transformed materials, energy, income, and information. We are clearly a living extension of the entire history of humankind, of change and development, and of the environment. To put it another way, we are also some billions of years old.

If we accept this world view (as Boulding and others appear to have done years ago) and the selected details in this big picture, different sets of implications can be derived from it. The first generation of implications--spheric models and the presentation of complex hierarchic systems models in ordinary textbooks[1]--largely resulted from partitioning the vast macro and micro universes in a special way and recognizing the relationships between things, events, and systems; greater and lesser systems; and completely different kinds of systems, constraints, and possibilities. It was thus apparent that simplistic solutions would not solve complex socioeconomic-ecologic problems. It also became apparent that some trade-off existed between total knowledge and actually making repairs or improvements to a system. Thus, the simplest yet most explanatory and predictive way to partition internal dimensions of the macro and micro world was to use stocks and flows (and transformations) of materials, energy, income, and information to and from both greater and lesser systems or responsive wholes.

These concepts were also generalized by the author into two least changing fundamentals. It was these generalizations which held true as principles or rules that constituted the foundation of wholistic analysis. The wholistic framework was based on the author's so-called First Law of Human Ecology, which states that "there is no such being as an independent individual, no such invention as an isolated technology, no such thing as a single resource, and no such place as an independent nation-state" since each is linked by flows of materials, money, energy, and information and interacts with external phenomena, environments, or other systems. The analytic framework was based on the author's so-called Second Law of Human Ecology, which states that "humankind is an organized ecosystem of flows and stocks of transformed and reconstructed materials, energy, information, and income," where organized refers to social, economic, political, physical, biological, and ecological structures of systems. It should also be noted that the process of breaking up a whole (analysis) to find out its nature and significance can conceptually differentiate relatively independent entities, subsystems, processes, linkages, and unknowns. This analysis should be done after the whole has been examined in case it embodies properties which cannot be derived from the examination and summation of components. Thus, from an economist's perspective, wholistic analysis is little more than n-dimensional modeling.

PROBLEM SHIFTING ANALYSIS

The second generation of implications arose out of the reexamination of problem shifting and the third "law" of human ecology. Problem shifts had already been defined as "solutions which became problems" because the problem had been shifted out of someone's area, perception, value system, or frame of analytical reference. Also four broad forms of problem shifts had been identified, namely:

a. Problem shifts associated with changing states of transformation, e.g., resources are processed, production is consumed, residuals and externalities result.

b. Problem shifts across generations, i.e., associated with the passing of time, the accumulation and application of information.

c. Problem shifts across countries, systems, or sectors, i.e., associated with changes in location or place. DDT is a classic example; its use to solve local insect problems also resulted in its accumulation in food chains, in animals and people in distant lands as well as the problems of persistence, biomagnification, resistance, nontarget kills, secondary pests, reduced effectiveness, and pollution.

d. Problem shifts associated with partial solutions to complex problems, e.g., inadequate data, poor models, tunnel vision, and the inadequacy of some current thinking, practices, and solutions for solving complex socioeconomic-ecologic problems.

Thus, the author's so-called Third Law of Human Ecology predicts that "one generation's, community's, or culture's answers, solutions, or opportunities become other people's problems." Or, in general, that we shift problems rather than solve them.

This generalization that we shift problems rather than solve them is weaker than the first two laws of human ecology because (in general) there are commonly two outcomes or longer-term consequences of solutions. One outcome is that the problem is solved and that the answer represents an optimal solution to both the individual or individuals involved _and_ to the society or wider community as a whole. The second likely outcome is that the solution itself will become a problem for other people (in the same area, in different regions, and/or over time, more noticeably over generations). Unfortunately, this second outcome seems to be a better predictor of human behavior. On this assumption, it makes sense to attempt to maximize the beneficial shifts of materials, money, energy, and information and to efficiently minimize the undesirable and detrimental shifts.

The third generation of implications are considerations that affect education and/or extension programs. There are a large number of these implications, some specific and others very general. Except for a proposed university course on systems economics, they are presented elsewhere (see Miles 1983, "Wholistic Analysis, Problem Shifting Analysis, and Systems Economics") and are therefore not discussed here.

SYSTEMS ECONOMICS

The term _systems economics_ was coined by the author as a direct result of his earlier work on wholistic analysis and problem shifting analysis. Some tentative definitions and concepts developed as a starting point for systems economics were included in a letter to potential contributors to this volume in

1981. The author had received inspiration, stimulation, and/or guidance from the writings, teaching, and/or research supervision of most of the invitees and knew that much of their current work could, in his view, be classed as systems economics. Nearly all were enthusiastic about contributing to a volume of this title. Their conceptions of systems economics are embodied in _Systems Economics_.

Systems economics is formally listed and taught (for the first time in 1985) as a component in the final year undergraduate course Environmental Economics 401 at the Muresk Institute of Agriculture. Muresk is a branch of the Western Australian Institute of Technology.

NOTES

1. See "Wholistic Analysis, Problem Shifting Analysis, and Systems Economics" by Don G. Miles (1983). Copies available upon request from Don Miles, Lecturer, Muresk Institute of Agriculture, Western Australian Institute of Technology, Northam, 6401, Western Australia.

REFERENCES

Bews, J. W. 1937. _Life as a Whole_. London: Longmans Green & Co.

Bradley, F. H. 1962. _Appearance and Reality_. Oxford: Oxford University Press.

Dewey, J. 1938. _Democracy and Education: An Introduction to the Philosophy of Education_. New York: The Macmillan Co.

Greniewski, H. 1955. _Elements of the Logic of Induction_ (in Polish). Warsaw: Polish Scientific Publications. Reprinted in O. Lange, ed. 1965. _Wholes and Parts: A General Theory of System Behavior_. Oxford Pergamon Press.

Hannah, B. 1971. _Striving Towards Wholeness_. New York: G. P. Putnam's Sons.

Lange, O. 1965. _Wholes and Parts: A General Theory of System Behavior_. Oxford: Pergamon Press. (Translated from Polish by E. Lepa; first printed by Polish Scientific Publishers, Warszawa, 1965.)

Lewin, K. 1951. _Field Theory in Social Science: Selected Theoretical Papers_. New York: Harper and Row.

Moulyn, A. C. 1957. _Structure, Function, and Purpose: An Inquiry into the Concepts of Biology from the Viewpoint of Time_. New York: The Liberal Arts Press.

Phillips, D. C. 1976. _Holistic Thought in Social Science_. Stanford, CA: Stanford University Press.

Smuts, J. C. 1926/1973. _Holism and Evolution_. Reprint. Westport, CT: Greenwood Press.

Spedding, C. R. W. 1979. An Introduction to Agricultural Systems. Barking, England: Applied Science.

Teilhard de Chardin, P. 1965. The Phenomenon of Man. New York: Harper and Row.

von Bertalanffy, L. 1968. General Systems Theory. New York: George Braziller Inc.

Weiss, P. 1967. "1 + 1 ≠ 2 (One Plus One Does Not Equal Two)." In G. C. Quarton et al., eds., The Neurosciences: A Study Program. New York: Rockefeller University Press.

APPENDIX 2
Some Classic Examples of Systems Thinking in Several Sciences: Comments and Recommended Readings

KARL A. FOX

The papers in this volume imply a broad scope for systems economics. The systems it deals with may be worldwide in extent (Boulding, Miles). They may incorporate economic, social, biological, physical, ecological, and environmental components (Johnson, Miles, Boulding). They may include comprehensive economic and social systems at local, regional, or national levels (Fox, Prescott, Sengupta).

Systems economists should be able to conceptualize the economic aspects of any system and to identify their interfaces with aspects requiring the expertise of other disciplines. Systems economists should be able to communicate and cooperate with workers from other relevant disciplines in delineating all components of systems required to solve problems or to model specified subject matter domains (Johnson).

To do these things, systems economists will need broader knowledge than is usually acquired in formal course work, and they will need this knowledge at a mature level. Where classic works of broad scope exist, they should be ideal for this purpose.

In this chapter we discuss and recommend a number of books of this nature. One is a masterpiece in world economic and social history by Braudel. Two others--by Ibn Khaldun and Vico--are among the most original efforts ever made to explain the historical development of societies and cultures. Several relate to the revolutions in astronomy and physics associated with Copernicus, Kepler, Galileo, and Newton, each of whom, like Aristotle and Ptolemy before them, sought to discover "the true system of the world."

We also comment on several classics in the biological sciences: Greene's historical study of the development of evolutionary thought from Ray to Darwin, Lotka's _Elements of Mathemat-_

ical *Biology*, Wright's *Evolution and the Genetics of Populations*, and Wintrobe's edited volume on the history of research in hematology, *Blood, Pure and Eloquent*. Psychology and social psychology are represented by Kurt Lewin's works on topological and vector psychology and on field theory in social science. The chapter concludes with comments on E. A. J. Johnson's *The Organization of Space in Developing Countries* and Richard L. Meier's *Planning for an Urban World* and *Science and Economic Development*.

SOCIAL AND ECONOMIC HISTORY FROM 1400 TO 1800: FERNAND BRAUDEL

During the past four decades, economists and agricultural economists have been vitally concerned with problems of economic development. The economic development literature has been relatively self-contained and relatively isolated from the literatures of economic and social history. When economists apply themselves to development projects in a particular country, they may try to learn something about the very recent history of that country, but it would be desirable to have a broader perspective in both time and space.

Fernand Braudel's (1981, 1982, 1984) three-volume history of civilization and capitalism during the 15th through 18th centuries is a masterpiece of scholarship, writing, and illustration. It is in effect an economic and social history of the world from the Middle Ages to the Industrial Revolution. Braudel (born in 1902) achieved worldwide eminence in 1949 with publication of his book *The Mediterranean and the Mediterranean World in the Age of Philip II* (roughly, the 16th century). He began work on his Civilization and Capitalism series in 1952.

Braudel published a version of Volume I in 1967 and substantially revised it while preparing the complete three-volume set for publication (in French) in 1979. The English translations of Volumes I, II, and III were published in 1981, 1982, and 1984, respectively.

Braudel's is not a political history; there is no clutter of names, dates, treaties, battles, and maps of national boundaries. It is not simply an economic history; it is also a social history. It is not limited to a particular nation or region. It is centered on Europe to the extent that the development of capitalism and the initiatives which led to the organization of a world economy were centered there, but Braudel's perspective is always worldwide and there is no evidence of national or cultural bias.

Two examples of insights that may be obtained from Braudel are

1. The population of the world more than doubled (from about 350 million to about 1,000 million) between 1400 and 1800. This growth was not confined to Europe as many scholars once believed; the population of China more than doubled from 1680 to 1800 (from about 120 million to 300 million). All the countries

in the world were, in a sense, "colonizing themselves at that time, settling their empty or half-empty land" (Vol. I, p. 48). Braudel cites Rene Grousset to the effect that China's history during those centuries involved "the conquest of immense virgin country by a race of tillers who found only a poor semi-nomad population there before them" (Vol. I, p. 48). Grousset compares this aspect of China's history with that of Canada and the United States.

2. Per capita real incomes in Europe as of 1400 were probably no higher than those in China and India at that time.

Volume I, *The Structures of Everyday Life: The Limits of the Possible*, emphasizes the material aspects of daily life. Braudel deals with food and drink, dress, housing, energy, technology, demography and family structure, and the growth of towns--in different parts of the world and as affecting different social classes and village, town, and city populations. The illustrations, all from contemporary drawings, paintings, and other sources, are copious and magnificent. There are 169 of them in this volume of 623 pages, not counting 29 maps and graphs. The book is a visual as well as an intellectual experience.

In the illustrations for Volume I, we see people in the acts of consumption and household production--in the terminology of eco-behavioral science (Fox, Chapter 7 of this volume), we see them *behaving* in *behavior settings*, using their customary *behavior objects* in the *circumjacent milieus* of their homes. Most of the activities of "material life" in Braudel's sense during the 15th-18th centuries would be excluded from our conventional national income accounts; however, they must have occupied well over 90 percent of the living-times of the people involved.

In Volume II, *The Wheels of Commerce*, Braudel leaves the ground level of material life and explores the upper storeys, representing what he calls "economic life," before moving to the highest level of all, the action of capitalism (Vol. II, p. 21). He begins with towns and markets and explains the emergence and proliferation of *shops*--first those of artisans, who sold the work of their own hands, and later of "real" shops run by middlemen, who inserted themselves between producers and consumers. The contact surface between material life and economic life is not continuous but "takes the form of thousands of humble points of intersection: markets, stalls, shops. Each point marks a break: on one side is economic life with its commerce, its currencies, its nodal points and its superior equipment--great trading cities, Stock Exchanges, and fairs; on the other 'material life', the non-economy, imprisoned within self-sufficiency. The economy begins at the fateful threshold of 'exchange value'" (Vol. II, p. 21).

Hence, in Volume II Braudel tries to analyze "the machinery of exchange *as a whole*, from primitive barter up to and including the most sophisticated capitalism" (Vol. II, p. 21). Within that range, he distinguishes between a normal and often routine exchange economy characterized by something approaching free competition and an upper level of calculations, speculation, and restricted competition which he calls capitalism. Chapter 3 deals with "production: or capitalism away from home" and Chapter 4 with "capitalism on home ground." Chapter 5 discusses social hierarchies and the state (i.e., government) under the general rubric of "society: a set of sets." Once again, the illustrations are profuse--129 of them plus 29 maps and graphs.

Volume III, _The Perspective of the World_, contains 106 illustrations plus 58 maps and graphs. In it, Braudel organizes his history around several world-regions which were relatively self-contained economically during portions of the 1400-1800 period. Four chapters deal with Europe, the center of action in the development of capitalism. Chapter 5 (150 pages) covers other world-regions: the Americas, black Africa, Russia, the Turkish Empire, and the Far East. Chapter 6 deals with waves of industrial development in various regions and sectors prior to 1640 and continues with the so-called Industrial Revolution in England during the 18th century. In a concluding section (pp. 619-632) Braudel discusses the implications of his historical analysis for the subsequent development of capitalism and the world economy.

SYSTEMS THINKING ABOUT HUMAN SOCIETIES, I: IBN KHALDUN (1332-1406)

Communication between economists and other social scientists is not easy, but it is important that systems economists develop an ability to think in terms of complete societies and cultures. We are so completely immersed in our own society that we lack perspective and objectivity about it. We can gain some insights from the works of writers who acquired vast knowledge about particular societies and then achieved detachment through time, distance, and reflection.

Ibn Khaldun's _The Muqaddimah: An Introduction to History_ has been appraised by an English historian as "undoubtedly the greatest work of its kind that has ever yet been created by any mind in any time or place."[1] Ibn Khaldun was born in Tunis in 1332. The family name originated in South Arabia, and one of his ancestors had migrated to Spain in the early years of the Muslim conquest (in the 8th century). The Khaldun family played a dominant role in Seville from about 1050 to 1248, when Seville fell to the Christians and many Muslims fled to northwest Africa. Seville had been the political capital and cultural center of a regime that included much of northwest Africa; Ibn Khaldun's immediate ancestors enjoyed high prestige as government officials and scholars in Tunis.

Ibn Khaldun himself was a brilliant scholar and also politically ambitious. At age 20, he was given a court position in Tunis which did not involve executive or administrative functions but which kept him informed about all important government business and enabled him to act in an advisory capacity. At age 22, he joined the court of another ruler in Fez; after three years, suspecting Ibn Khaldun of intrigue, the ruler imprisoned him for nearly two years. That ruler was murdered and replaced by his brother, who gave Ibn Khaldun an important position (roughly equivalent to attorney general and chief justice of the supreme court). Ibn Khaldun had supported the brother but became completely disillusioned with his weakness, shortsightedness, and tyrannical behavior.

At age 30, Ibn Khaldun moved to Granada, the capital of Muslim Spain. Its young ruler, having delegated most of his responsibilities to an outstanding vizier, was interested in Ibn Khaldun's ideas and had a series of long private sessions with him. Ibn Khaldun had high hopes of educating the young man to become a philosopher-king, but the vizier became suspicious and virtually forced Ibn Khaldun to leave. Back in North Africa at age 33, another ruler put him in charge of the affairs of the city of Bijaya; within a year that ruler was overthrown by his cousin.

Ibn Khaldun had tried two approaches to fruitful political action and both had failed. In Granada he had tried to educate a ruler; in Bijaya he had tried to be an adviser to a tyrant and create an efficient state based on moderation--but without absolute control of power, that proved impossible. He had to admit to himself that he really did not understand the concrete social forces at work in the community he had tried to reform. During the next few years, Ibn Khaldun spent most of his time in research and teaching in Baskara and Fez. North Africa was in turmoil. He visited Granada again and found that the ruler who had been so receptive and forward-looking a decade earlier had become a cruel tyrant. He had arranged the murder of his outstanding vizier; when the ruler learned that Ibn Khaldun had sympathized with and tried to help the vizier, he ordered Ibn Khaldun to leave.

Ibn Khaldun finally managed to spend four years (1373-1377) in a secluded castle away from the centers of political activity. His intent was to write a history of contemporary western Islam (North Africa and Muslim Spain); he had known many of the principal figures personally, had studied official documents and archives in all the important cities, and knew all the major scholars who might conceivably address themselves to such a task. He concluded that he was the only person who could, and would, do it properly, but he discovered that he could not proceed with his history until he had solved some major philosophical and scientific problems.

Mahdi (1957/1964, pp. 48-50) puts it this way:

> His (Ibn Khaldun's) early training in the philosophic sciences had taught him that the understanding of a subject requires an investigation that progresses from the external

data, transmitted from the past or acquired through personal experience, to the explanatory and demonstrable knowledge of their cause and nature. This means that there is behind the external data an internal rational structure which, if understood, could explain the whys and wherefores and render the external data intelligible. Therefore, if history is to be truly understood, it must be subjected to the same enquiry as any other rational field of knowledge. The external data pertaining to it should be collected and classified; and then their causes and nature ascertained.

He found that the two aspects of history are intimately related: To understand the causes and nature of historical events, one must start from correct information; but in order to be able to rectify information about events and distinguish the correct from the false, one must know their nature and causes. In order to write an accurate history of contemporary western Islam, it was, therefore, necessary for Ibn Khaldun to know the internal aspect of history.

Ibn Khaldun found that no previous Islamic historians had possessed, or claimed to possess, such knowledge; for the most part they had simply transmitted information received from their informants. He found that other disciplines--politics, rhetoric, religious law--had touched on his problem only in an accidental fashion. He decided "that he himself would have to create a new science to deal specifically with this problem, and to define its principles, method, subject matter, and end . . ." (Mahdi, p. 49).

Ibn Khaldun spent the next two years thinking about his new science, which he later called the "science of culture." He decided that the new science, to be comprehensive, had to be based on data from the world as a whole and not simply from western Islam. In its final form, his great work consisted of three books: Book One containing the new science; Book Two, a universal history down to his own time; and Book Three, the history of western Islam.

We are concerned here only with Book One, which came to be known (and read) separately from the other two under the title of *Muqaddimah* ("introduction"). Thus, the complete English translation by Franz Rosenthal of Book One is entitled *The Muqaddimah: An Introduction to History*. Only a few excerpts from Book One were available in English prior to 1950, when Issawi translated a number of important passages. Rosenthal's is the first, and we believe the only, English version of Book One as a whole.

We suggest the following approach to Ibn Khaldun's "science of culture":

1. Read Chapters I, IV, and V of Muhsin Mahdi (1957/1964), *Ibn Khaldun's Philosophy of History: A Study in the Philosophic Foundation of the Science of Culture*. We have based our comments so far on Chapter I, "Historical background and fragments of a biography." Chapter IV deals with the subject matter and prob-

lems of the science of culture and Chapter V with its principles and method.

2. Read the translator's (Rosenthal's) introduction, especially pp. lxviii-lxxxvii, in Volume 1 of _The Muqaddimah_ (Ibn Khaldun 1377/1958).

3. Read the table of contents of _The Muqaddimah_, which occupies pp. v-xvii of Volume 1 but covers all three volumes of Rosenthal's translation.

4. Read Ibn Khaldun's own foreword, pp. 6-14.

The chapters of primary interest to systems economists are Chapter II: Bedouin civilization, savage nations and tribes and their conditions of life (Volume 1, pp. 247-310); Chapter III: On dynasties, royal authority, the caliphate, government ranks, and all that goes with these things (Volume 1, pp. 311-481 and Volume 2, pp. 1-231); Chapter IV: Countries and cities, and all other forms of sedentary civilization (Volume 2, pp. 233-307); and Chapter V: On the various aspects of making a living, such as profit and the crafts (Volume 2, pp. 309-407).

The states with which Ibn Khaldun was personally familiar were dynastic states in western Islam. In the 13th and 14th centuries, when such a state reached the peak of its power, its total population apparently ranged from 500,000 to 2,000,000 and that of its capital city from about 70,000 to 250,000. A considerable part of the total population was made up of nomads and settled agriculturists with strong tribal loyalties, _solidarities_ (Mahdi), or _group feelings_ (Rosenthal). When the ruling dynasty in the capital city began to slip, the recognized leader of the strongest tribe _not_ associated with the dynasty began to build up a coalition based largely on desert and rural people. These people were tough; they had grown up in small groups related by blood or marriage, and they had shared vicissitudes. Their face-to-face groups had been too small to achieve significant specialization and division of labor; hence, they had been able to produce only necessities. They wanted luxury and a soft life, their recognized leader wanted power, and they were jointly willing to fight for these objectives.

What happened when they succeeded in displacing the ruling dynasty? Ibn Khaldun's analysis is as follows (Volume 1, pp. 353-355):

> It should be known that a dynasty goes through different stages and encounters new conditions. Through the conditions that are peculiar to a particular stage, the supporters of the dynasty acquire in that stage traits of character such as do not exist in any other stage. Traits of character are the natural result of the peculiar situations in which they are found.
>
> The conditions and stages of a dynasty are as a rule no more than five in number.
>
> The first stage is that of success, the overthrow of

> all opposition, and the appropriation of royal authority from the preceding dynasty. In this stage, the ruler serves as a model to his people by the manner in which he acquires glory, collects taxes, defends property, and provides military protection. He does not claim anything exclusively for himself to the exclusion of his people, because such an attitude is what is required by group feeling, and it was group feeling that gave superiority to the dynasty. . . .
>
> The second stage is the one in which the ruler gains complete control over his people, claims royal authority all for himself, excluding them, and prevents them from trying to have a share in it. . . .
>
> The third stage is one of leisure and tranquillity in which the fruits of royal authority are enjoyed. . . . Throughout this and the previous stages, the rulers are independent in their opinions. They build up their strength and show the way for those after them.
>
> The fourth stage is one of contentment and peacefulness. . . . (The ruler) adopts the tradition of his predecessors . . . and imitates their ways most carefully. He thinks that to depart from tradition would mean the destruction of his power. . . .
>
> The fifth stage is one of waste and squandering. In this stage, the ruler wastes on pleasures and amusements the treasures accumulated by his ancestors, through excessive generosity to his inner circle and at their parties. Also, he acquires bad, low-class followers to whom he entrusts the most important matters of state. . . . In addition, the ruler seeks to destroy the great clients of his people and followers of his predecessors. Thus, they come to hate him and conspire to refuse support to him. . . . Thus, he ruins the foundations his ancestors had laid and tears down what they had built up. In this stage, the dynasty is seized by senility and the chronic disease from which it can hardly ever rid itself, for which it can find no cure, and, eventually, it is destroyed. . . .

Typically, these five stages would involve five different generations--perhaps 125 to 150 or more years. Ibn Khaldun is by no means simplistic or mechanistic in applying this model to particular cases. He describes the social and economic changes associated with various stages in such detail that it is tempting to think of representing them with mathematical models.

In Chapter VI (Volume 2, pp. 409-463, and Volume 3, pp. 3-481), which we do not particularly recommend, Ibn Khaldun describes the various sciences (i.e., branches of higher learning) that existed in his time, noting that these sciences and their practitioners, teachers, and students were numerous only in the largest cities. Ibn Khaldun spent the last 24 years of his life (1382-1406) in Cairo, at that time a city of 450,000 and the leading cultural center of the Islamic world. Cairo had the library resources he would need for his universal history (Book Two); he had collected most of the materials for his history of North Africa before moving to Cairo.

Ibn Khaldun states that he wrote the original version of Book One, now called The Muqaddimah, in a period of five months ending in November 1377! He revised and corrected it later, but the original version must rank among the more remarkable achievements in the history of scholarship.

SYSTEMS THINKING ABOUT HUMAN SOCIETIES, II: VICO (1668-1744)

Ibn Khaldun acquired his understanding of the dynastic states of North Africa through active participation and travel. His detachment came partly from the fact that his roots were in Muslim Spain, which had enjoyed a much higher level of culture and scholarship than North Africa before his ancestors were driven out of Seville, and partly because he had served several different dynasties. From about age 35 on, he was not psychologically committed to any ruler or state.

Vico never traveled far from his native Naples, the largest city in Italy during his lifetime (population 200,000 to 300,000). In his autobiography (Vico 1725/1944, p. 111), he says he grew up with "a melancholy and irritable temperament such as belongs to men of ingenuity and depth, who, thanks to the one, are quick as lightning in perception, and thanks to the other, take no pleasure in verbal cleverness or falsehood." He attributes his temperament to a fractured skull suffered at the age of 7, which left him unconscious for five hours and gave rise to a large tumor (presumably from internal bleeding) which required many deep lancings. The surgeon predicted Vico would either die or grow up an idiot.

Whether or not this trauma was the cause, Vico's temperament evidently limited him to a very low-salaried professorship. He became an intellectual "loner" and acquired further detachment by concentrating on the early history and prehistory of Greece, Rome, and other societies rather than on the contemporary scene. Before taking up his professorship at age 31, Vico had done an enormous amount of self-directed reading in many fields. He "blessed his good fortune in having no teacher whose words he had sworn by" (p. 133).

Fisch and Bergin regard Vico as the greatest of Italian philosophers. They describe his achievement as follows:

> Modern historiography . . . rests on the discovery of man as a peculiarly historical being, subject to a development transcending the life of any individual, nation or race. . . .
>
> Wherever the impact of this discovery is felt, the interest in history shifts from personal feats and exploits, wars, treaties, alliances, and dynastic successions, to customs, laws, institutions, forms of economic and social

> organization, languages, arts, religions, sciences, climates of opinion. . . . (History) has acquired an end of its own, which emancipates it from theology, morals, and politics. In pursuit of that end, it calls into being a corps of auxiliary disciplines: anthropology, genetic and social psychology, sociology, comparative mythology, comparative law, philosophy of history.
>
> So far as this discovery and the adumbration of these auxiliary disciplines can be ascribed to a single man or book, the man is Vico and the book is the *New Science*. (Vico 1725/1944, pp. 46-47)

Vico published successive editions of the *New Science* in 1725, 1730, and 1744. Its title was evidently inspired by Francis Bacon's *Novum Organum* and still more by Galileo's *Dialogues Concerning Two New Sciences*.

The accessibility of manuscripts relevant to the study of history had increased greatly during the 16th and 17th centuries, and one of the greatest advocates of the study of history, Leibniz, held that its chief purpose was "to teach prudence and virtue by examples, and to exhibit vice in such a way as to arouse aversion and lead to its avoidance" (Fisch and Bergin's Introduction to Vico 1725/1944, p. xxiii). As Galileo's "new sciences" of mechanics and physics gained momentum, Descartes and others came to believe that science must consist only of rational knowledge of the mathematical type and that the study of Greek, Latin, and history was a waste of time.

Vico (born in Naples in 1668) was repelled by both of these attitudes. In the 1600s, Latin was the international language of science and scholarship. Most if not all of his schooling had been conducted in Latin, and he had read virtually all the available works of Greek and Roman philosophers, scientists, poets, dramatists, and historians in their original languages. At age 31, he became a professor of Latin eloquence, preparing students for their advanced courses in the law school. In line of duty, Vico acquired a vast knowledge of Roman law and institutions and the etymologies of legal terms associated with property and the rights of persons of different social statuses.

When Vico was about 50, a very lucrative professorship in the law school became vacant. Vico tried to position himself for it by writing a treatise on *Universal Law*. In doing so, he greatly extended his knowledge of comparative law; the job went to another candidate who had better political connections, but Vico now had all the ideas he needed for the first edition of his *New Science*.

Vico concluded that the extant histories of Greece prior to the Peloponnesian War (430 B.C.) and of Rome prior to the Second Punic War (218 B.C.) dissolved into fables and fragments. In each case, he identified two earlier stages, which he called a *divine age* (reflected in fables of the gods) and a *heroic age* (reflected in myths of the heroes--Hercules, Achilles, and so on).

The divine age in Vico's system dates from perhaps 2000 B.C.[2] It is "divine" in that people are not able to think in terms of cause and effect but attribute all events to gods (one scholar claimed to have found references in Greek and Roman fables to some 30,000 different supernatural beings). Authority resides in the fathers of families. Speech is "poetic"; writing is unknown, but pictures (hieroglyphs) may be used to represent objects or words. Territorial units are small, and strangers are regarded as enemies.

The heroic age grows out of the divine age as the family-fathers band together to keep their dependents (slaves, serfs) in subjection. In Rome, the two groups are called _patricians_ and _plebeians_. In Greece, the "heroes" are members of the dominant class; speech and poetry reflect their values, exploits, and ideals. There are no written laws; arguments between heroes are settled by personal combat (duels). Heroic poetry consists of epics that are composed orally and transmitted orally by illiterate bards or rhapsodes.

The third or _human age_ grows out of the age of heroes as the common people demand certain rights previously withheld from them and reserved to the patricians. The common people (plebeians) demand written laws, which are to be interpreted mildly with attention to equity and special circumstances rather than literally and vindictively. Speech and writing become rational and prosaic (or matter-of-fact); events are understood in terms of cause and effect. Vico does not give calendar dates for the beginning of the human age, but our guess is that Greece would have qualified in about 600 B.C. and Rome perhaps two centuries later.

In addition to describing the evolution of civil or political society in terms of these three stages, Vico asserts that other major aspects of culture evolve with them. According to Fisch and Bergin (Vico 1725/1944, pp. 58-59), Vico finds

> three kinds of "natures" (ways of apprehending the nature of the world and of man)--animistic, mythopoeic, scientific; three kinds of customs--religious, punctilious, humane; three kinds of natural (i.e., customary) law; three kinds of language expressed in three kinds of characters; three kinds of jurisprudence employing three kinds of authority and as many of "reasons"--divination, reason of state, natural equity--in as many of judgments.

The leading humanistic scholars of the 17th century showed no awareness that the writings of ancient poets and philosophers were conditioned by the particular cultures in which they lived and worked or that cultures evolved and changed. They believed that Homer was not only a great epic poet but also a great philosopher on a par with Plato and Aristotle. Vico asserted that it was not possible for an epic poet to think like a philosopher; in fact, it was not possible for _anyone_ to think like a philosopher in the societies reflected in Homer's epics, the _Iliad_ and the _Odyssey_.

The epics describe events which ostensibly took place during the Trojan War (the _Iliad_) or during the return of Ulysses from that war (the _Odyssey_); hence, both epics should reflect the same attitudes, customs, and modes of thought existing in a 20-year period around 1200 B.C. Vico (1744/1968, p. 325) concluded that the epics reflected drastically different customs and attitudes and that "the Homer who was the author of the _Iliad_ preceded by many centuries the Homer who was the author of the _Odyssey_." Moreover, the Homer of the _Iliad_ came from the northeastern part of Greece (not far from Troy) and the Homer of the _Odyssey_ from the southwestern part (which included Ulysses' kingdom).

Further, Vico found that both epics contained episodes and passages in different dialects or local idioms; passages varied in terms of their more or less strict adherence to meter, the crudity of their comparisons, the vulgarity of the customs described, and the brutality of the attitudes assumed. He concluded that both epics in their complete forms, as finally written down in the 6th century B.C., were the cumulative products of many generations of oral (and illiterate) poets or rhapsodes from many different localities, each poet contributing improvisations of his own. Moreover, he emphasized and retained those materials which were most pleasing to the audiences of his own time and place; he sang or recited what they wanted to hear. In this sense, Vico concluded that "the true Homer" was the people of Greece over a period of several centuries!

The two epics

> should henceforth be highly prized as being two great treasure stores of the customs of early Greece . . . the Homeric poems, having been regarded as works thrown off by a particular man, a rare and consummate poet, have hitherto concealed from us the history of the natural law (culture) of the gentes (peoples) of Greece. (Vico 1744/1968, p. 328)

Vico regarded this (at the time) mind-blowing discovery as an illustration of the explanatory power of his "new science." For theological reasons, Vico said that his science did not apply to the Hebrews, but he thought it did apply to all other peoples--the "gentile" nations. He believed that each of these peoples had gone through the same three stages (though not necessarily at the same times) as the result of the same endogenous social, institutional, and psychological forces. Other scholars assumed that the first written laws of the Romans (the Twelve Tables, about 450 B.C.) were borrowed from Athens; Vico proved that these laws were developed completely independently in response to specifically Roman conditions. An ancient writer had observed that some 40 different peoples (independent city-states or small kingdoms) each had their own Jove and their own Hercules--under a variety of different names and referring (in Vico's view) to endogenous legendary figures. Thus, Vico had a conceptual model which he thought would be found to apply to all the gentile peoples--a sort of "ideal eternal history."

Vico was a devout Catholic and his objective was to elevate history to the status of a true science. In fact, he believed history could achieve a higher standard than the natural sciences. Since social institutions had been created by men, they could be understood by men; but nature had been created by God and hence, in an ultimate sense, could only be understood by God. To understand institutions, it was essential to go back to their very beginnings to see how and why men created them. The institutions men created in one generation shaped the attitudes and customs of their children in the next.

Marx was enthusiastic about Vico's contribution. However, Marx separated primary activities (production) from secondary activities which conformed themselves to the mode of production--something Vico had not done or thought of. Vico sought to revolutionize the _study_ of history and, by implication, all future sciences concerned with the _study_ of social and cultural change; he had no desire to change history itself.

We suggest the following sequence of readings by and about Vico:

1. Vico (1725/1944), _The Autobiography of Giambattista Vico_, translated by Fisch and Bergin. Read especially pp. 8-14 and 20-60 of the translators' introduction.

2. Vico (1744/1968), _The New Science of Giambattista Vico_, translated by Bergin and Fisch. Read especially the translators' introduction, pp. xix-xlv; in the text, pp. 3-26, 60-68; the topic sentences in the sections numbered XXIII through CXIV on pp. 68-95; Book Three, Discovery of the True Homer, pp. 301-328; Book Four, The Course the Nations Run, pp. 335-393; and Book Five, The Recourse of Human Institutions Which the Nations Take When They Rise Again, pp. 397-415.

In addition, Leon Pompa's (1975) book, _Vico: A Study of the 'New Science,'_ may be scanned. Pompa emphasizes the philosophical theories in Vico's text. Pompa's chapter headings include the structure of the _Scienza Nuova_; critique of current historiography; human nature and social change; human nature and historical change; providence; the character of Vico's metaphysics; the problem of knowledge; the problem of methodology; the ideal eternal history: (1) its theoretical character, (2) its deductive character, (3) its sociological content, (4) its historical content; philosophy and historical interpretation;

philosophy and historical confirmation; theory of knowledge; and the character of Vico's theory of knowledge.

SYSTEMS THINKING IN ASTRONOMY AND PHYSICS: ARISTOTLE, PTOLEMY, COPERNICUS, KEPLER, GALILEO, AND NEWTON ON "THE SYSTEM OF THE WORLD"

There is a story about a 20-year university alumnus who happened to drop in on his old professor during test week and was shown the final exam. "Why, those are the same questions you asked us 20 years ago!" "Yes, but the answers have changed."

In the present case, the questions remained the same for 2000 years. The orthodox answers prevailed over scattered opposition for nearly 1900 of those years but were then succeeded by four new ones within a century and a half! As a problem in mathematical astronomy, "the system of the world" consisted of only eight moving parts, did not change, and was plainly visible to the naked eye. (The moving parts included the sun, the moon, five planets, and the fixed stars regarded as a unit.) The earth was assumed to be motionless. Aristarchus offered an alternative solution to the astronomical problem within 50 years after Aristotle's death but was laughed down by contemporary physicists. The physicists were wrong, but they didn't know it; and they were impressively unanimous.

Copernicus put forward the same basic solution in 1543; this time the physicists were reinforced by the theologians. A further breakthrough in mathematical astronomy was achieved by Kepler, but it was not convincing until Galileo made an independent breakthrough in experimental and theoretical physics. Newton was then able to show that Kepler's proposed solution to the astronomical problem was perfectly consistent with Galileo's (and his own) newly discovered laws of physics.

The system of the world is a fairly simple problem in systems analysis in that only two disciplines are involved. It offers a useful introduction to more complex problems whose "solutions" may change in response to new discoveries in any of several sciences.

As might be expected from Vico's demonstrations, the systematic development of Greek philosophy, science, and mathematics began sometime after 600 B.C. and reached a high point with Aristotle around 360-320 B.C. Further developments in Greek science and mathematics occurred during the next five centuries (many of them in the Hellenistic city of Alexandria), but Aristotle's masterful synthesis of the knowledge accumulated down to his time became the basis for most scientific instruction in European universities from 1300 to 1600 or later.

One of the great problems of philosophy was the origin and mode of operation of the system of the world--the earth, sun, moon, planets, and fixed stars. Aristotle concluded that the fixed stars were embedded in a crystalline spherical shell and that each of the five planets then known (Mercury, Venus, Mars,

Jupiter, and Saturn), the sun, and the moon was embedded in a similar shell--eight concentric shells in all. These shells were in contact with each other; a ninth shell outside of and touching the sphere of the fixed stars was the "prime mover," and its motion was transmitted by friction to the other shells.

The earth was a sphere (tiny in relation to the system as a whole) located at the exact center of the universe. It was natural for heavy bodies or elements to move as nearly as possible to the center of the universe, so "earth" in the generic sense--rocks, dirt, other solids--would come together as a sphere. The next heavier element, water, would overlie the solids; the third, air, would overlie earth and water; the fourth, fire, was even lighter than air. It was natural for fire and air to move "upward" from the surface of the earth in all directions and for solids and water to move "downward"--toward the center of the universe, which was also the center of the earth.

Thus, linear motion (up or down) was natural to the four elements found on earth and circular motion was natural to the heavenly bodies. Aristotle further believed that the heavenly bodies were formed of a kind of matter not found on earth and that the crystalline spheres consisted of an exceedingly light element, aether, which was nevertheless strong and impenetrable. The heavens were unchanging and incorruptible; change and corruption were confined to the earth, sometimes called "the sublunary sphere."

This system was rational and logical--a tremendous advance over the origin myths of Vico's first two stages. Moreover, it was, and is, extremely useful for navigation and surveying. Kuhn (1957/1959, p. 38) says that most handbooks of navigation or surveying open with some sentence like this: "For present purposes we shall assume that the earth is a small stationary sphere whose center coincides with that of a much larger rotating stellar sphere"--i.e., the shell containing the fixed stars. The essential features of this two-sphere model can be committed to memory once and for all. The model has great conceptual economy; it summarizes an enormous amount of observational material and must be regarded as a most successful theory.

It was the inner shells that caused problems. The solar year was not an integral number of days, so the calendar kept getting out of whack. Adding a "leap day" every fourth year helped, but even that was inexact. The lunar year didn't agree exactly with the solar year. Eclipses of the sun and moon were regarded by many as omens or portents--disconcerting if unexpected. Rulers and generals became much interested in the ability of astronomers to predict such events accurately. The planets also were believed by some to carry divine messages by their (apparent) close approaches to one another "in" (i.e., against the background of) particular constellations.

The Hellenistic astronomers worked out separate models for forecasting future positions of each of the seven heavenly bodies, subject to two assumptions: (1) the earth was at the center of the universe and (2) circular motion was natural for heavenly bodies. None of the orbits could be described by a single circle centered on the earth. A much better approximation could be obtained by combining *two* circular motions: a *deferent*, centered on the earth, and an *epicycle*. The center of the epicycle moved along the deferent; the planet (or sun or moon) occupied a position on the circumference of the epicycle, which revolved in such a way that the planet was sometimes inside and sometimes outside the deferent. The sizes of the two circles and their relative rates of movement were adjusted until the predicted path of the planet agreed as closely as possible with its observed path.

Alternative models assumed that the center of the deferent was displaced to some distance from the earth and/or that the center of the deferent moved in a circular orbit around the earth. Still another adjustment, called an equant, required that the rate of rotation of the deferent be uniform not with respect to its own geometric center but with respect to a point (an *equant* point) displaced from that center.

Four centuries of research by Hellenistic astronomers in this tradition were summarized in Ptolemy's *Almagest*, written in the 2nd century A.D. (An excellent English translation has been published by Toomer in 1984.) The *Almagest* displaced nearly all earlier works; as with obsolete textbooks today, there was no longer a market for those works so the existing copies decayed and no new ones were made. Ptolemy's work was translated into Arabic in the 9th century and into Latin in the 12th; it was *the* book on astronomy into the 1500s and was not completely superseded until the middle or late 1600s.

The method of least squares was not known in Ptolemy's time, but our guess is that each of his calculated orbits would have explained at least 99 percent of the variance in his observed data. As time went on, his models predicted less accurately.

Copernicus (1543/1976) objected to Ptolemy's system on aesthetic grounds. He found it more reasonable to assume a daily rotation of the earth, the stars remaining fixed, than to assume a daily rotation of the heavens (implying fantastic velocities) about a stationary earth. Copernicus also concluded that the movements of the sun, moon, and planets relative to the earth could be explained much more simply by placing the sun in the center of the universe and assuming that the earth and the planets moved in circular orbits around the sun. *However*, a system of perfect circles centered on the sun did *not* fit the observed data, or predict, nearly as well as did Ptolemy's more complex (and unaesthetic) models, so Copernicus ended up keeping most of Ptolemy's eccentrics and epicycles. His complete system was nearly as cumbersome as Ptolemy's and equally accurate, but not more so.

Tycho Brahe (1546-1601) did not agree with either Copernicus or Ptolemy. In 1563 he observed a conjunction, or overlapping, of Jupiter and Saturn and found that tables based on Copernicus were several days off in predicting this event. During the next 35 years he made the most accurate, continuous, and sustained astronomical observations that were physically possible before the invention of the telescope. His pupil and assistant in Brahe's later years, Johannes Kepler, inherited Brahe's data.

Kepler (1571-1630) accepted the Copernican system, but for a long time he clung to the view that the planets, being perfect like all other heavenly bodies, could only move in circular orbits. He tried to fit the orbit of Mars to Brahe's data, using every combination of circles his ingenuity could devise. But his best model missed some of Brahe's observations by 10 minutes of arc (one-sixth of a degree), and he knew Brahe was accurate to within 4 minutes. At that point, it struck him that Copernicus had treated the earth like a planet with respect to its orbiting around the sun. The earth was imperfect and therefore need not be limited to circular motion. If the planets were like the earth, and therefore imperfect, they too might move to other-than-circular orbits.

Kepler tried various noncircular paths until he found the true solution: the orbit of Mars was an ellipse with the sun occupying one of the two focuses. The orbits of the other planets and the earth also proved to be elliptical, as did the orbit of the moon around the earth. By 1619 he had formulated three laws of planetary motion that applied to all of these bodies: the uniformity of circular motion was replaced by other principles of uniformity, but the "lawfulness" and uniformity of the solar system was preserved. Kepler also tried to deal with the next question, Why do planets move in elipical orbits? but Newton was the first to arrive at a satisfactory answer.

Galileo (1564-1642) was the first to study the skies with a telescope (in 1609). He identified mountains and craters on the moon, demonstrating that it, like the earth, was not a perfect, polished sphere. He observed spots on the sun (imperfections), and their motion implied that the sun rotated on its axis, as did the Copernican earth. He observed at least four of the moons of Jupiter, their movements suggesting a solar system in minature. He showed that Venus had phases, which could only be explained by assuming it revolves about the sun.

Galileo accepted the Copernican system but got into big trouble for supporting and disseminating it. His studies of motion on or near the earth's surface (the motions of projectiles, pendulums, falling bodies, bodies rolling down inclined planes) caused him less trouble with the religious authorities and also contributed to Newton's grand synthesis in 1686. Galileo was the first scientist to clearly grasp the concept of force as a mechanical agent.

Newton (1642-1727) concluded that the moon was sustained in its orbit by two offsetting forces. One of these would cause the moon to fly off in a straight line tangent to its orbit and perpendicular to a line drawn from the center of the earth. The other force would cause the moon to fall toward the earth along the line just described. It seemed plausible that a given force radiating from the earth to the inner surface of a spherical shell with area $4\pi r^2$ would impinge on any square foot (say) of its area in proportion to $1/r^2$--the "inverse square" of its distance from the center of the earth. On this assumption, Newton calculated that the force causing the moon to "fall" toward the earth was of the same kind Galileo had identified in his experiments with falling bodies and projectiles at the earth's surface.

With his principle of universal gravitation and his laws of motion, Newton accounted simultaneously for the motions of the earth, moon, and planets and the motions of ordinary objects on the earth. Some minor deviations from Kepler's elliptical orbits could now be explained by such considerations as the following:

1. The moon does not merely orbit around the earth (since the earth attracts the moon); the moon also attracts the earth, so the two-body system rotates about the center of gravity of the system, some distance from the earth's center.
2. Similarly, all other bodies in the solar system exert gravitational forces on the sun, so the actual location of the sun's center in space should deviate somewhat from its average or expected location.
3. Planets exert attractions on each other, which also cause some minor irregularities in their orbits.

From a predictive standpoint, Newton's gravitational model worked impressively. In 1845-1846 two astronomers independently noted minor irregularities in the orbit of Uranus (a "new" planet discovered by telescope in 1781); they computed the implied position of a suspected additional new planet (Neptune) and found it within one degree of the computed position.

However, Newton himself was quite uncomfortable with the concept of gravity. What was it? How did it operate? How is it possible for one body to act on (move, displace) another body millions of miles away? Einstein offered an alternative explanation of such apparent actions in the early 1900s, but this takes us beyond our intended story.

On the surface, the system of the world is a very simple one. It consists of eight spherical bodies, each of which traces out a smooth, continuous path in space, and some fixed stars which form a spherical map against which the apparent motions of seven of the bodies are viewed from the eighth.

We can only speculate as to how long it might have taken mathematicians to arrive at Kepler's solution if they had been psychologically free to consider all types of closed curves to represent the conjectured motion of each of the eight bodies. Apollonius of Perga (262-190 B.C.) wrote a great treatise on conic sections and introduced the terms parabola, ellipse, and hyperbola. Archimedes (287-212 B.C.), the most talented mathematician of antiquity, also wrote a treatise on the solids generated by the revolutions of circles, ellipses, parabolas, and hyperbolas about their axes. Several generations of Hellenistic mathematicians and astronomers down to and including Ptolemy were familiar with these works.

Further, Aristarchus of Samos (fl. 270 B.C.) maintained (as did Copernicus 1800 years later) that the earth rotates on its axis and revolves around the sun. Eratosthenes (276-194 B.C.) made an estimate of the circumference of the earth that was somewhere between 83 and 100 percent of its true value. Aristarchus estimated the distance of the moon at about 2/3 and its diameter at 4/3 of the true values, and he estimated the sun's distance at 19 times that of the moon. These first generation estimates could certainly have been improved if they had been given high priority on the Hellenistic research agenda.

Cleanthes, leader of the Stoic school of philosophy from about 260 to 230 B.C. and a zealously religious man, may have expressed a widely held attitude when he declared that Aristarchus should be indicted for impiety. Physicists may have rejected Aristarchus's theory out of hand because the assumed daily rotation of the earth posed a problem in physics: if the earth under their feet were revolving eastward at nearly a thousand miles per hour, objects tossed vertically into the air should land far to the west of them and/or everything movable should be swept to the westward by a tremendous wind. These things didn't happen; therefore the earth did not rotate. If it did not rotate, it could not revolve around the sun because people on the side facing the sun would fry and those on the dark side of the earth would freeze. At any rate, Apollonius, the greatest authority of his time on ellipses, was the person who introduced the systems of epicycles and eccentrics to explain planetary motion with combinations of circles.

There are many constraints on a scientist's ability to see "the whole truth." Kepler lost a great deal of time because he assumed that a planet's path had to be a perfect circle, "as it was taught on the authority of all philosophers, and consistent in itself with Metaphysics" (cited by Hall, 1966, p. 124). The Ptolemaic universe was gradually invested with religious significance. As part of the Aristotelian world view, the Ptolemaic system became part of the intellectual capital and teaching repertoire of a great many university professors in 16th century Europe. Galileo's ideas threatened the prestige and even the livelihoods of such professors, and they resented him on those grounds--though it seemed more dignified and expedient to charge him with heresy.

Personal rivalries between scientists also delayed the acceptance and dissemination of new discoveries. Newton was almost psychotically concerned about priority and leveled charges of plagiarism against Hooke and Leibniz, whose discoveries were clearly independent of his own. Matters of intellectual style also created delays and frictions: Descartes wanted to derive everything from first principles and dismissed Galileo's experimental work as mere empiricism.

We suggest the following readings in this area:

1. Kuhn (1957/1959), The Copernican Revolution: Planetary Astronomy in the Development of Western Thought.

2. Toomer's translation of Ptolemy's Almagest (Ptolemy 2nd cent./1984), pp. 35-47; also scan some of the many excellent diagrams in table-of-contents sections referring to epicycles and/or eccentricities of the orbits of moon, sun, and planets.

3. Galileo (1632/1953), Dialogue on the Great World Systems, in the Salusbury translation revised, annotated, and with an introduction by Giorgio de Santillana; read especially the historical introduction, pp. xi-li; the dedication, pp. 3-4; the author's preface, 5-8; the summaries on pp. 11, 118, 290; and "an astronomical note on the two systems," pp. 475-496; scan portions of the text.

4. Galileo (1638/1933), Dialogues Concerning Two New Sciences, translated by Crew and DeSalvio; scan pp. 153- 294; "the second new science, treating of motion": uniform motion, pp. 154-159; naturally accelerated motion, pp. 160-243; and the motion of projectiles, pp. 244-294.

5. Newton (1731/1969), A Treatise of the System of the World, 2nd edition, with an introduction by Cohen; read the table of contents and the preface and scan the text (about 150 small pages).

6. Newton (1687/1934), Mathematical Principles of Natural Philosophy, translated by Motte in 1729, revised by Cajori; read the table of contents; scan the italicized statements of laws or axioms, corollaries, etc., in the text: Book I, the motion of bodies; Book II, the motion of bodies in resisting mediums; and Book III, the system of the world in mathematical treatment.

SYSTEMS THINKING IN THE BIOLOGICAL SCIENCES: GREENE (ON DARWIN AND HIS PREDECESSORS), LOTKA, WRIGHT, AND WINTROBE

John C. Greene on the Development of the Evolutionary View of Nature from Ray to Darwin

John C. Greene's 1959 book, The Death of Adam: Evolution and Its Impact on Western Thought, is a fascinating history of the rise of evolutionary views of nature and the decline of static creationism during the two centuries from Newton to Darwin. Greene, like Vico, illustrates the interweaving of many branches of human thought. The various sciences could not develop independently within neat disciplinary boundaries. Fossils presented mind-blowing problems for geologists *and* biologists; biblical chronology was first breached by the former. Physical anthropologists tried to explain the origins of different human groups; comparative anatomists puzzled over the similarities and differences among apes and men. The distribution of species, genera, and families among continents raised questions of "separate creation" in different parts of the world and of the emergence and subsidence of land bridges between continents and large islands. Darwin's synthesis was an effort to reconcile the findings of all the relevant disciplines in so far as they bore on the origins of species.

A very recent book by John Greene (1984), American Science in the Age of Jefferson, surveys the activities in nearly all branches of science in the United States from about 1780 until the 1820s.

Alfred J. Lotka on the Elements of Mathematical Biology

Alfred J. Lotka (1880-1949) published his classic Elements of Physical Biology in 1925. It was reissued in 1956 as Elements of Mathematical Biology. We believe economists and agricultural economists will find it surprisingly modern, surprisingly comprehensive, and surprisingly mathematical.

Part I, General Principles, defines evolution as "the history of a system in the course of irreversible transformation." It discusses the statistical meaning of irreversibility; evolution considered as a redistribution, among the components of a system, of the material of which the system is built up; and the program of physical biology.

Part II, Kinetics, presents the fundamental equations of kinetics of evolving systems in the general case and in the special cases of one, two, and three dependent variables; it also includes two chapters on analysis of the growth function.

Part III, Statics, presents general principles of equilibrium, chemical equilibrium as an example of evolution under a known law, discusses interspecies equilibrium in general and for aquatic life, and describes "the stages of the life drama" involving the atmosphere, the ocean, and the upper 10 miles or so of the earth's crust. Several chapters describe the circulation of the elements within this global system: the water cycle, the carbon dioxide cycle, the nitrogen cycle, and the phosphorous cycle. Other chapters deal with moving equilibria, displacement of equilibrium, and the parameters of state.

Part IV, Dynamics, deals with the energy transformers of nature, the relation of the transformer to available sources, the correlating apparatus, the adjustors, consciousness, the function of consciousness in the living organism, energy relations of consciousness, and review of the correlating apparatus. There is a final chapter of conclusions (retrospect and prospect) and a synoptic chart of physical biology.

Lotka was an unusually versatile and original scientist. Spengler (1968, p. 475) says that Lotka

> anticipated many of the ideas of cybernetics and did original work in demography, evolutionary processes, and self-renewing aggregates. Born in Austria of American

> parentage, he spent his boyhood in France, and acquired his advanced education in England, Germany, and the United States. He was employed as a chemist, physicist, mathematician, and biologist until 1924, when he joined the Metropolitan Life Insurance Company. . . . He held the office of president of the Populatlon Association of America and of the American Statistical Association and several posts in the International Union for the Scientific Study of Population. . . .
>
> Probably most representative of Lotka's thought is Elements of Physical Biology (1925). Appearing when few social scientists used mathematics, it informed some of them of the uses of differential equations, the mechanics of systems and subsystems and the uses of systemic theory, and an essentially cybernetic view of organismic behavior (Simon 1959, p. 494). Even today it contributes to the study of statics and dynamics.

Sewall Wright on Evolution and the Genetics of Populations

Sewall Wright's Evolution and the Genetics of Populations (four volumes: 1968, 1969, 1977, 1978) is among the most impressive works ever written by a single scientist.

Born in 1889, Wright became one of the "Big Three" of population genetics, along with R. A. Fisher (1890-1962) and J. B. S. Haldane (1892-1964). Wright published his first scientific paper in 1912. The fourth volume of his great treatise was published in 1978, and he has continued active well into his nineties.

Gregor Mendel (1822-1884) discovered the simple rules of heredity in his experiments with garden peas and reported on them in his landmark article, "Experiments with Plant Hybrids," in 1866. Unfortunately, his article was overlooked until 1900, when his principles were rediscovered independently by three different botanists, de Vries, Correns, and Tschermak, who also rediscovered his paper. It was immediately recognized that Mendelian heredity was a phenomenon that should throw new light on the theory of evolution.

Wright (1968, Volume 1, p. 10) says that

> About a decade before the rediscovery of Mendel's principles of heredity came the initiation of the statistical study of resemblances among related individuals by Galton (1889) and later by Karl Pearson (1894). The viewpoint of this "biometric" school came into violent conflict with that of Mendelian genetics after the rediscovery of Mendelian heredity in 1900. Population genetics arose from the attempts to reconcile these viewpoints.

Volume 1 deals with genetic and biometric foundations, Volume 2 with the theory of gene frequencies, Volume 3 with experimental results and evolutionary deductions, and Volume 4 with variability within and among natural populations.

A special feature of Volume 1 is an exposition of the theory of path analysis and the interpretation of path analysis models. This method was developed by Wright during 1918-1921 and became the method of choice for estimating sociometric models in the mid-1960s. Wright's treatment of the problems of causal ordering and identification anticipated the simultaneous equations approach of Haavelmo and others by more than 20 years; it influenced the work of Fox from 1941 on and was enthusiastically advocated by Goldberger in the early 1970s.

Volume 2 includes such topics as inbreeding, effective size of population, simultaneous inbreeding and recombination, inbreeding and selection, assortative mating, and population structure. Volume 3 discusses the course of directional selection, artificial selection, natural selection in the laboratory, mutation and selection; also, theories of evolution based on mutation and mass selection, shifting balance theories of evolution, genetic load and genetic variability, and the evolution of dominance.

Volume 4 is exclusively concerned with natural populations. Topics include species and subspecies, effective sizes of local populations, genetic variability in natural populations: methods, chromosome polymorphisms, deleterious genes in natural populations, conspicuous polymorphisms, biochemical polymorphisms, quantitative variability in nature, variability within human populations, racial differentiation in mankind, speciation, the higher categories, and general conclusions.

Maxwell M. Wintrobe (Editor) on the History of Research in Hematology

Blood, Pure and Eloquent, edited by Maxwell M. Wintrobe, is a carefully planned monograph describing the history and cumulative findings of research on various components, functions, and diseases of the blood. The preface states that

> The present monograph is designed to tell how the study of the blood began, how understanding developed, and what degree of comprehension we have today. Circulating as it does throughout the body and being at the same time that part of ourselves that can be most easily sampled and analyzed, the blood has yielded to research facts of profound significance concerning its components, the blood-forming organs, and the so-called blood diseases, and also about the human organism as a whole.
>
> And what have we learned? Far more than we had ever dreamed of. But in addition we have discovered that everything is vastly more complicated--and more wondrous--than we had imagined. Moreover, each solution has opened the door to still more areas for exploration, more questions to

> answer and this has made it all that much more exciting. (Wintrobe 1980, p. xxi)

The 19 contributors are all distinguished medical scientists, 13 located (as of 1980) in the United States and 6 in England, Canada, and Australia. Five of the U.S. contributors are members of the National Academy of Sciences.

The chapters are primarily historical and expository and unusually well written; some read like scientific detective stories. Several lines of research stemmed from cases encountered by practicing physicians. Efforts to understand a specific phenomenon often led researchers into several disciplines: genetics, biochemistry, bacteriology, molecular biology, physiology, and others. Sometimes the answers were a long time coming; sometimes correct answers were found by young scientists and shunted aside by older "authorities," delaying acceptance and even rediscovery for decades.

It is hard (impossible?) to imagine a more complex "system of systems" than the human blood. It is interrelated with all other systems involved in our functioning, health, and longevity and conditions our responses to shocks and "invasions" from our external environments.

SYSTEMS THINKING IN PSYCHOLOGY AND SOCIAL PSYCHOLOGY: KURT LEWIN ON FIELD THEORY IN SOCIAL SCIENCE AND ON TOPOLOGICAL AND VECTOR PSYCHOLOGY

Kurt Lewin (1890-1947) was primarily a psychologist and made his major contributions in that field, but the influence of his work has extended well beyond the bounds of traditional psychology. Cartwright (1951, p. vii) says:

> When the intellectual history of the twentieth century is written, Kurt Lewin will surely be counted as one of those few men whose work changed fundamentally the course of social science in its most critical period of development. During his professional life of only about thirty years, the social sciences grew from a stage of speculative system building, through a period of excessive empiricism in which facts were gathered simply for their intrinsic interest, to a more mature development in which empirical data are sought for the significance they can have for systematic theories. Although the social sciences are only barely into this third stage of development, Lewin's work has accelerated greatly the rate of development.

The best point of entry into Lewin's work for systems economists is Lewin (1951), _Field Theory in Social Science: Selected Theoretical Papers_. It is important to begin with the foreword and preface by Dorwin Cartwright, who edited the volume. As Cartwright (p. xi) sees it:

> The most fundamental construct for Lewin . . . is that of field. All behavior (including action, thinking, wishing, striving, valuing, achieving, etc.) is conceived as a change of some state of a field in a given unit of time, ($\frac{dx}{dt}$). In treating individual psychology, the field with which the scientist must deal is the "life space" of the individual. This life space consists of the person and the psychological environment as it exists for him. In dealing with group psychology or sociology, a similar formulation is proposed. One may speak of the field in which a group or institution exists with precisely the same meaning as one speaks of the individual life space in individual psychology. The life space of a group, therefore, consists of the group and its environment as it exists for the group. It is the task of the scientist to develop constructs and techniques of observation and measurement adequate to characterize the properties of any given life space at any given time and to state the laws governing changes of these properties.

The essays in Lewin (1951) include formalization and progress in psychology; constructs in field theory; defining the "field at a given time"; field theory and learning; regression, retrogression, and development; field theory and experiment in social psychology; psychological ecology; frontiers in group dynamics; behavior and development as a function of the total situation; and an appendix on analysis of the concepts whole, differentiation, and unity.

The appendix is a very important contribution to systems theory. Economists may be surprised at the mathematical and logical texture of Lewin's definitions and derivations.

Pages 234-237, the concluding pages of "Frontiers of Group Dynamics," are particularly important to systems economists. Some excerpts are:

> Many aspects of social life can be viewed as quasi-stationary processes. They can be regarded as states of a quasi-stationary equilibrium in the precise meaning of a constellation of forces the structure of which can be well defined. . . .
>
> The scientific treatment of social forces presupposes analytical devices which are adequate to the nature of social processes and which are technically fitted to serve as a bridge to a mathematical treatment. The basic means to this end is the representation of social situations as "social fields." Some aspects of social processes can be treated by way of systems of coordinates called "phase space.". . .
>
> The analytical tools used are equally applicable to cultural, economic, sociological and psychological aspects of group life. . . .

> . . . From what I have been able to learn recently about the treatment of equilibria by mathematical economics, I am convinced that this treatment . . . is also fully compatible with our considerations. . . .
>
> The analytical tools of mathematical economics should be of great help for carrying through the task of measuring social forces. . . .
>
> For economics, the fusion implies the possibility of taking into account the cultural and psychological properties of the population involved. . . .
>
> The fusion of the social sciences will make accessible to economics the vast advantages which the experimental procedure offers for testing theories and for developing new insight. The combination of experimental and mathematical procedures has been the main vehicle for the integration of the study of light, of electricity, and of the other branches of physical science. The same combination seems to be destined to make the integration of the social sciences a reality.

Unfortunately, Lewin died a few weeks before this article was published, and we see no evidence that his message reached the economists for whom it was partly intended or that it elicited the desired response from psychologists.

Lewin had good early training in mathematics and in the philosophy of science and published several papers (in German) comparing the methodologies of physics and biology. In the 1920s he became convinced that topology, then a relatively new branch of mathematics, could be developed into an ideal tool for the representation of psychological forces. He published two monographs on these ideas in the 1930s. Our impression is that these ideas were respected but not followed up by other psychologists.

Currently, many economists have the mathematical equipment to understand Lewin and to follow up on some of his suggestions for cooperation between economists and psychologists (including social psychologists). It may be that Lewin's ideas will have a major influence on the development of systems economics.

Principles of Topological Psychology (Lewin 1936) has the following major divisions: the task of psychology and the foundations of topological and vector psychology, concepts of topology that are fundamental for psychology, topology of the psychological environment, topology of the person, and dimensions of the life space.

The chapter headings are the present state of psychology; formulation of law and representation of situation; general considerations about representing life space; content and extent of the psychological life space; causal interconnections in psychology; the psychological life space as space in the sense of mathematics; psychological space and psychological dynamics; the psychological worlds and the physical world; mathematical representation and psychological theory; concepts of topology fundamental for psychology; psychological regions, locomotions, and communications; boundaries of psychological regions; the relative positions of two regions; structural changes; the life space as finitely structured space; the person as a differentiated region in the life space; fundamental concepts and coordinating definitions for the representation of the person; and the dimensions of the life space.

Lewin's (1938) _The Conceptual Representation and the Measurement of Psychological Forces_ was designed as the first part of a "vector psychology," which should be viewed together with his _Principles of Topological Psychology_ as an outline of a conceptual framework of psychology. Its major headings are the position of the construct of force in psychology, the geometry of direction in psychology, psychological examples illustrating the application of hodological space, the determination of psychological forces, and examples of the measurement of forces.

Alfred J. Marrow's (1969) book, _The Practical Theorist: The Life and Work of Kurt Lewin_, is an informative and readable biography.

SYSTEMS THINKING ABOUT THE SPATIAL ORGANIZATION OF HUMAN SOCIETIES, THE DESIGN OF RESOURCE-CONSERVING CITIES, AND THE INTERACTIONS BETWEEN NEW TECHNOLOGIES AND STRATEGIES FOR SOCIAL AND ECONOMIC DEVELOPMENT: E. A. J. JOHNSON AND RICHARD L. MEIER

E. A. J. Johnson on the Organization of Space in Developing Countries

E. A. J. Johnson, author of _The Organization of Space in Developing Countries_, was for many years a professor of economic history at Johns Hopkins University and editor of the journal _Economic History_. He lived more than 10 years in Korea, Greece, Italy, Yugoslavia, and India in connection with economic development programs and (in some cases) reconstruction in the aftermath of World War II. He became convinced that the focus of most economic development efforts on "core region urbanization" was misplaced; in his book he suggests how "a more benevolent spatial distribution of enterprise, employment, and creative effort can be achieved." His study, as he says, "lies somewhere between economic history and economic theory, somewhere between micro and macrogeography, interblending description and analysis, prescription and policy" (Johnson 1970, p. vii).

Johnson was nearly 70 when he completed his book. It was written during 1965-1969, but he brings to bear his extensive knowledge of economic history as well as of current situations. Topics covered include the nature of landscapes in human geography: purposes underlying the organization of terrestrial space, the early organization of space in countries now considered "developed," market systems and spatial design, central-place theory and regional organization of space, great cities and the macroeconomic consequences of dual economies, the critical role of market towns in modernizing the landscapes of underdeveloped countries, spatial reconstruction: some policy aspects, functional economic areas as spatial entities, spatial experiments: areas of progress, spatial experiments: tentative and partial, and some guidelines for spatial policy.

Richard L. Meier on Planning for an Urban World and Designing Resource-Conserving Cities

Richard L. Meier's (1974) book, _Planning for an Urban World: The Design of Resource-Conserving Cities_, is an outstanding example of systems thinking. Meier chose a biological analogy as the most appropriate way to describe the dynamics of the worldwide growth of urban concentrations in a period of decreasing resources.

The city itself is seen as an ecosystem of interacting populations--dominant and subdominant human populations, domesticated assemblages of plants, animals, machines, and automata. The system as a whole processes inputs of raw materials, energy, and information to produce self-sustenance and material and cultural outputs.

The topics treated include redefining urban ecosystems, crises of resource scarcity, surviving all challenges, processes of transitional urbanization, farsighted strategies for organization, the Green Revolution and its aftermath, energy and water supply, the uses of space and time, spectrum: the ultimate resource, what cities produce from natural resources, growing the global metropolis, and steady-state urbanism.

Richard L. Meier on the Relation of New Technologies to Strategies for Social and Economic Development

Richard L. Meier is a remarkably versatile scientist and urban planner. In his first book, _Science and Economic Development: New Patterns of Living_, Meier (1956; 2nd edition, 1966) traced out a new path for economic development, which was suggested and shaped by post-World War II discoveries in science and technology. He had completed a Ph.D. in organic chemistry in 1944, which prepared him for the appraisal of technological developments and prospects in the physical and biological sciences. The logic of his research on new foods and new fuels also led him to acquire a wide acquaintance with the social and behavioral sciences and with urban planning.

His 1956 book discusses the present world predicament, new foods, new fuels, and new patterns of living, displaying an unusual combination of breadth and sharpness. The _American Journal of Sociology_ called it "a book of magnificent scope and broad vision." The _Quarterly Review of Biology_ described it as "an excellent survey of all phases of world development." The _American Economic Review_ appraised it as "a remarkable book: a weighty contribution to the theoretic solution of the excruciating dilemma facing the majority of mankind who inhabit the underdeveloped countries."

The 1966 edition is to be preferred.

NOTES

1. Arnold J. Toynbee, A Study of History (2nd ed.; London: Oxford University Press, 1935), Volume III, p. 322.

2. Vico accepted the biblical tradition of a universal flood and a chronology that placed it in about 2200 B.C. His divine age begins about 200 years after the flood.

REFERENCES

Braudel, F. 1949/1973. The Mediterranean and the Mediterranean World in the Time of Philip II. Translated by Sian Reynolds. New York: Harper and Row. Originally published in French in 1949.

__________. 1981, 1982, 1984. Civilization and Capitalism, 15th-18th Century. Volume 1, 1981: The Structures of Everyday Life: The Limits of the Possible. Volume 2, 1982: The Wheels of Commerce. Volume 3, 1984: The Perspective of the World, translated by Sian Reynolds. New York: Harper and Row. Originally published in French in 1979.

Cartwright, D. O. 1951. "Foreword." In K. Lewin, Field Theory in Social Science, pp. vii-vx. New York: Harper. Reprinted in 1975 by Greenwood Press, Westport, CT.

Copernicus, N. 1543/1976. On the Revolutions of the Heavenly Spheres. Translated from Latin by A. M. Duncan. New York: Barnes and Noble.

Galileo, G. 1632/1953. Dialogue on the Great World Systems. Translated into English by Thomas Salusbury, 1661. Translation revised by Giorgio de Santillana, 1953. Chicago: University of Chicago Press.

__________. 1638/1933. Dialogues Concerning Two New Sciences. Translated by H. Crew and A. DeSalvio, 1914. Reissued in 1933. New York: Macmillan.

Greene, J. C. 1959. The Death of Adam: Evolution and Its Impact on Western Thought. Ames: Iowa State University Press.

__________. 1984. American Science in the Age of Jefferson. Ames: Iowa State University Press.

Hall, A. R. 1966. The Scientific Revolution 1500-1800: Formation of the Modern Scientific Attitude. 2nd ed. Boston: Beacon Press. First edition published in 1954.

Ibn Khaldun. 1377/1958. The Muqaddimah: An Introduction to History. Three volumes. Translated from the Arabic by

Franz Rosenthal. New York: Pantheon Books. Published for Bollingen Foundation, Inc.

Johnson, E. A. J. 1970. The Organization of Space in Developing Countries. Cambridge: Harvard University Press.

Kuhn, T. S. 1957/1959. The Copernican Revolution: Planetary Astronomy in the Development of Western Thought. New York: Vintage Books. Originally published in 1957 by Harvard University Press.

Lewin, K. 1936. Principles of Topological Psychology. Translated by F. Heider and Grace M. Heider. New York: McGraw-Hill.

__________. 1938. The Conceptual Representation and the Measurement of Psychological Forces. Contributions to Psychological Theory, Volume I, No. 4. Durham, NC: Duke University Press.

__________. 1951. Field Theory in Social Science: Selected Theoretical Papers. Edited by Dorwin Cartwright. New York: Harper. Reprinted in 1975 by Greenwood Press, Westport, CT.

Lotka, A. J. 1925/1956. Elements of Mathematical Biology. New York: Dover Publications. Originally published in 1925 as Elements of Physical Biology.

Mahdi, M. 1957/1964. Ibn Khaldun's Philosophy of History: A Study in the Philosophic Foundation of the Science of Culture. Chicago: University of Chicago Press (Phoenix Books). First published in 1957 by Allen and Unwin, London.

Marrow, A. J. 1969. The Practical Theorist: The Life and Work of Kurt Lewin. New York: Basic Books.

Meier, R. L. 1966. Science and Economic Development: New Patterns of Living. 2nd ed. Cambridge: MIT Press. First edition published in 1956.

__________. 1974. Planning for an Urban World: The Design of Resource-Conserving Cities. Cambridge: MIT Press.

Newton, I. 1687/1934. Mathematical Principles of Natural Philosophy. Translated into English by Andrew Motte in 1729; translation revised by Florian Cajori, 1934. Berkeley: University of California Press.

__________. 1731/1969. A Treatise of the System of the World. 2nd ed. With an introduction by I. B. Cohen, 1969. London: Dawsons of Pall Mall. First edition was published in 1728.

Pompa, L. 1975. Vico: A Study of the 'New Science.' Cambridge: Cambridge University Press.

Ptolemy, C. fl. 2nd century/1984. Ptolemy's Almagest. Translated and annotated by C. J. Toomer. New York: Springer-Verlag.

Spengler, J. J. 1968. "Lotka, Alfred J." In International Encyclopedia of the Social Sciences, Volume 9, pp. 475-476. New York: Macmillan Company and the Free Press.

Vico, G. 1725/1944. The Autobiography of Giambattista Vico. Translated by M. H. Fisch and T. G. Bergin, 1944. Ithaca,

NY: Cornell University Press. Originally published in Italian in two parts, 1725 and 1728.

__________. 1744/1968. The New Science of Giambattista Vico. Revised translation of the third edition (1744) by T. G. Bergin and M. H. Fisch, 1968. Ithaca, NY: Cornell University Press.

Wintrobe, M. M., ed. 1980. Blood, Pure and Eloquent: A Story of Discovery, of People, and of Ideas. New York: McGraw-Hill.

Wright, S. 1968, 1969, 1977, 1978. Evolution and the Genetics of Populations. Volume 1, 1968: Genetic and Biometric Foundations. Volume 2, 1969: The Theory of Gene Frequencies. Volume 3, 1977: Experimental Results and Evolutionary Deductions. Volume 4, 1978: Variability within and among Natural Populations. Chicago: University of Chicago Press.

NAME INDEX

SUBJECT INDEX